ALSO BY JEANNE MARIE LASKAS

Concussion

Hidden America

Growing Girls

The Exact Same Moon

Fifty Acres and a Poodle

We Remember

The Balloon Lady and Other People I Know

TO: Cynthia
♡ Happy Mama's Day!
~ May this book take you
on a journey of
nostalgia + grace +
HOPE
I love you!
Shelley

To Obama

To Obama

With love, joy, anger, and hope

JEANNE MARIE LASKAS

 Random House | New York

Published in the United States by Random House, an imprint and
division of Penguin Random House LLC, New York.

RANDOM HOUSE and the HOUSE colophon are registered trademarks
of Penguin Random House LLC.

Originally published in hardcover in the United States by Random House,
an imprint and division of Penguin Random House LLC, in 2018.

LIBRARY OF CONGRESS CATALOGING-IN-PUBLICATION DATA
Names: Laskas, Jeanne Marie, author.
Title: To Obama : with love, joy, anger, and hope / by Jeanne Marie Laskas.
Description: New York : Random House, [2019]
Identifiers: LCCN 2018023502 | ISBN 9780525509394 (Paperback)
| ISBN 9780525509400 (ebook)
Subjects: LCSH: Obama, Barack. | Presidents—United States—Correspondence. |
American letters. | United States—Politics and government—2009–2017—Sources.
Classification: LCC E907 .L35 2019 | DDC 973.932—dc23 LC record available at
https://lccn.loc.gov/2018023502

Printed in the United States of America on acid-free paper

randomhousebooks.com

9 8 7 6 5 4 3 2 1

For Anna and Sasha

Contents

To Obama

Samples, 2008-2009

Gold Hill, OR

November 10, 2008

President-Elect Barack Obama
United States Senate
713 Hart Senate Office Building
Washington DC 20510

Dear President-Elect Obama,

My name is Benjamin Durrett. I am 18 years old. This was my first time voting, and let me tell you it was not a fun experience. I fought with my father over this election so much that I didn't get my ballot filled out till the morning of the election. It was not until that night when the Democrats had a chance to get sixty chairs that I saw some of the things my father was talking about. He showed me how the Democratic Party now has majority control over all branches of the government. He even went as far as to say that we may not have an election in 2012. After he had finished his rant he looked at me, and said "I pray that you are right and I am wrong." Voting for you in this election was truly the first time I have done something that went against my father. I feel that this has been a big step in becoming the person I am meant to become. I truly believe that you are the man who can make this place we call home a great one again. If we are doomed to collapse then so be it, I will look like a fool along with all of my friends, and my father will tell me its okay and that I never could have predicted this. I don't know what you have to do to fix this place we live in. I don't even know if you can. All I ask is that you give it everything you have. If you do that I will know that I made the right choice.

Sincerely,

Benjamin Durrett

38/SAMPLE

MK

June 3, 2009

Dear President Obama,

I saw a report that you take 10 randomly selected letters each day to prepare a response. I hope mine is one of them. I really need to hear from you.

The country I once knew and deeply cared about is disappearing. The capital that I and other generations before me built is being squandered. I have played by the rules thinking my family and I would be secure and that the preparation for old age would be safe in a country that would continue to honor the values of integrity (being a person of your word), fairness (you reap what you sew), self reliance, and discipline(forgoing short term reward for long term gain). All this is crumbling. It started before your watch but is accelerating during your administration. I am saddened.

Let me tell you why I think this way. Like you, I was raised by a single mom of very modest means. My Dad was killed in a plane accident when I was 11. My mom had saved enough to start me in college. I paid for most of it and for all of my MBA which I earned after serving as a US Army Officer. I worked for AT&T/Lucent for 28 years and through a lot of discipline (see definition above) I paid for 2 daughter's undergraduate degrees and helped them with their Masters in Social Work. I have been married for 40 years. I carry no debt except a mortgage. I have served as a church officer, been president of my national fraternity and now tutor, run a business, provide SCORE counseling and serve on a non- profit board. In short I have done my part as a patriotic American and have saved for my retirement without being a burden to my fellow countrymen. I have done all this without government help except for the little I received from the GI bill.

Unfortunately, it appears I have been a sucker. I could be getting transfer payments for being irresponsible i. e. borrowing beyond my means to buy creature comforts, taking extravagant vacations and manipulating the weak to enter agreements they could not afford. I could have avoided the Army. I could have spent all my kid's college money on myself. Instead, I am rewarding this behavior today through my tax dollars and your decisions. Not only that, but I believe the dollar will fail under your wasteful spending and transfer payments to the least productive among us. My savings will be worthless. All my hard work and sacrifice to no avail. All that American capital (moral and physical) from generations past will be spent.

What's more, you make all these decisions knowing that you and your family will never be affected by them. You will always be protected when social unrest and collapse destroys the rest of us.

Here is my request. Reward integrity (people who keep their word), let people reap what they sew (the good and the painful), recognize citizens who have been self reliant and preserve the system that allowed them to become that way, show discipline and demand it of others.

Also, on a personal note, fight against hubris. To be human is to be prone to that condition. I see signs that it is affecting you on the Brian Williams White House report and in your decision to go to NYC on a personal trip using my tax dollars. I think you are probably a decent man but even you can be destroyed by hubris.

I remain a loyal American who at least wrote a letter,

Reply.

Richard A Dexter

Dover, NH

Richard —

THE WHITE HOUSE
WASHINGTON

Thanks for your letter, and for your service to our country. I applaud your life of responsibility, but frankly am puzzled as to why you think I don't share in those values. The only transfer payments we have initiated were to states to prevent wholesale cuts in teachers, police officers, firefighters etc. in the wake of the financial crisis, and short term measures to prevent the banking and auto sectors from collapsing. (over)

You may disagree with some of these policies, but please know that all I want to see is the hard work of individuals like you rewarded.

Again, thank you for your thoughtful note.

Richard A. Dexter
Dover, New Hampshire

JUN 2 2 2009

Jeri LeAnne Harris
Alger, MI

November 5, 2008

President-Elect Barack Obama
John C. Kluczynski Federal Office Building
230 South Dearborn St.
Suite 3900 (39th floor)
Chicago, Illinois 60604

Reply

Dear President-Elect Obama,

I'm not quite sure why I am writing to you, but as I feel compelled to do so – here goes! I am a 'dyed in the wool' republican. I didn't vote for you and felt with my whole heart that you should have been defeated (Not the best start for a letter – smile).
HOWEVER, my country didn't agree with me and therefore, you are going to be the 44th President ... my President of these great United States. As of 12pm last night – my heart changed. I wanted to tell you that even though I did not cast my vote for you, I respect the race that you ran and I will commit to you today – that I will pray for you and your presidency each and every day.
I have voted since I was 18 (the last 8 elections) and even, in all my years of voting – I have never made that promise – or written a letter to a President but, as I stated before, I feel compelled. Your acceptance speech was gracious, and showed the makings of a true leader. I, like many others, am part of the fabric of this country and that I am going to be one of your constituents. I am proud to be an American each and every day and I'm proud that we have a due process that spelled out most definitely that America wants Senator Barack Obama as our next President.
I realize you may never receive this, but I hope you do. I hope you know that there are voters – who like you said last night "Didn't vote for you – but you will be our President" – I may have not committed millions to your cause, I may have not supported you before, but as of today, I am committed to serving you as a citizen and to praying for you daily. I can only hope that there are millions more like me – who will make that commitment to you.
Thank you for your honest campaign and as you said last night – May God Bless the United States of America.

Best Regards,

Jeri Harris

Jeri L. Harris

THE WHITE HOUSE

Dear Teri —

Thank you for the wonderful note.
It is most gracious, and please do keep
praying for me, my family, and most importantly,
the country!

Jeri L. Harris
Alger, Michigan

FEB - 2 2009

$\frac{11}{4}$/2008

DEAR MR. PRESIDENT ELECT:

You HAVE MY SUPPORT UNTIL I DRAW MY LAST BREATH.

GOD BLESS YOU AND YOURS.

RESPECTFULLY,

[signature]

J. MARTIN BALL

RICHTON PARK IL
USA

MK

April 6, 2009

Peggy

Spring, TX

Mr. President:

I am an average American woman. I am fifty-five years old. I am a wife, mother and a grandmother of two beautiful little girls, age seven and eleven. I love my country (The USA) and for what it stands.

My husband and I both work very hard to earn our living. Each month we pay our mortgage, bills, TAXES, buy our food and take care of our own business. We are blessed because on top of that we are able to support our local church and various other organizations that feed the hungry, give water to the thirsty and clothe the naked (the simple things that God wants us to do). Please don't make this harder for us to do by reducing our tax deductions.

I also want you to know that life has not always been so easy for me. I was a single mom for several years. Things were hard some of the time, but I say to you that God met my every need and the government never had to "bail me out".

Mr. President, you are to represent the people of this nation. I can honestly say that I DO NOT feel represented by you. I am so disappointed and angry that you and many of the current representatives are trying to lead our nation into socialism. You should know from observing other countries with socialistic governments that this does not work and will not work in the USA.

I, as one of the WE in "WE THE PEOPLE" say to you STOP this terrible debt that you are telling us to take on. This is not the future that I want to leave to my children and my children's children.

Mr. President, as an average citizen of The United States of America, I ask to you STOP what you are doing (NOW), admit that you are on the wrong path and move forward in governing our country with it's original intent and in a way that would be pleasing to God.

Sir, I know that you are very busy, but I feel that if you have not done so in a while you should read the Constitution of the United States and the Bill of Rights. Please remember this is to be a government for the people and by the people.

Thank you for reading my letter.

Sincerely,

Peggy

Reply.

may we never forget what it took & what sacrifices were made to win freedom for our country!!

Peggy —

THE WHITE HOUSE

WASHINGTON

Thanks for your letter. I wanted to respond briefly.
First, no one is moving the country towards socialism.
I have tried to deal with an unprecedented economic
crisis by increasing government investments in roads,
bridges, schools and other infrastructure to encourage
jobs creation until businesses in the private sector
get back on their feet.

Second, rather than raise taxes, I have actually cut

taxes for 95 percent of working families. I have
proposed to increase taxes on those making over
$250,000 per year to pay for the tax cut for everyone
else, but those increases don't go into effect until
2010, and the rates will still be lower than they
were under Ronald Reagan.

We do need to get control of government spending
over the long term, and I am committing all of my
team to find places to cut our waste, fraud, and
abuse. But please rest assured that I take my
oath to uphold the Constitution seriously.

Sincerely,

CHAPTER 1

The Letters

It felt almost like a secret, the way Shailagh was talking about the letters; she wanted me to know how important they were, and she seemed frustrated, or perhaps just exhausted, like a soldier in some final act of surrender, tossing off the keys to the kingdom right before the village blows up.

This was October 2016. Hurricane Matthew had just rolled out to sea, Samsung phones were abruptly catching fire, and Republican presidential candidate Donald Trump was tweeting—"Nothing ever happened with any of these women. Totally made up nonsense to steal the election. Nobody has more respect for women than me!"— and I suppose Shailagh was feeling as wistful as anyone tumbling inside the gathering awareness of sweeping cultural change in America.

She had served six years in the Obama administration, the past two as a senior advisor, and we were in her office in the West Wing, where she was reaching toward a bookcase filled with thick three-ring binders. Inside the binders were letters to Obama that dated back to the beginning of his administration. They were from constituents. Ordinary Americans writing to their president. "They became a kind of life-force in this place," Shailagh said. She had her shoes off and a woolly sweater wrapped around her; she had a raspy voice and an unfussy Irish look, a person you might sooner find wiping the counter at a pub in Dublin than sitting comfortably across the hall from the Oval Office.

At that point Hillary Clinton was still up by double digits in the national polls, and the unthinkable was still unthinkable. Clinton campaign staffers were jockeying for position in what everyone believed would be the new administration, and Shailagh had no designs on being part of it; two terms in the White House were enough. Her job helping to lead the administration's communications strategy was to act as the gatekeeper between Obama and the people who wrote about him, and it appeared to have taken its toll. "I will not miss the bros," she said. With Obama just a few months away from leaving office, journalists were reaching peak bravado, she said. They wanted exit interviews; they wanted them now; they wanted to be first, biggest, loudest. She was sick of the egos, the same old questions, the lack of imagination, and Trump was tweeting, and it seemed like the world was going haywire.

The letters, she said, served as a kind of respite from all that, and she offered to show some to me. She chose a navy-blue binder, pulled it off the shelf, and opened it, fanning through page after page of letters, some handwritten in cursive on personal letterhead, others block printed on notebook paper and decorated with stickers; there were business letters, emails, faxes, and random photographs of families, soldiers, and pets. "You know, it's this dialogue he's been having with the country that people aren't even aware of," she said, referring to Obama's eight-year habit of corresponding with the American public. "Collectively, you get this kind of American tableau."

Obama had committed to reading ten letters a day when he first took office, becoming the first president to put such a deliberate focus on constituent correspondence. Late each afternoon, around five o'clock, a selection would be sent up from the mailroom to the Oval Office. The "10LADs," as they came to be known—for "ten letters a day"—would circulate among senior staff, and the stack would be added to the back of the briefing book the president took with him to the residence each night. He answered some by hand and wrote notes on others for the writing team to answer, and on some he scribbled, "SAVE."

Everyone on the senior staff knew the importance of the letters, but Shailagh had taken an interest in the story they told in the aggregate, what they said about the country and her boss. She told me she would sometimes put her feet up and devour the material, as if it were a history project and she were a scholar intent on mastery.

"So this is January 23, 2009, right after the inauguration," she said, choosing a letter at random from the binder. "'I'm a seventy-three-year-old owner of a manufacturing company. My husband and I started from nothing . . . put every dime back into the business. We've had no orders or inquiries for over three months now . . . still recovering from open-heart surgery. . . . We've got this house. Our mortgage is nine hundred seventy-nine dollars and seventy-one cents. We still owe a hundred twenty thousand dollars. What are we going to do?'

"You know?" she said. "That kind of stuff. All these signs. Because at that point, it wasn't clear. The job losses hadn't really started yet. There's page after page after page of people venting about the big banks. I mean, that's the other thing: You see the rage. You see the terror. Just the vulnerabilities that people are feeling that so transcend at that point what the fundamentals even looked like. So right at the beginning when Obama took office, he's hearing—he's hearing, like, Larry Summers, the director of his National Economic Council, and then he's hearing, you know, Francis and his wife Collette from Idaho. You know? It's like a running dialogue with the American public.

"You know?" Shailagh said, as if she was pleading with me to *get this.*

I told her I did, or at least I was trying to.

"Did I tell you about the letter from the guy in Mississippi?" she asked.

No, she hadn't.

"Oh my God—"

She stood, headed back to the bookshelf to get a different binder. "Wait till you see this one."

Presidents have dealt with constituent mail differently over the years. Things started simply enough: George Washington opened the mail and answered it. He got about five letters a day. Mail back then was carried by foot or on horseback or in stagecoaches—not super high volume. Then came steamboats, then rail and a modernized postal system, and by the end of the nineteenth century, President William McKinley was overwhelmed. One hundred letters *every day*? He hired someone to help manage the flow, and that was the origin of the Office of Presidential Correspondence. It wasn't until the Great Depression that things got crazy. In his weekly fireside chats, Franklin D. Roosevelt began a tradition of speaking directly to the country, inviting people to write to him and tell him their troubles. About a half million letters came pouring in during the first week, and the White House mailroom became a fire hazard. Constituent mail grew from there, and each succeeding president formed a different relationship with it. By the end of his presidency, Nixon refused to read anything bad anyone said about him. Reagan answered dozens of letters on weekends; he would stop by the mailroom from time to time, and he enjoyed reading the kid mail. Clinton wanted to see a representative stack every few weeks. George W. Bush liked to get a pile of ten already-answered letters on occasion. These, anyway, are the anecdotal memories you get from former White House staff members. Little hard data exists about constituent mail from previous administrations. Historians don't focus on it; presidential libraries don't feature it; the vast majority of it has long since been destroyed.

President Obama was the first to come up with a deliberate practice of reading ten letters every day. If the president was home at the White House (he did not tend to mail when he traveled), he would be reading constituent mail, and everyone knew it, and systems were put in place to make sure it happened. The mail had currency. Some staff members called it "the letter underground." Starting in 2010, all physical mail was scanned and preserved. Starting in 2011, every word of every email factored into the creation of a daily word cloud, its image distributed around the White House so policy makers and staff members alike could get a glimpse at the issues and ideas constituents had on their minds.

In 2009, Natoma Canfield, a cancer survivor from Medina, Ohio, wrote in, detailing her staggering health-insurance premiums in a letter Obama framed and had hung in a corridor between his private study and the Oval Office: "I need your health reform bill to help me!!! I simply can no longer afford to pay for my health care costs!!" It stood in for the tens of thousands of similar letters he got on the healthcare issue alone. They saw spikes in volume after major events like the mass shootings in Newtown, Connecticut, and Charleston, South Carolina; the Paris terrorist attacks; the government shutdown; Benghazi. You could see these spikes in the word clouds. "Jobs" might grow for a time, or "Syria," or "Trayvon," or a cluster like "family-children-fear" or "work-loans-student" or "ISIS-money-war" surrounding a giant "HELP"—the most common word of all. After a gunman opened fire on police officers in Dallas in 2016, the word "police" ballooned, surrounded by "God-guns-black-America" with a tiny "peace" and even tinier "Congress."

At one point during my visit to Shailagh's office that day, there was some commotion out in the hallway, and I followed her to the doorway to see what it was.

"Hey! How you doing?"

"Hey, man!"

"*This guy!* How you doing?"

"There she is. *How are you?*"

It was Biden. The VP zooming through the West Wing, zooming toward us, flanked by serious-looking men in black suits. "Hey, how you doing?" he said to me in his Joe Biden way. He shook my hand in his Joe Biden way—the net effect is always like you're a neighbor who just won some big bowling tournament, and he's *so pleased*! He gave Shailagh a quick hug and kept on zooming.

"Yeah, I know," Shailagh said when we sat back down in her office. Neither of us even needed to say it out loud. Biden may have been behaving like . . . Biden, but he didn't look like the person we were used to seeing. He looked thin. Brittle. Pale and exhausted. I wondered if perhaps that was just the look of a seventy-three-year-old man who had decided to pass up a lifelong dream to be president.

"I'd say it's more complicated than that," Shailagh said, and for a moment we reminisced.

Biden was how Shailagh and I had become friends in the first place; she was his deputy chief of staff and communications director back in 2013 when I was profiling him for a magazine. She invited me to fly on Air Force Two to Rome for the pope's inauguration, where she and I and a team of patient reporters watched Biden in his aviator sunglasses hobnob with world leaders. I was grateful for the opportunity, but afterward I told Shailagh I didn't really have anything to write about beyond: Here is what it feels like to stand with a bunch of patient reporters watching Biden in his aviator sunglasses hobnob with world leaders. That's how those press trips work. There's a rope: the powerful on one side, the curious on the other, everybody smiling and waving. You couldn't get at how anyone thought, what gave them nightmares, what private moments anybody cherished or even cared about. You couldn't get close.

Shailagh thought about that. "We should go to Wilmington," she said. "Let me ask the VP."

And so that's what we did, the three of us, romping through Biden's Delaware hometown as he relived his childhood there. "It's really muddy back here," Biden said, plowing through the woods to find the old swimming hole, the Secret Service guys trying to keep up. "Shailagh, you will not believe— Come here, Shailagh. I told you about this, didn't I, Shailagh?" He took us past his first girlfriend's house, his second girlfriend's house, his *favorite* girlfriend's house; we stopped at his high school and the hoagie shop he loved, and we sat together on the neighborhood stoop where, as a kid, he'd filled his mouth with rocks, attempting to cure his debilitating stutter. We went to the cemetery where his first wife, Neilia, and his baby Naomi were buried—he didn't want to get too close—and we found ourselves peeking into the front window of his boyhood home so we could see the dining room hutch where his sister, Valerie, used to hide. "Do you see what I'm talking about, Shailagh? Now, if only these people were home, I could show you my room." All day long the two of them laughed and bickered like father and daughter; it was a privilege to witness the tenderness and to begin to see the ways in which a White House operates like a family. Or at least this part of that one did.

I remember asking Shailagh back then if there was a chance Biden would make a run for president in 2016. "Oh, he would never get in the way of Hillary," she said, and that was that—nothing worth talking about. It seemed kind of sad, a guy spending his whole life aiming for the presidency and getting so close but now answering a call to duty that involved shutting up and not mucking up the chance for the country to finally see a woman serve.

That day in her office, after we saw Biden zooming down the hall, Shailagh told me about the toll Beau Biden's brain cancer had taken on everyone; the vice president's son had lost the battle and died at forty-six on May 30, 2015. Shailagh said that was why Biden looked the way he did; she said anyone urging him to launch a presidential bid during his time of grief, as some were doing all the way up through the 2016 primaries, didn't know him or didn't love him.

She let it go at that, like you would if it were your dad suffering.

"God, this early stuff," she said, returning to the letters. She flipped through a red binder. "Oh, I remember this woman. Yeah, we ended up inviting her to a speech."

I suppose nostalgia was the main reason Shailagh thought to tour me through some of the letters that day. The administration ending, everyone getting ready to pack up and leave, all those letters left over. What would become of them? History is . . . big. History is sweeping. History is supposed to be a record of *momentous occasions,* not so much the tiny, insignificant ones.

"These are the voices in the president's head," Shailagh said. And I suppose that got to the heart of the matter. "He internalizes these things. Some of these letters he carries around and stews over. Especially the critical ones. It's a private space he's been able to preserve. Which suits him, you know?"

I got the sense that the letters were kind of Obama's Wilmington. A path toward understanding. A back door swinging open. Here was a chance to get to know Obama in a way most people hadn't. The tiny stories that stuck. The voices that called. The cries and the howls of the people he had pledged to serve. Here was the raw material of the ideas that bounced through his mind as he went about his days in cabinet meetings, bilateral summits, fundraisers, the Situation Room, and to his bed at night.

"Foreclosure, foreclosure, foreclosure," Shailagh said, flipping through some early letters. "I mean, the housing crisis just kind of unfolds in real time in these things. People were coming up against these balloon mortgages that they didn't even know they had. You can see the confluence of the economic crisis and the healthcare crisis happening at the same time. The loss of faith that people have in everything. The banks are collapsing; the Catholic Church is reeling. It's like all these institutions are letting them down. And here's this new president, this person who comes in on a change mandate, that has established a connection with them."

Some of the letter writers would turn into iconic heroes to staffers, Shailagh told me, their stories the stuff of speeches and State of the Union addresses. "As time went on, we often had letter writers at events; letter writers often introduced him. When the president's out traveling around the country, he visits places and has lunch with letter writers. I mean, we didn't want to turn it into a schlocky thing. It's—we tried to be respectful of it. Because it's essentially a series of private relationships he had with these folks. And I think that's what makes them so impactful. The private nature, the vulnerability of these people."

She yanked her glasses off, propped them on her head, stood to get a different binder. "The guy in Mississippi," she said, "I really need to find you that one. He wrote about the calluses on his hands. How the journey of his hands was actually this whole journey of the country at that moment. I'll find it—

"You don't see the cynicism, you know? You don't see the kind of dystopian view of government in these letters that we're so used to seeing. They're almost from another time, like conversations from another era, when people looked to government and to their leaders not just for *stuff* and not just to vent, but because they really wanted the president to understand what their problems were. They really wanted him to understand what their lives were like. And so it's very—you know, against the backdrop of all the polarization and cynicism and negativity and just the onslaught of opposition that we face day to day in the White House, these letters are a constant reminder that some people do view government as essentially a force for good. Or want it to be a force for good, want it to be better at what it does. Want it to serve veterans better, want it to deliver better healthcare.

"So that's been really kind of spiritually uplifting, seriously. In a period, against a backdrop, of just this brutal, you know, day-to-day combat."

I asked her if she thought the letters served a similar purpose for Obama.

"I just think letters suited him," she said. "I mean, the Obamas are, you know, a lot like the Reagans were and the Bushes were, for that matter. They are, like, inherently conservative, normal, traditional people, right? They fully occupy the office. They are as big as the office. They fit it. You know? You know what I mean? It's like the suit fits."

And the letters fit. Like mothballs, and good posture, and proper table manners, and no swearing. "The letters have this kind of otherworldly feel to them that doesn't seem part of the moment that we're in," she said, "even though what people are saying is very much in the moment. But the format feels otherworldly to me. It feels old to me. It feels very . . . Evelyn Waugh."

Like the letter from the guy in Mississippi. She was still looking for it. She had moved on to a green binder. "I know it's here. . . . It was just so well written. It felt like a page falling out of a novel. It's so interesting that people take the time. What compelled him to write that letter, that perfectly crafted little one-page letter?"

I told her that's what I was wondering. Who writes to the president? Not since my Santa Claus days would it have occurred to me to do something like that. Who were all these people? What did they get out of it? Moreover, I wondered about the nature of the experiment itself. Whose idea was it to have Obama read ten letters a day? I wondered what the letters meant to him, and I wondered how, if at all, constituent mail influenced his presidency.

My initial impulse was to meet some of the letter writers, to hear their stories firsthand. And while I would do plenty of that, what I didn't count on was the journey inside the mailroom itself. The people who kept the machine in motion. You couldn't tell one story without the other, an interdependent relationship that serves to tell the story of the Obama administration through the eyes of the people who wrote to him.

Shailagh didn't find the letter she was looking for that day. She promised me she would. The letters came in by the millions, and those in the binders in her office were but a tiny sample, a few thousand of her favorites she liked to occasionally revisit. "You should go to the mailroom if you want the full effect," she said. "Just sit there and read. You'll see what I'm talking about."

I asked her where the mailroom was. She sat back, thought for a moment. "There's a person there who runs it. Her name is Fiona. You'd have to get past her."

I asked if perhaps she could introduce me? She nodded but not convincingly, more as if a scheme was forming in her head.

I made the point that if she could get me on Air Force Two to go to the pope's inauguration with the vice president, surely she could score me a visit to the mailroom.

"You don't know Fiona," she said.

Martha C. Dollarhide

Oxford, MS

MEMPHIS TN 381

18 APR 2009 PM 1 T

President or Mrs. Obama
1600 Pennsylvania Ave.
Washington, D.C. 20500

SG
MAY 16 2009

✓ #139

Bobby Ingram
Oxford, MS.   Reply
   APR. 16, 2009

Mister Obama - My President,

    In 2007 I was proud of my hands.
They had veneered calluses where my palms
touched my fingers. Cuts and scrapes
were never severe. Splinters and blisters
merely annoyed me. With a vise-like grip
and dextrous touch my hands were heat
tolerant and cold ignorant. I was nimble
when whittling or when sharpening an axe.
I could exfoliate with an open palm when
my wife's back itched or my cat arched for
a rub. My nails were usually stained
after a chore; they were tougher, not cracked,
seldom manicured. My hands defined my
work, passions, my life.
    After 23 years as a land surveyor and
nearly 2 years unemployed, I miss my
career and my old hands. I kneel nights
and clutch new hands together, praying we
all can recover what seems lost. May
God guide your hands to mould our future.

Thank you for listening to the Citizen
    I am,
                    Bobby Ingram

CHAPTER 2

Bobby Ingram,
April 16, 2009

OXFORD, MISSISSIPPI

That last line and the closing are important. Notice the line break in between? That was intentional. Without that you could read it as "Thank you for listening to the citizen *that* I am," which would throw everything off. He didn't mean it that way. He didn't mean to tell the president thank you for listening just to him, Bobby Ingram of Oxford, Mississippi. He wrote "Citizen" with a capital *C* to suggest the citizen in general, the collective—everyone in the United States of America—in a way, he determined, that only a capital *C* could accurately indicate. But is that even a *thing*, grammatically speaking? He stressed over that, sitting there in his den, at that ancient tower computer (we're talking floppy drive) in the old armchair, with Babbitt, his cat, in his lap. *Probably not,* he thought. *That is probably not grammatically a thing.* You can't imagine how many drafts he wrote of that letter. How important it was that he got it just right. This was 2009, sort of at the bottom of things. Yeah, you could say he had hit bottom. He was glad about Obama coming in. Maybe something good would happen. Obama would be a president who would listen to the Citizen. Bobby wanted the president to know he believed that. (He did.) When he'd first conceived of the letter, his plan was that it be the first one Obama got when he reported to work at 8:35 A.M. on

January 21, 2009. He wanted Obama to know: Hey, here's a guy who is not like him, not Ivy League, not from Chicago, not African American. Hey, here's a skinny white guy from rural Mississippi without a super impressive education whose life is pretty terrible at the moment. Here's this guy out here; he's, like, the last kid in the class you'd expect to raise his hand to be called on, but his hand is up for him to say: "Dude, I like you. I want you to do well."

In between drafts (this was over a period of months) and sometimes just to clear his head, Bobby studied the postal route the letter would likely take, and he ticked off days on his calendar, working on the timing so the letter, when he sent it, would have the best chance of being the first thing Obama got when he sat down at his desk. Well, of course he studied the postal route. *You are talking about Bobby Ingram here.* He knows a little bit about everything. More precisely: He knows a lot about everything. That was the way of life his grandfather instilled in him, on his deathbed, when he called the grandbabies in one by one to give them each their personalized goodbye message. "Do everything" was what he told Bobby. "Try it for six months. If you like it, continue."

Anyway, with the whole grammar thing. Martha, his wife, usually gets the final say. They go over most things together. Ethical dilemmas and such. Fortunately, she's loose. Not like her mom, Atomic Betty. Martha understands that being incorrect is not, in itself, always an undesirable outcome. Witness: Michael's deplorable grammar. Michael is Bobby's baby brother, a long-haul trucker who usually writes while waiting his turn for a shower at the Pilot or the Flying J. His letters? You should see his letters. Oddest syntax, misspellings all over the place. The errors have a way of adding nuance to the sentences, Michael's signature *nuance,* that makes you feel his presence on the page. "He's flowing, Martha!" Bobby will say, marveling at the way Michael's letters *move.* The feeling he gets on the page. "He's flowing good now, Martha!" Bobby knows he'll never be the writer Michael is. But it's okay. It's okay.

Letters, Bobby thinks, are important in a man's life. He also writes to his sister, his dad, his friend Brian who's stuck in prison, and to a family of stamp collectors—good people. Letters are emotion on the page. Letters are a gift. When you write to someone, and they write back, you establish a bond. It validates both of you. He likes to throw in big words, but only if they're beautiful. Like when he said "dextrous touch" in the president's letter. Bobby is not sure, to this day, if he nailed that one. A hand can be dextrous, but a touch? Should it have been a "light touch"? But see, that doesn't do it. He needed some syllables. Some rhythm. "Let it go," Martha said. "Let it go." Bobby's favorite word of all, by the way, is "éclaircissement," which means the experience of being enlightened by a subject. See how you got "clarity" as your root word there? That is a hell of a word.

For Bobby, letter writing started with Michael. They began corresponding maybe fifty years ago, back when Bobby went off to basic training. Do you know how hard it is to enlist in the army when you're a Quaker? How many forms, how many *variances?* The army thinks if you're a Quaker, you're a conscientious objector, and you're going to poison the troops. That was not Bobby's intention. He was curious about the concepts he had been protesting along with all those elders in his church marching in antiwar rallies. It started to feel hollow—protesting others doing something you had never even tried. He became curious about war and politics—to say nothing of bugs, spiders, birds, turtles, sign language, antique cars, poetry, kilts, bamboo, bridges, and forestry. Everything. Do everything.

The army sent him to Munich, and he learned how to put rotors on helicopters, and he wrote to Michael to tell him about it. Michael wrote back about converting a Volkswagen to a dune buggy. They never stopped writing after that.

A letter is brotherhood. You start off by extending your hand. That is exactly what Bobby did with the president. *Literally.* He sat at that computer with Babbitt in his lap, and he extended his hand, and he saw how pathetically soft it was, and he needed to explain why. Not to overdramatize, but honestly, the collapse of his entire being, his psyche, his sense of self, his body, and his soul is captured in that image of his hands devoid of calluses.

Maybe you don't think calluses when you think land surveying. You probably don't know about the sledgehammer—eight pounds— and the way to swing it, around and around, bam, bam, just so, banging the stake six inches in. The sledgehammer is his second favorite tool. He bought it in 1983. His first favorite tool is the bush axe. Here again it's the swinging motion; if you stand back, he will demonstrate. Then there is the plumb bob. You hold it like this, and when it stops swinging, it tells you where the center of the earth is. *The center of the earth.* That is an ancient tool. That's just your plumb bob. Between all his tools, he carried eighty pounds of equipment on him every day. Walking through the woods, swamps, all kinds of terrain. He was doing what George Washington did. He was doing what Lewis and Clark did. Land surveying was connecting yourself to somebody from long ago. Getting to know the intent of the landowners. The deeds. You had to read these things and follow. Like that one time he traced the property back to a King George land grant. "Start at the post on the first crest past the water's edge." Well, which water's edge? Which post? "Ride four days by mule to the next corner, head north, sun to your cheek, two days by mule." Well, how fast can a mule walk? He had to figure out the speed of a mule of the size available at the time of King George. And the weather at the time they were surveying it. He figured it out. It was 110 miles. Basically two hours by car. He found that post. Oh, he found it! And then it was just good math to figure out the boundaries of the tract of land. Close the box for that tract of land. Good math. Mind you, when he first started, this was all by slide rule. Tangent. Cosine tables. You looked up the cosine of an angle. Multiplying by *that* would give you *that* tangent distance, and *that's* the angle you need to calculate to match this triangle. Fantastic. Fantastic. Five increments of pi, check it against the radius of the arc. All that stuff, it just meshed with him. He would slop through the swamps with his slide rule doing math and finding hundred-year-old locust posts, and he would think about why the Egyptians, the ones who figured out all this stuff, were of course mystical people.

That's how good land surveying was. It was just *that good.*

Anyway, by now you're probably wondering about that sound. The bark? Then the trill? That is a pileated woodpecker. A lot of people don't pronounce that right. Pi-lee-ay-ted. That's the tallest woodpecker in Mississippi. Eighteen inches. Bark-bark-bark, bark-bark-bark, then too-too-too-too-too-too. His favorite bird is the summer tanager. His favorite tree is the mimosa (a.k.a. Persian silk tree). Martha hates the bamboo down back here. Also, Martha has a spider phobia. Nevertheless, she tolerates his having this spider habitat out here. That's love. The common brown wood spider's web is larger than Bobby's kitchen table. The southern box turtle is also an important species to promote. That turtle on the rock there is named BooHiss. Among the varieties of snakes Bobby promotes are the eastern hognose, the puff adder, and the speckled king. Lizards, of course. This whole yard is about promoting certain species. Indian pink, that's a perennial weed. He's promoting it. Same with swamp irises, chives, lilies, thistles, garlic.

A lot of this knowledge comes from land surveying. You're out there with nature all day, every day.

Until one day they tell you to go home. When the recession hit in December 2007, people all across America lost their jobs. Construction was among the hardest hit industries. No more building, no more properties bought and sold, no more land disputes, no more land surveying.

Bobby was out. He and Martha could get by for a while on Martha's admin work at the university, but that was hardly the point.

He'd lost his purpose. The grief was like if someone had died. Or a divorce. Just any of those big ones that suck all the air from your lungs until you're doubled over. Two years of doubled over. *Two years.* He applied for jobs everywhere, offered to relocate to Texas. He was fifty-two years old. Nobody needed him.

He followed the news. Barack Obama appealed to him. The idea of hope. But the main thing he saw with Obama was, *Wow, this guy is inheriting a shit show. A mess of a country.* He needed help. Everyone needs help. It was like, let's do this together. That's how Bobby started the letter in his mind.

Extending his hand. That was hello. That was: It's me. The guy who used to have the calluses. Middle- to lower-class. Not so much education. That guy. Who is also—this guy. Curious, constantly questioning, a self-taught renaissance man. An enigma. A contradiction. *I'm both guys.* "I am large, I contain multitudes," Walt Whitman said. Don't forget that, Mr. President: multitudes.

Bobby missed the chance at getting his letter to the president on January 21, 2009. He wasn't done writing the letter until April.

After he got it just right, he sat back, exhaled, scooted the cat, and reached for the loose-leaf paper. Printing it in his own hand was paramount. A letter is a part of you. He wanted it to fit on one page, fit exactly, and he wanted it to be block style. It took many attempts. (He has five trash cans in his den.) Then he sent it. Then he forgot about it. Sending it was the main thing. He got it said. In that way, it was like every letter he's ever written. A letter is a prayer.

He came out of his depression shortly after he sent the letter. A switch. *I can't live like this.* Just a switch. Martha needed him. Atomic Betty was dying, which was an incomprehensible concept. The life-force of that woman. He was good with her. Just holding her hand all those days when nobody else could bear it. Then he started with his LOLs. The Little Old Ladies who needed help with daily chores. They needed him. He can soothe people. (He can put a cat to sleep in seconds.) Then of course, BooHiss and all the habitats outside. My God, the birds alone. Pretty soon Jeff was calling. He needed help rebuilding a boat. Everybody needs help! He and Jeff work together now. Jeff does the talking. Bobby can carry six two-by-fours in one go, up a ladder, in the worst heat imaginable.

He's that guy in the background with the bandana, sweating his brains out. You know that guy. But he's this guy too. He's got poetry in his head, and he knows which bird is singing, and he has math equations going on, and now he's trying to solve the hydrology problem down at the lake.

Some months after he sent the letter to the president, he got a response, on a white note card labeled, "The White House."

THE WHITE HOUSE
WASHINGTON

Bobby —

Thanks for the powerful letter. I'm working as hard as I can to make sure that hard working Americans like you have the opportunities you so richly deserve.

He and Martha stood together in the den scrutinizing that thing to determine if it was written in Obama's own hand. Martha said yes, holding it up to the light from the window. He said maybe, squinting over her shoulder. And then he stepped away, and it was like, well, hold on a second there, Martha. The president *writes back*?

Samples, 2009-2010

MK.

reply.

TO: ANYONE WITH ANY COMMON SENSE AT THE WHITE HOUSE,

Bonuses?? BONUSES??? For what? Losing the companies money at a record pace??

A.I.G. ....Freddie Mac....Fannie Mae....Morgan Stanley....Wells Fargo....Merrill Lynch....The list goes on & on!!

I realize I'm not the sharpest knife in the drawer, but for the life of me, I cannot understand what in the world is going on in our business sector! And in our Gov't.!! Can just ONE of you up there please explain to me how in the world this can be justified?? And please, don't start with the "best minds in the biz" routine...heard it all before. If that's the best we got, we're all in a world of hurt!!

Is this what we're teaching our kids to do when they move into the world by themselves...steal? Scam?? All in the name of the almighty dollar??

Since when do we reward incompetance?? Please tell me so I can pass it on to my boss!! Perhaps he's missing something! Since this "recession" showed it's ugly face, I have been cut back to working only 4 days a week. I struggle to pay my bills, gas the car, put food on my table. We watch every dime. I pay my taxes on time and mind my own business, but I now realize I've been doing wrong this whole time. What I really need to do to get ahead in the world is put on a coat & tie, get a wig, and smile like I'm everybodies best friend then SCAM the Hell out of them for all they got!!

And now, not only do you guys give my money away to the greedy ones who made
the very mistakes that put us in this mess, but you GIVE THEM BONUSES?????

I, for one, have had enough. It's time the citizens of this country take back our Gov't. & find someone who will not only tell us the TRUTH, (remember that word??), and who will not reward these idiots because they're the BEST WE GOT!!

BONUSES?? Come on...WAKE UP WASHINGTON!!!!!!

Timothy H. Mullin

LYNCHBURG, VIRGINIA

COPY FROM
ORM

THE WHITE HOUSE
WASHINGTON

Tim —
Thanks for your letter. I share your
sentiments, and we are moving as quick
as we can to restore some common sense
to the financial system.

Mr. Timothy Mullin
Lynchburg, Virginia

APR - 3 2009

#21   11258603 - Linette Jones, In ID: 6858341, Out ID: 6696164

From:
Date: 9/29/2009 10:05:18 AM
Subject:Foreign Affairs

President Obama, I am very disappointed that you believe campaigning for the Olympics to be hosted in your home town is more important than my childs safety in Afghanistan! I did not care for George Bush, but at least I felt safe when he was in office. I cannot say the same now that you are President. I fear for my childs safety serving in the military in Afghanistan, I fear for me and my familys safety here in the United States. Your lack of decision making ability is putting us in jeopardy for attacks from terrorists. Please stop campaigning and do your job!

==== Original Formatted Message Starts Here ====

Date of Msg: September 29, 2009

reply

```
<APP>CUSTOM
<PREFIX></PREFIX>
<FIRST>Linette</FIRST>
<LAST>Jones</LAST>
<MIDDLE></MIDDLE>
<SUFFIX></SUFFIX>
<ADDR1></ADDR1>
<ADDR2></ADDR2>
<CITY></CITY>   North Yarmouth
<STATE></STATE>  ME
<ZIP>       </ZIP>
<COUNTRY></COUNTRY>
<HPHONE></HPHONE>
<WPHONE></WPHONE>
<EMAIL>            </EMAIL>
<ISSUE>W_POTUS</ISSUE>
<ISSUE>W_POL_FA</ISSUE>
<ISSUE></ISSUE>
<MSG>
```
President Obama, I am very disappointed that you believe campaigning for the Olympics to be hosted in your home town is more important than my childs safety in Afghanistan! I did not care for George Bush, but at least I felt safe when he was in office. I cannot say the same now that you are President. I fear for my childs safety serving in the military in Afghanistan, I fear for me and my familys safety here in the United States. Your lack of decision making ability is putting us in jeopardy for attacks from terrorists. Please stop campaigning and do your job!
```
</MSG>
</APP>
```

COPY FROM ORM

THE WHITE HOUSE
WASHINGTON

Dear Linette —

I received your note. I am grateful for your child's service, and have no more important job than keeping America safe. That's why I am puzzled that you would think a one day trip on the Olympics — a trip in which I met with General McCrystal, our commander in Afghanistan, to discuss war strategy — would somehow distract me from my duties as (over)

Commander-in-Chief. You may not like all my policies (that is something you quickly get use to as President), but rest assured that I wake up in the morning and go to bed at night thinking about our soldiers and my responsibilities to them.

Sincerely,

DEC - 9 2009

Pdf emailed to Mike Kelleher

11-30-2009

President Barack Obama
The White House
1600 Pennsylvania Ave, NW
Washington, DC 20500

Dear President Obama;   20/Jan/09

    Hello, my name is Michael P. Powers, and I was born in Waukegan, Illinois on July 4, 1954...Enclosed is a picture of my father, and I have carried it for almost 30 years now...His name was Benjamin Maurice Powers Sr. and like me he was born in Waukegan, Illinois on April 1, 1929...Now the reason I have sent you this picture of my father,(You may keep it if you like), is that he smoked 3 packs of cigarettes a day, and on August 21, 1979 at the age of 50 he died from smoking 3 packs a day...I was 25 years old at the time, and since than their has been roughly about one million times that I wanted, and needed to talk to him...I remember watching you on TV in Grant Park when you won, as you walked out I heard one of your daughters almost scream,"Hi Daddy" and at that moment I missed my father more than I think I ever have, because I did the same thing when I was a kid, and he would get home from work...He was and always will be my best friend... If you always want to be there for your girls, than stop smoking NOW! Someday they are going to need you for something,(we all do need our parents for something at sometime or another), and I want you to be there for them, and also I think The United States, and the World need you now more than ever, and I want you to be there for all of us...I just know you are going to do a knockout job for the next eight years, so like Red Skeleton used to say,"Good day and May God Bless"...

                                                   Sincerely, Your Friend

                                                   Michael P. Powers

THE WHITE HOUSE

Michael —

Thank so much for the wonderful
letter, and the good advice. I am
returning the picture, since it must be
important to you, but I will remember
your dad's memory.

Barack Obama

From: Ali Hazzah
Hobe Sound, Florida
September 16, 2009

I lost my job in 2001, after the tech meltdown. Was a senior IT manager for an Internet company in NY that went belly up. I applied to hundreds of jobs, after this disastrous event - nothing. I was never able to get a full time job, I guess due to my age (I am now 58), but got by on my considerable savings, and some minor real estate transactions. Of course I hade to take out private insurance. I was assured by the sales agent that rates rarely went up. Since 2001, my insurance premiums have gone up exactly one hundred per cent - and i have never had a serious illness of any sort. In the last 8 years, I have paid almost ONE HUNDRED THOUSAND DOLLARS in insurance premiums, for my wife and I, to Blue Cross Blue Shield of Florida. I believed in then Senator Obama, when he said it was time for a change, that yes, he could be the one we could believe in to change things. I was one of the few where I live who put up Obama/Biden election signs (at my own expense, and at some personal risk from Republican goons, who tore them down every night) up and down US1 and did other things (such as contributing $100 to the Senator;s campaign, and working with the local democratic party) to help him get elected - this in a conservative, often bigoted, religion-obsessed county, a place where Rush Limbaugh is actually taken seriously by many. Three month ago, my wife had to have minor arm surgery. Our insurance premium immediately went up 30 per cent, and this is the first claim we have ever put in. I now have to make do without insurance - I can longer afford it - and I am, I repeat, 58 years old, not exactly in my prime. But I guess people like my wife and I dont really matter to you, President Obama, or the rest of the Washington crowd; we are just disposable, powerless losers who will be forced to go through everything we own before we can one day qualify for Medicaid. Thank you, Mr. Obama, thank you so much for reminding me what Washington is really about, and how much my wife and I mean to you. I just have one question: how could you put aside what your own mother had to go through? Sorry for taking up your time. After all, I am nothing but a disposable old fool in your world, right? Good luck getting our vote next time around. I am even going to vote Green or sit out the midterm elections to teach you and your cynical coterie of advisers a very very small lesson about keeping one's promises. You betrayed me, Sir: shame on you. I will never forget it.

THE WHITE HOUSE
WASHINGTON

Dear Ali —

Thanks for your letter. I confess I was confused
by the anger directed at the Administration, since
we are working every day to get a strong health care
bill passed. Of course I wish it would come
quickly, but change is never easy.
And I am convinced we will get
it done before the end of the year.

Dear Mr. President,

I was watching your State of the Union address a few nights ago on television. There was a part in your speech where you alluded to the many letters you receive from people throughout the United States. I'm writing because I thought that you might somehow get to read mine.

I am a 21 year old college senior at East Stroudsburg University of Pennsylvania majoring in elementary education. My home is farther South, in the small town of Walnutport. That is where I reside with my family when I am not living at school. My father is in his fifties and has been laid-off from his job as a union construction laborer for many months. He is receiving some money through unemployment, but not nearly as much as he would receive if there were a job available to him. My mother is in her late forties and has a job in a screen printing factory. Her hours are cut frequently without notice. My 18 year old brother graduated from high school last year and has opted to work two jobs, one at a local grocery store, and the other at UPS. I recently had to take a few months off of my jobs as a swim coach for two teams to ensure that I can put all of my energy into student teaching.

The reason I am writing to you is to ask for some advice. I want to help my family. We are lower middle class and very hard-working, especially

my mother and father. We are certainly not
at the top of the food chain, but we have always
been thankful for the things that we do have,
knowing there are others with larger needs.
My father is used to experiencing temporary
lay-offs, as it is typical of the construction
industry. Because of that, we have always been
an efficient and frugal family. We've also been
able to make it through past financial hardships
by sticking together and waiting patiently for
things to get better. But I'm starting to really
worry. My parents have always kept their concerns
hidden by telling my brother and me that they
were the adults and there were not problems
for us to worry about. Well, I am an adult
now, so I have a decent idea of what our status is.

Throughout my life, my father has always been
positive about everything. He works incredibly hard
and is very good at what he does. But since he has
been out of work for so long, I can see a marked
change. It is mainly in his eyes. They seem much
more sullen. He does not laugh nearly as much. He
seems smaller somehow. I can tell by the way he
acts that he feels responsible for all of our current
worries. Will my mom have enough gas to make it to
work? Which car will break down this week that he
will need to fix? Out of all of the important bills,
which is most important to be paid first? How
long until his benefits run out? What if one of
us gets sick? What groceries will we be able to
afford this week? Will he have a pension when he
is finally able to retire? The list goes on and on.

I can see it all eating away at him. He can't sleep. And I wonder... if even he is starting to break, what can the rest of us do?

And my mom, she tries hard as well. She stayed home with my brother and me for most of our lives because her job couldn't pay for child care, and she hated the idea of strangers raising us. She went back to work a few years ago. Now, after getting sent home early due to lack of work, I've seen her come inside, a long while after hearing her car park, only to enter the house with red eyes from the tears she just cried to herself in the car.

Please don't get the impression that I am searching for an apology or pity. Those things are never necessary or useful, and there are others who are far worse off than I can imagine. I know action is the only way we can move forward. But I feel so insignificant and helpless. I don't know what I can say or do to help my family. I know the usual answer, "Just wait, things will get better." I have to be honest though, I don't know how much longer we can wait. I don't know how much longer I can bear to look into my father's eyes and see the deep-seeded sadness that has replaced his positive demeanor and posture. I don't know how much longer I can watch them be told to "just wait, it will be OK," just to see their hopes be smashed again and again. I don't know how much longer I can listen to the subtle note of defeat that is invading my mother's words. And I don't know how much longer I can deal with the guilt of putting additional financial strain on my family by trying to be the first of us to attend and graduate college. And now, I am realizing that the chances of me being able to get an honest job as a teacher is more like a fairy tale than a reality.

I guess the advice I am searching for is "What do I do?" I know that as the president, you have a lot of expectations placed on you. A lot of the things that people are expecting of you are not even things you have direct control over. I also understand that all of the things contributing to our country's problems will not and cannot be fixed overnight, or even over four years. It's not your job to respond to me, or even to read this letter. But for some reason, I felt that I needed to try. Maybe my mind finds comfort in the fact that I took some sort of an action.

Anyway, I don't care about having enough money to buy a new car, or a laptop, or a smartphone. I just want to be able to walk back into my home and see my mom smile the way she used to, or hear my dad laugh without it sounding like it is coming from someone else. I miss that more than anything.

Name withheld
Walnutport, Pennsylvania
March 17, 2010

Ellen F. Crain, MD, PhD
Professor, Pediatrics and
Emergency Medicine
Network Director,

Reply.

January 23, 2009

The Honorable Barack H. Obama
President of the United States
The White House
1600 Pennsylvania Avenue NW
Washington, D.C. 20500

Dear President Obama:

I want to share with you a story from our pediatric emergency department which demonstrates the impact of your Presidency on our young people in a way that might not otherwise be apparent. Both the patient and her mother have given me permission to share this story with you as well as their names and address.

On January 21, 13-year-old _____ was brought to our pediatric emergency room by her mother, _____, after being punched in the face by other youths on her way home from school. She had two lacerations just below her right eye that needed suturing, but she was crying and trembling so much that we couldn't treat the wounds without risking injury to her eye. Nothing anyone said could calm her down. Then I asked if she had watched the inauguration and President Obama's speech. She said yes, and I asked her, "What would President Obama want us to do right now?" She replied, "He would want us to do what we have to do and do our best." She took a deep breath and became still, and we were able to successfully and close her wounds. I told her President Obama would be very proud of her, and she beamed. I know she would treasure a communication from your office. Her address is below:

Ms. _____

More impressive than the many remarks we heard from citizens about your inauguration's meaning to them was to see how your election and inaugural remarks could give a young person the strength to successfully deal with a personally frightening situation.

Sincerely,

Ellen F. Crain, MD, PhD
Medical Director,

THE WHITE HOUSE
WASHINGTON

Your doctor, Ellen Crain, told me about your recent difficulty. I'm proud of how you handled things, and have confidence you will do great things in the future.
Be well!

MAR 17 2009

THE WHITE HOUSE

WASHINGTON

Dr. Crain —

Thanks for the note. I wrote to Ms. ████, and appreciate your interest!

[signature]

Dr. Ellen F. Crain
Medical Director

MAR 17 2009

11/25/09
MC

Reply

Support 2

Kenny Jops

Chicago, IL

Dear President Obama,

I heard that you are good at correcting homework.
I was wondering if you could take a look at
this (particularly the highlighted portion on the
back). How did I do?

Thank you,
Kenny Jops, Beaubien School
Chicago, IL

Kenny Jones

-wants you to look
at his homework

Send back with the
vocabulary list.

Kenny Jops
Beaubien

Vocab Lesson 2

1	dubious	c	d	precariously	c
2	vacillate	a	c	qualms	c
3	qualm	d	b	conclusively	a
4	precarious	d	c	unequivocally	b
5	indeterminate	b	d	apprehensiveness	d
6	apprehensive	c	b	tentatively	c
7	tentative	a	b	categorically	d
→ 8	categorial	d	d	dubiously	d
→ 9	unequivical	d	c	indeterminate	c
10	conclusive	b	b	vacillation	a
11		c	F		
12			T		
13			T		

- apprehensive, anxious, uneasy. Bill was apprehensive about sky diving.
- categorial, absolute. Her categorial boycott of Cheese Flavored Cheese Snacks left her yearning for cheese.
- conclusive, decisive, ending uncertainty. His colclusive report on cells changed the science world.
- dubious, unsure. This report left no one dubious.
- indeterminate, vague. Even slightly indeterminate statements made by the president seemed to fascinate FOX news.
- precarious, This puts Obama in a precarious position. ⤶ dangerous.
- qualm, a sense of doubt. He is probably in a qualm as to why this is happening.
- tentative, uncertain or provisional. FOX is probably tentative as to what to do when he makes good decisions.
- unequivocal, perfectly clear. Some believe that it is unequivocal that during this scenario FOX will run around like a headless chicken and scream death panels.
- vacillate, to switch opinions. They always seem to vacillate drastically so as to disagree with him.

THE WHITE HOUSE

WASHINGTON

Kenny —
Nice job on the homework. I caught only two words misspelled on the vocabulary list. Dream big dream.

COPY FROM
ORM

Kenny Jops

Chicago, Illinois

✳ Encl. Original homework
    vocab list.

DEC 14

June M. Lipsky

East Meadow, NY

March 4, 2009

Dear President Obama:

I have not been able to contain myself over the news I have been hearing in the last few days.

I voted for you in the last election and I was very excited about the change you promised. I watched the presidential debates. I remember hearing you say that you would stop the special pork that has plagued every bill passed in Washington for the last several years. I remember you saying that your presidency will be marked by putting an end to special interest groups. I was so excited about the prospect of these changes.

Newsday reported this week that Lobbyists are gearing themselves to help special groups to seek the distribution of the billions of dollars that the Stimulus Package and the Proposed Budget make available contrary to what you promised for CHANGE.

You have nominated and sworn individuals who have been part of the problem in Washington for many years, and while you indicated in your speeches before being elected that you will CHANGE. It sounds like more of the same.

I am a Democrat and I have always voted with the Democratic Party. I am a regular citizen, part of the middle class. I have worked all of my life, living within my means. Never collected unemployment insurance, never applied for Medicaid, never asked for financial assistance. My mortgage is paid off. I have been saving regularly for my retirement and invested to have a comfortable retirement.

I hear that your program will serve the needs of many taxpayers that earn less than $250,000, that I will receive a sum of money $800 if I remember correctly.

Frankly, I am very disappointed. The $800 will hardly do me any good. You have provided bail out money for large companies who have a history of failing, continue to fail, and you continue to bail them out. Typically the automobile manufacturers, the insurance companies like AIG, the banks, who by the way are licensed to steal money from hard working folk like myself.

If my business had failed, I would have gone bankrupt without credit and without a helping hand such as the one your government is providing these large companies.

03/04/09 WED 10:31 FAX   EPILEPSY

Where is the fairness?. I have lived within my means all of my life. I sent my children to
school without public assistance, paid my taxes and penalties when required.
In the meanwhile some of the people you appointed are known to have failed to pay their
fair share. Even in Congress, Mr. Rangel, head of the Ways and Means Committee has
been accused of failing to pay his fair share among other pending accusations that the
Ethics committee has failed to investigate. Yet, Mr. Rangel continues to serve.

How would you like me to react when I see that manufacturers, banks, insurance
companies, and individuals who have acted irresponsibly are being rewarded while
people like me are not reaping the reward of having acted responsibly.

Is this what our sense of justice is?

Thieves such as Bernard Madoff, who have been indicted for stealing 50 billion dollars
from hard working folk as well as rich companies, pension plans, rich individuals,
retirees, has the gall of requesting that 62 million dollars in his wife's name not be used
to compensate the victims of his fraud. Where did a middle class person from Laurelton,
Queens, NY get to accumulate such vast sum of money? Now he wants his wife to
keep the reward of this Ponzi scheme to keep it while he serves out his time in jail? How
do you expect honest working people to feel when we see so much injustice being
committed.

No, Mr. President it is not about republicans or democrats, it is about fairness. We the
middle class have been denied the opportunities by previous administrations. We have
been holding the bag while banks and powerful politicians in Washington continue to
steal our hopes and dreams.

You, Mrs. Pelosi and Mr. Reed are not really trying to work in a bipartisan way, and in
the process we the hard working middle class is paying for your vendetta against each
other.

Mr. President, it is time to stop the bickering. Your stimulus package and your present
budget proposal have violated the promises you have made during the presidential
debates and continue to reward a sector of society that hardly contributes to the wealth of
this nation.

Wall Street is reacting to the insecurity exhibited by your appointees and by your failure
to keep your promises. If you want us to trust you, you must keep the promises you made.
You are serving the same interests you spoke against during the presidential campaign,
and like in the past, went the same as many other politicians. This, for the Americans is a
policy of NO CHANGE!

Like always, in Washington business is as usual, and so far you have not CHANGED
anything. Please restore the faith and trust I put in you when I voted for you in

November. When I argued with my friends and yes, even my father and my children, that things would be different if you got into office. So far, they were right and I was wrong. Nothing has changed.

Sincerely,

June M. Lipsky

THE WHITE HOUSE
WASHINGTON

June —

Thanks for the letter. Please know that the only thing I spend my days thinking about is how to help hard-working Americans like you. I share your outrage about the big banks, and the only reason we are helping them is to make sure that the whole banking system doesn't collapse and result in even more hardship for ordinary Americans.

As for as keeping promises, the budget I've outlined only gives tax breaks to middle class folks, and moves us in the direction of health care reform and energy independence. That's what I campaigned on, and that's what I intend to deliver.

I understand your frustrations; I'm frustrated too. But don't give up hope — we will get this done!

Sincerely,

[signature]

Ms. June M. Lipsky

East Meadow, New York

MAR 17 2009

MK

1.28.2009   Reply

Dear President Obama,

 I am in 6 graid, I am a girl, I am elevin years old, I am the only child.

I live with my mom in ▮▮▮▮▮ and my dad livs in ▮▮▮▮▮

I am a artist, I draw cartoons. my dad werks on the boats, and my mom werks at the marina. somtimes I pick up trash at the beach.

my contry is the u.s.a, and its fine. my contry is grait be cawse we all are safe, my contry is beautiful, we all runto the beatch and pick up sheals, I run to the beatch with my dog rozi. I want to cainch my contry into...somthing thats in the future in 3001.

me and my mom are homeless. I want a circle house with a bedroom upstears, my mom and me would live thear. the kitchen is supposed to be big. the house neads to be in the forest near a big lake.

ail, see you laiter!

sincerely.

E▮▮▮▮

THE WHITE HOUSE
WASHINGTON

E▓▓▓ —

Thanks for the beautiful letter, and the great
cartoons!
   I will be working hard so that all families
have a nice place to live, and I will keep you
and your family close to my heart.

8/9/2009

Subject: Health Care

Dear President Obama -

I am very concerned about what I am hearing about your new Health Care Plan. My wife and I care for our only child, an 8 yr. old boy, Mason, who has a form of muscular dystrophy is wheelchair bound, ventilator dependent and feeds through a g-tube. Needless to say he is a very happy little boy and the love of our lives. I work full time and am blessed to have health insurance through my employer. This insurance pays for all of our sons care and the medical equipment we use in the home. Our son requires in home nursing care which is also covered by our health insurances and MediCal. My recent concerns are rumors that I am hearing about our proposed health care plan that would no longer allow children like my son to be cared for in our home and lead to he and children like him being institutionalized in order to contain health care costs. Please help me to alleviate these concerns. I have faith in you as our President and truly appreciate all you do.

Thank you,

Scott, Staceyanne & Mason Fontana

Chico, CA

THE WHITE HOUSE

WASHINGTON

Scott, Stacey anne & Mason —

Thank for your note. I promise — nothing in our health care plan would take away Mason's care. In fact, we are trying to strengthen the system so care will always be there for him.

ample/Hardship

10/29/09
MK

Mr. Barrack Obama
The President
The White House

September 25, 2009

Reply

Dear Mr. President:

Congratulations on your election. It has been very interesting to watch your
Administration grow and move forward. I am writing to you today as a concerned citizen
from middle class America, because I know I am not alone and I want to enlighten you to
what happens in the real world to people who have been working hard to see this country
prosper.

Three years ago, my family was living a comfortable life. We had a home, cars, a boat,
and were able to pay our bills and still provide the little things for our two growing boys.
Then my husband lost his job. While he finally found employment in January 2008, it is
at about one third of his previous earnings.

We began to fall behind on our bills and I was forced to draw from my retirement and
credit to keep us afloat. All the while, my husband, a highly successful salesperson, was
trying to get a job and couldn't even get an interview with a local discount store. To make
a long story short, after about a year and a half struggle, the repossessions of a vehicle
and a boat, and numerous attempts asking for help from our Mortgage Holder, we lost
our home in March of this year. We were too late for your help as much as we desperately
wanted it.

So, now we are in a rental unit. We are living paycheck to paycheck. Trying to stay afloat
in that two year time frame cost me $80,000 out of my retirement and approximately
$200,000.00 of debt and credit card debts we incurred through
that period. Now we can barely pay to put food on our table or clothes on our kids for
school. We need to file bankruptcy—it is the only solution. The problem is we cannot file
for Bankruptcy protection without $2000.00 to pay for it. If we were able to file, we
could make it and start again, but there is no money to file and we have run out of
options for loans.

Mr. President, I make a good living and I have been at my job for 14 years. While my
husband's income trickles in we have to live off an income that was never designed to be
the main income. I just am at a loss as to what to do. We are not buying extras—no new
clothes for me in two years, not eating out, and no extra amusements for the kids- and
yet we cannot get a leg up. I know there are people out there in worse shape. Recently,
when I called the power company for help paying a past due bill to keep the power on at
my home, I was directed to a number of charities to ask them for help. I could not bring
myself to do it, knowing I make a lot more than most people.

We are not the only people in this situation. We are willing to accept responsibility for
our actions and take the hit of filing bankruptcy, but we can't afford to do that and keep a
roof over our head, so it seems like a catch 22. I cannot sleep and have developed
medical conditions over this. I live in constant fear every morning of waking up to find
all the money in my checking account—what little there is—gone from a garnishment
from which I cannot defend myself.

After all this, I have a very important question to ask you: What does a person who is trying to recover in this economy supposed to do when they can barely afford to pay their bills and need to file bankruptcy, but they cannot afford to do it? I am not condoning bankruptcy, but it is the only solution for us. Where do we go for help? We did nothing wrong and tried to make good on our obligations, but no one will help us. My husband was even fortunate enough to find some work, but it just isn't enough.

My 13 year old son asked me to write to you. He asked me why you won't do anything to help people who are struggling like us. What do I say to him Mr. President? When he cannot have the new school clothes he needs and I have to explain to him that we cannot afford what we used to take for granted, what do I tell him? No child should worry about money or offer to find a way to work to help his family. But, at 13, he is well aware of the stresses on our family despite our efforts to shield him. How do I prove to him that you are the person and lead an administration that will help us?

I am very interested in your reply. My guess is you will never see this letter and some staffer will respond on some form letter. But, I am trying to show my son that our leaders are hearing our pain and responding. You probably have no way to help us either—I have pretty much given up hope and just hope I don't lose my job because I am in financial danger---you see, I work for Bank of America where associates are held to higher standards and cannot even receive help with Overdraft fees because we should know better. They also hold the second mortgage note that we had to default on, so I just hope I can keep my job. The stress never stops   I just pray a lot and hug my kids a lot and hope we can have a roof over our heads as winter comes.

Thanks for taking the time to read the rambling of a frustrated and scared citizen. I know you have bigger and better fish to fry. If I get a reply I will make sure my son knows it. It is important for kids to respect the President and to know he cares.

I would like to leave you with a quote of inspiration as you plow through the many issues you deal with each day, as it sometimes gets me through my day, "A river cuts through rock, not because of its power, but because of its persistence." (Jim Watkins).

God Bless you and America

COPY FROM
ORM

THE WHITE HOUSE
WASHINGTON

Dear

I know how tough things are, and I am doing everything in my power to speed up the recovery. The economy took a big hit from the financial crisis, but the steps we have taken have halted the slide into Depression, and I'm confident that if we persist, your family and the country will see brighter days!

God Bless,

CHAPTER 3

The Mailroom

Fiona was an old lady with a beehive hairdo, tiny glasses at the end of a drooping chain resting on a magnificent bosom, and a bulbous chin sprouting random whiskers that shook as she barked, "No trespassing!" through a brass mail slot from which only darkness and the musty smell of mold spores could be detected.

Or something like that. In my mind I had Fiona out to be a menacing gatekeeper, and so I felt somewhat cheated when she appeared as a perfectly pleasant young woman, early thirties; she had a delicate stature, absorbing dark blue eyes, and the precise diction of a literature professor.

"We will begin with a tour," she said upon welcoming me at the White House security gate on a cool autumn morning. In emails she had said I would have to agree to certain terms before I would be allowed into the mailroom. These mostly had to do with understandable privacy concerns—I couldn't disclose the contents of any letter I read unless it was cleared with its author—but the fortitude with which she announced the rules made the larger point: Fiona cared deeply about people who wrote letters to the president.

It would be some time before I would appreciate the astonishing fullness of Fiona's zeal.

She led me to the loading dock of the Eisenhower Executive Office Building or "EEOB," as people called it, a massive block-long structure that never seems to appear in press photos or cable news backdrops when they show the White House. Which is strange because it's so hard to miss. The EEOB sits just steps away from the door to the West Wing. It's an annex of the most extreme variety, a humongous creation with dramatic pavilions, ornate crestings, elaborate chimney stacks—architecture so exuberant that when it was built back in the late nineteenth century, a lot of people complained that it looked like a big cake. Mark Twain said it was the ugliest building in America; historian Henry Adams called it an "architectural infant asylum." This went on for a while—Truman would later call it "the greatest monstrosity in America"—and its architect, Alfred B. Mullett, would end up killing himself. Nowadays, people take the EEOB for granted, like you would any big old awesome courthouse in a midsize city. It houses more than five hundred government offices, everything from the National Security Council headquarters to the Secret Service locker rooms to the vice president's ceremonial office.

The mailroom was on the ground floor, just off the loading dock. The door says, "Office of Presidential Correspondence." If you send a letter to the president, it ends up here—after having first been screened off-site, at some secret location, to make sure it doesn't contain anything that would blow up or poison people. "So it arrives already opened, flat, the envelope stapled to the back," Fiona told me as she opened the door to an office they called the "hard-mail room." It was a sprawling space that had the tired, unkempt look of a college study hall during finals—paper everywhere, files stacked along walls, bundles under tables, boxes propping up computer monitors dotted with Post-its, cables hanging. Hushed young men in ties and hushed young women in sweater sets and hose—you dress up if you work for the White House—held pencils between their teeth or behind their ears, most of them with their heads bent, reading. There was an equally crowded work space, "the email room," in a satellite office just outside the White House gates on Jackson Place. In total, the Office of Presidential Correspondence—"OPC" was what everyone called it—required the orchestration of fifty staff members, thirty-six interns, and a rotating roster of three hundred volunteers to keep up with about ten thousand letters and messages every day. As the director of the entire operation, Fiona was the one who kept it all humming along.

"Why don't you sit down and read?" she said. It felt more like a command than a question. Ten interns were crowded around two long tables, but there was an extra seat.

Grab a bundle, sit down, and read. It was pretty straightforward: Read.

A girl doesn't want her mom to be deported, and can the president please help? A guy finally admits to his wife that he's gay, and now he would like to tell the president. A car dealer writes to say his bank is shutting him down, and thanks for nothing, Mr. President. A vet who can't stop seeing what he saw in Iraq writes a barely intelligible rant that makes his point all the more intelligible: "Help." An inmate admits to selling crack, but he wants the president to know he is not a lost cause: "I have dreams Mr. President, big dreams." A man can't find a job. A woman can't find a job. A teacher with advanced certification can't find a damn job. A lesbian couple just got married; thank you, Mr. President. A man sends his medical bills; a woman sends her student-loan statements; a child sends her drawing of a cat; a mother sends her teenager's report card—straight As, isn't that awesome, Mr. President?

Dear Mr. President,

. . . YOU, sir, are the PRESIDENT of the United States. YOU, sir, are the one person that IS supposed to HELP the LITTLE PEOPLE like my family and others like us. We are the ones that make this country what it is. You say that jobs are up and spending is up. YOU, sir, need to come to my neck of the woods and see how wrong that is. Because here in Spotsylvania County, it's not. I live in Partlow, a rural community of Spotsylvania, and I tell you what . . . jobs are few and far between. My husband and I just want to be able to live and be able to buy a cake or a present for our kids when it's their birthday or for Christmas. That's another thing—my boys didn't even have a Christmas because we did not have money to buy them

presents. Have YOU ever had to tell your girls that Santa isn't com-
ing to your house? . . .

Sincerely,
Bethany Kern
Partlow, Va.

This pile, that pile, another pile over there; pull from the middle if
you want. The narrative was sloppy and urgent, America talking all
at once. No filter. The handwriting, the ink, the choice of letterhead—
every letter was a real object from a real person, and now you were
holding it, and so now you were responsible for it.

Mr. President,

*My wife and I very recently lost our 22-year-old son, David Jr. He
took his life with a handgun that he purchased. Our son was precious to us. He could have done anything he chose to do.*

*I am writing because our son was suffering from mental illness yet
still was able to purchase a gun. He had been involuntarily hospital-
ized when he was 17, yet Pennsylvania allows people with this on
their record to purchase a gun.*

*The sadness we are feeling is overwhelming us. We are trying to be
strong for our other three sons, but we are breaking down every
day. . . .*

Thank you.
David Costello
Philadelphia

"You'll need a pencil," said a woman seated next to me. She looked
like an intern, but it turned out she was one of Fiona's deputies,
Yena Bae. She was in her midtwenties, and there was a lightness to
her, a welcoming glow, like your first kindergarten teacher. I noticed
Fiona had disappeared; apparently she had passed me off to Yena.

There would be a whole lot of orchestration like that going on during all my time at the White House, somebody always keeping watch.

On a whiteboard at the far end of the room was the countdown: "You have 99 days to make a difference in the life of a letter writer," someone had written, referring to January 19, 2017, the last full day of the Obama administration and the last day for this OPC staff, nearly all of whom were political appointees and would no longer have a job at the White House when the new administration took office. The election was less than a month away. "Our time is, like, ticking," Yena told me. "We want to put our letter writers in good shape for the next administration. We want them to be in good hands.

"Team little people," she said. "That's what we call ourselves." She said the mailroom might seem like the least prestigious place to work in the White House, yet the ethos here was that it held a kind of secret superpower. "You'll see."

Ten letters from this room would, after all, land on the president's desk that night. Part of the work of the mailroom staff was to sift through the thousands of letters that had just come in that morning and pick which ten Obama should see.

"The 10LADs," Yena said, handing me a pencil.

"You have to code," one of the interns said.

The first task in the hard-mail room was to code each letter with a "disposition" on the top left corner (in pencil). What was the person writing about? Gun Violence, Healthcare, Drone Strikes, Domestic Violence, Ukraine, Taxes. Put your initials under the code. Code a stack, then stand to stretch your neck and your legs and take your stack over to "the wall," a tan shelving unit stuffed with paper, shelf after shelf labeled with corresponding dispositions. Gitmo, Mortgage Crisis, Immigration, Bees. (*Bees?*) The codes corresponded to more than a hundred different form-response letters from the president that the OPC writing team, a group of nine, worked to constantly update. In the meantime, all the letters from kids went into a separate bin to be picked up by the kid team upstairs; requests for birthday, anniversary, and baby acknowledgments went to the greetings team; gifts went to the gifts team. A casework team of six across the hall handled letters that required individual attention from a federal agency. Maybe someone needed help getting benefits from the Department of Veterans Affairs, for example; a caseworker could step in and investigate. There were a few more codes to be aware of. Sensitive meant someone was writing to the president about a loss, a sickness, or other personal trauma. Those went over to Jack Cumming, a quiet guy in beige who spent his days reading letter after letter about small and large tragedies suffered by strangers across the country and who often needed a break from the unbearable sadness, and so he liked to hang out in the hard-mail room. "It's nice to come in here and just . . . read," he said.

A lot of people who worked in OPC would tell me that. The hard-mail room was where you went when the rest of your job got difficult, or annoying, or boring. It had a way of re-centering you, reminding you why you were here. Sit down and read. The bins were never empty. America had a lot to say, and without you, there would be no one to listen.

Interns in the hard-mail room were expected to get through three hundred letters a day, and this group had learned to move quickly, everybody scribbling on the corners, distributing into piles.

I told Yena I was still stuck on the first one I'd picked up. A guy in Colorado. He had some problems with heroin. He was writing to the president to say he'd gotten clean.

"Yeah, we get those," Yena said.

He relapsed. He was not comfortable with his own sexuality. His father died. He contemplated suicide. His mom never gave up on him. It was a long letter. The deeper I got into it, the more uncomfortable I felt reading it, as if I were intruding on a private friendship.

"He got clean again," I told Yena. I looked at the stack of letters she had to get through and the piles in front of all the others reading. Were all the letters going to be like this?

"If you want to, you can just go ahead and sample that one," Yena said.

"Sample" was shorthand for: Put the letter in the pile for consideration to be included in the 10LADs, the ten letters that would go to Obama that evening.

I thought about Obama reading about this guy's heroin problem. Should he? Who was I to say? Who were any of these people to say?

"You just write 'Sample' on it," Yena said when I asked her how to sample a letter. You wrote it on the top left corner. In pencil. Small print. (Respect the letter.) You then took it and dropped it in the wooden inbox with a sticker on it that said, "Samples." Fiona would collect them at the end of the day, sift through, and decide. About 2 percent of the total incoming mail, two or three hundred letters a day, ended up in the sample bin.

I tapped my pencil, looked at the letter again. It was typed. The grammar was precise. The guy seemed to have put a lot of time into it. He said he'd been meaning to write for a long time but had wanted to wait until the time was right. He wanted Obama to know he'd been sober a year. Which was great. But did Obama need to know that? Did this stand for something larger? Was someone going to have to prepare a brief asking for more funds for the opioid addiction crisis or something to go along with this letter?

"Don't overthink it," Yena said.

She told me that Fiona kept the bar deliberately low. Does the letter move you in some particular way? Don't overthink it. Sample it. These were *people* writing, and you were a *person* reading, and the president was a *person*. "Just keep remembering that, and you'll be fine," Yena said.

Dear President Obama,

. . . I am an undocumented immigrant. I came to the United States when I was 14 years old. . . . In my mind I am as American as it comes. I still have my first pair of Air Jordans. There are very few pop cultural references I do not understand.

. . . I did not become aware of my status until I was finishing up college and had gotten accepted to medical school and realized I did not qualify for funding.

. . . Until recently with the passing of the Deferred Action for Childhood Arrivals I basically walked on eggshells every day and truly was not sure how safe I was or what path my life would follow. . . .

I would like to say although I did not vote for you . . . mainly because I could not . . . I feel like you voted for me with DACA and all your efforts with the DREAM act. Thank you.

Sincerely yours,
Dare Adewumi, M.D.
Redlands, California

"You get attached," the intern sitting next to me said. Her name was Jamira. She had her hair bundled tightly on top of her head and wore a pretty print top. She said that one time she had opened a letter from a woman who was writing the president to say she had lost a family member to gun violence. "She had enclosed photos. Just blood all over in a car . . ." She tapped her eraser on the table, up and down on the table.

"Everybody has that one letter," Yena said. Letters could take a toll. Unlike most other shops at the White House, OPC offered monthly counseling sessions to anyone who felt the need.

The most important code everyone needed to know about was Red Dot. Red Dots were emergencies. These were from people writing to the president to say they wanted to kill themselves or someone else, or they seemed in some way on the edge. You wrote "Red Dot" on the top of the letter if you got one of those, and then you immediately walked it across the hall and gave it to Lacey Higley, the woman in the back corner more or less in charge of rescuing people.

"Do you need a break?" Yena asked me. "Do you need cookies? We have cookies." She reached for a tub of oatmeal-raisins and slid it over.

I asked her if she had ever red-dotted a letter.

"Oh my," she said. Some two hundred letters a day were red-dotted.

I asked her if she had a letter like Jamira's, one that haunted her.

"It was an email from a mother who missed her son," she said. She pushed her hair behind her ears as if having to prep herself for this one. She said in the email the mom explained that her son had been kidnapped overseas, and at the time the investigation was still under way. Yena read the letter a dozen times, stunned by details in it that, for reasons of OPC confidentiality—and national security—she could not reveal to me. "Everything was hush-hush." She alerted the authorities, then felt helpless because there was nothing more she could do. Weeks later, she was watching CNN, and that was how she learned the son had been killed. It was national news. It was an international incident, and his mom had reached out, and Yena had been on the receiving end of her desperate pleas. And now he was dead.

"I just lost it," she told me. "I sobbed and sobbed and sobbed." It was a Sunday. She came in to the office and sat at her computer. "What if his mom wrote again?" She told me the experience changed the direction of her life and her sense of her place in the world.

Jamira was leaning in to hear Yena tell the story of the mother and the lost son. She had put her pencil down. "It's weird. I'm going to go from this to being back at school," she said. "It's hard to explain all this to my friends."

"You can't," Yena said.

"I never thought about how powerful a letter was."

"Did you even know we had a correspondence office before you came here?" Yena asked her.

"I had no idea."

"You think you're going to be the mail lady or something."

"We're in the mailroom."

"The mailroom."

In the end I didn't sample the letter from the guy who had conquered his heroin problem; I didn't sample any of the ones I read, in part because I wanted to sample all of them and then got overwhelmed by the weight of the responsibility. I surrendered my stack, adding it back in the pile for reconsideration by the group. Later when I saw Fiona, I told her about the guy with the heroin and about some of the other letters I had read, and I wondered if there was something I could do to put my finger on the scale so that if any of them ended up in her daily sample pile, she would give them special attention when she sat down to pick the day's 10LADs.

I learned that pretty much everyone felt that way. You got attached. You became an advocate for your letter. And if yours got picked as one of the 10LADs, it would make your day. And if the president actually wrote back to the person, you felt high. And if something from one of your picks ended up in a speech or a policy decision, well, it was time to throw a party.

When Fiona interviewed people for jobs in OPC, one of the tests she had them do was writing their own letter to the president. Not for her to find out what they had to say. But so they got a chance to know what writing a letter to the president felt like.

The capacity to occupy a stranger's head and heart—that was the key competency needed to land a job in Fiona's mailroom.

Dear President Obama,   January 21, 2009

   My name is Thomas J. Meehan III, the father of Colleen Ann Meehan Barkow, age 26, who perished on September 11 2001 at the WTC. Colleen was an employee of Cantor-Fitzgerald, working on the 103rd Floor. Her upper torso was found September 17th, 2001, the date of her first wedding anniversary. In the days and months afterwards there were to be additional discoveries of her, a total of six, which still did not amount to a whole body, but was more than what some other families affected have been given back, Families still speak in terms of body parts found and not found, and what will never be found.

   In the past seven years, my wife and I have been committed to the issue of the ashen remains of those lost that day, which have been interred (bulldozed) into the 40 acres of land known as the Fresh Kills landfill on Staten Island, New York. For the one thousand families who did not receive any remains, this is the final resting place, an un-holy, un-consecrated landfill. The lives lost are there with garbage beneath them and construction fill above them, an unbefitting resting place for those we called heroes and took an oath never to forget.

While this issue has been before the courts, and the remains may in fact be permanently interred at the landfill, parents, spouses, siblings, extended family members must live with the knowledge that their loved ones lie in what was the world's largest dump. How we as a society will be judged in the treatment of those lost, only history will record.

   My wife and I mourn the continued loss of American lives in the war in Iraq and Afghanistan while we still await the apprehension and trial of those we hold responsible for the death of our daughter and almost 3000 other American and international citizens.

   While we understand the reasons for the closure of the detention facility at Guantanamo Bay, we urge you to allow the trials of those defendants charged in connection with the attacks of September 11, 2001, to go forward, and complete the judicial process and give some small measure of Justice to all of the 9/11 family members, while we still await the capture of Osama Bin Laden.

   Our lives have been forever changed by the events of September 11,2001, and yet life goes on, we now have two granddaughters, Brett Colleen ,age four an and Ryann Elizabeth, age two ,we hope that their lives will be in a better world that the one which claimed their aunt. And they will have the opportunities to live their lives to the fullest and live in a safer world, free of the threat of terrorism.

   I share these facts with you so that you will understand why these issues mean so much to us, and ask that you not forget the promise "Never To Forget", and will bring to justice those responsible for September 11, 2001.

God Bless You and You're Family,
May the Peace of the Lord Be Upon You and Remain With You,

Respectfully,
Thomas J. Meehan III & JoAnn Meehan
Thomas J. Meehan III & JoAnn Meehan

Toms River, New Jersey

CHAPTER 4

Thomas and JoAnn Meehan, January 21, 2009

TOMS RIVER, NEW JERSEY

Thomas Meehan started writing letters soon after the towers came down. He needed an outlet. One of the first letters he wrote was to the navy. He remembers this part so well. A lot of other things are fuzzy. He is seventy-four years old, and the main thing lately is to get everything recorded before his memory goes altogether south.

JoAnn, his wife, lets out a polite chuckle, as you do. But she knows it's true about Tom's memory. The stents, the tranquilizers, the strokes—they've taken a toll.

They're sitting at the dining room table on a hot July morning in their home in Toms River, New Jersey, not far from the ocean and the Pine Barrens. The little dog's name is Chewy. JoAnn has a piece of white marble from Tower 1 she would like to show you. It's from the floor of the lobby, a gift from first responders. "Always remember Colleen. Ground Zero. 9/11/01," they wrote on it. She also would like to show you a piece of window glass they gave her.

"Look how thick," she says. "Maybe an inch thick, for the air pressure."

"It's so thick," Tom says.

One time Colleen took them to watch the fireworks from her

floor. The 103rd floor. You would not believe the elevators. The time it took to get all the way up there. Three separate elevators.

"I was like, 'Where are we going, to heaven?'" JoAnn says.

The whole reason Colleen left college to work in New York was because she got to work in the World Trade Center. That's how JoAnn remembers it. ("Also a romance played a part.") JoAnn was not in favor of Colleen's quitting college; a straight-A student leaving school made no sense. But Colleen told her mother an opportunity like that might never come again. The company needed women. Colleen learned how to read blueprints when they sent her to Ohio to train, and they sent her to London a few times to learn design. She was young and in love and basking in the hustle-bustle. Her job was in facilities. She designed a cafeteria for the 103rd floor of Tower 1 so everyone didn't have to go all the way down all those elevators for lunch. She even made a smoking room with big fans sucking out the smoke. She was extremely proud of that cafeteria.

"We looked *down* at the fireworks," Tom recalls. "That was the whole point. We saw fireworks from the top down."

"The top down!" JoAnn says.

Colleen got married and her husband worked in the city too, and they bought a car. Some days they would drive together into work, and some days they would take the train. Fifty-fifty. If they took the train, they got in early, and if they took the car, they got in late.

So that whole crystal-blue Tuesday morning of September 11, 2001, with all the phones in the region down, and the electricity out in the Carteret, New Jersey, neighborhood where they lived then, and her one neighbor running down the street with that TV from her camper that ran on batteries, JoAnn was pacing on the porch saying, "Please tell me you took the car, please tell me you took the car, please tell me you took the car."

But Colleen had taken the train that day.

Seeing the footage on TV of the smoke, over and over the way they showed it—that alone drove a lot of the families into madness.

"A lot of people forget," Tom says.

The first seventy-two hours was calling hospitals. Nobody knew anything. Nobody had her. By the end of the week, it was evident that she was gone. JoAnn took off work at the school for three months after that. They were extremely understanding, and when she got back, they adapted her position to one-on-one assistance rather than teaching a whole class. She was having bleeding ulcers, and they would get exacerbated by the sight of turbans, which some people did wear at the school.

"Even though they were lovely, nice people," JoAnn says.

"They were Sikhs," Tom says.

"They had nothing to do with 9/11," she says. "Nothing whatsoever."

She would get violently ill when she saw turbans. It wasn't something you could put logic to.

They met other families. A lot of the conversation in the beginning was just about body parts. What you got back. One woman received part of her husband's scalp; the other received a testicle. Some people didn't get anything back; some got a finger. People might say it's gruesome to talk that way. But if it becomes part of your everyday . . . People who got body parts back felt lucky, and people who didn't kept hoping, and so the people who did felt guilt. When they found Colleen's torso, it was among the debris from the north side of the building. The cafeteria was on the north side.

"I think Colleen was in the cafeteria," JoAnn says.

Fresh Kills Landfill on Staten Island was full; it had been officially closed a few months before 9/11, but then the state reopened a section for the sorting of the Twin Tower rubble. Hills 1 and 9 where they did the sorting were adjacent to the neighborhood where Tom and JoAnn lived, just over the river. The mound was like fifty acres. They brought in conveyor belts. And the trucks started coming. For weeks after the attack, the trucks would keep Tom and JoAnn up at night, the engine roars, the backup beeps, the clumping sounds of dumping.

"And the seagulls would attack it, and they would move the body parts," JoAnn says.

"So they put up tents," Tom says.

"The machines would sift it and remove whatever they could, and what was left was bulldozed into the landfill," JoAnn says. "And then on top of that is the fill."

"Industrial."

"Construction fill. Computers. Computer parts. Wires. Concrete."

"I'm sure people would debate, why are you arguing about minuscule elements?" Tom says. "What we are really talking about are bone fragments less than a quarter inch. But for me it doesn't matter the size."

When the sifting was done and they closed Hills 1 and 9 as a crime scene, the people at the sanitation department who ran the landfill would let people in if they wanted to come look, which a lot of families still did. You signed a paper, and a guy would take you to the dump site in a garbage truck.

Eventually, they put up a flagpole.

JoAnn finished out her thirty years with the district, and then she and Tom moved down here to Toms River to be near Daryl and the grandbabies. Daryl is the oldest; then JoAnn had another son who survived only one day, and then she had Colleen. One time when Colleen was two, she was in her crib for a nap, and JoAnn was outside shoveling snow, and suddenly here comes Colleen, fully dressed in her snow gear, out to help.

"I was like, 'What are you doing!'" JoAnn says. "She put all that gear on and figured all that out by herself." Colleen always had pigtails. She would put everything in her mouth. Their house was the one all the kids came to. Sleeping all over the rec room. You never knew who you'd bump into.

Anyway, Tom would like to get back to the letter he wrote to the navy. He says he also wrote to President George W. Bush. Actually, that might have been before the navy.

"No, definitely after," JoAnn says.

It's such a jumble.

Tom wrote to President Bush in anger, asking why he had not sent a note of condolence about Colleen. He figured something like that should have come. Tom got a letter back from the White House explaining that New York kept the list of victims' names, not the White House.

Tom starts wheezing.

"Who was in charge was a big question in the aftermath," JoAnn says, adding that later they did get a sympathy card from Vice President Dick Cheney.

"We have it somewhere here," Tom says. Wheezing is a symptom of chronic obstructive pulmonary disease, which he has, along with diabetes. His computer and the Internet were the keys to his sanity in the aftermath. That was how he managed. He wrote so many letters. The letter to the navy was the first one, definitely among the first. This was, gosh, within days. He was angry and he wanted somebody to do something immediately to get the people who had done this. So he googled, you know, "navy." He picked a ship that was deployed in the Far East. He picked the USS *Carl Vinson,* and he found an email address, and he wrote about Colleen. Within weeks he heard back. Who expects to hear back? The email was from a lieutenant who talked about not forgetting the victims, and he included an attachment. Tom opened the attachment, and it was a photo of a guy in a flight suit leaning over a bomb. "LASER," it said on the bomb. The guy had a pen, and he was writing something on the nose. "COLLEEN ANN MEE—" He was working on the second *E.*

Tom would like to show you the picture.

The *Carl Vinson* had been headed east around the tip of India on September 11, 2001, when, in response to the attacks back home, it abruptly changed course and advanced toward the Arabian Sea. On October 11, 2001, it launched the bomb with Colleen's name on it, one among hundreds the navy dropped in the first air strikes over Afghanistan targeting al-Qaeda and the Taliban in support of Operation Enduring Freedom.

Tom puts the picture of the bomb away and then folds his hands like an obedient schoolboy. JoAnn thinks Chewy is being remarkably quiet. Usually he's bouncing off the walls by now. He's still a puppy.

At the landfill, investigators were able to identify just 300 people (2,753 died in the attacks) out of the 4,257 human remains they recovered. The rest, the remains of more than a thousand victims, have not been identified. "You remember seeing the funerals on television with all those caskets," JoAnn says. "But they were all empty. There was nothing in those caskets."

"People don't remember," Tom says.

People don't know about the way they just covered everything up when they were done. They did not consult the families. They just put dirt and construction debris on top. They did put that flagpole in.

"I know there are parts of my daughter there," JoAnn says.

Tom: "You can argue till doomsday about the legal rights, but the simple fact that they didn't acknowledge it to the families—"

The Ground Zero memorial is a love-hate thing for Tom and JoAnn. It took ten years and $700 million to build. You would think there would be resources set aside for asking the families what they wanted done with the remains of their loved ones. The Office of the Chief Medical Examiner in New York had more than eight thousand body parts they couldn't identify, couldn't complete the DNA on. Somehow the decision had been made to put the body parts in plastic pouches—and then put the pouches in the basement of the museum.

A museum is not a memorial site.

"It costs twenty-four dollars to get into the museum," Tom says.

"Families get in for free," JoAnn says.

"Families are allowed to look in the basement."

"You look through a glass wall. It's a storage facility. It's lockers in rows."

Tom and JoAnn got involved in a lot of activist things with the other families. They got involved with WTC Families for Proper Burial Inc. They got involved in public remembrances, and there were so many nice things people did. Quilts, presents, like this slab of marble and this piece of window from the first responders. In the first few months, Tom wore a badge with Colleen's picture on it. He was in a gift shop, and a woman saw the badge, and she bought him a glass angel in remembrance of Colleen. It's an example. There were poems people wrote. Jewelry people made. Rosaries. Pictures of Colleen people drew. A CD with a song someone wrote. The Flag of Remembrance. Mountains of gifts. "I could start my own mini-museum," JoAnn says. They had to rent a unit at one of those storage places. It's so nice what everyone did.

Every year on the anniversary they have a ceremony at Ground Zero, and they read out the name of every victim. There's a lottery to pick who gets to read. If you get picked, you read twenty names. One year Daryl got picked, and then JoAnn got picked. It's the highest honor to get picked. Now they're talking about doing away with the name reading.

Tom is particularly upset about that one. The whole issue with memory. Tom says there's a saying he's heard veterans use: People die twice. "Once when they leave their physical form and the second time when their name is spoken for the last time."

Now Chewy is acting more like himself. He's skittering around and around the table, and his feet are so tiny the pitter-patter sounds like rain.

"Okay, Chewy," Tom says.

JoAnn is stuck back on a few points she made earlier. "The thought of going to visit where your daughter is buried and you have to call the sanitation department to get an appointment to ride on a garbage truck," she says.

"The issue of the remains and all of that—it's the best kept secret of 9/11," Tom says. "So to speak."

"I do think Colleen was in the cafeteria," JoAnn says.

"People not directly involved in the event have a certain view from the outside of what the families have endured," Tom says.

One day here at the local library, they were putting together a little exhibit, and they asked Tom and JoAnn to contribute mementos of Colleen, and so Tom and JoAnn were arranging the items in the glass cabinet.

Two women walked by. *"Can't these people just get over it?"* the one said.

Clear as day. Tom was ready to pounce. JoAnn gave him the look that said, *Ignore it.*

Tom couldn't.

He came home and wrote a letter. Obama had just gotten elected, so he wrote to him. When he sat down, he thought about what he wanted to say to the new president, and it was the same thing he wanted to say to the lady in the library. In a way the letter was for both. For everybody. Tom wanted everybody to know some of what the families went through. He wanted to say the issue wasn't whether or not the families ever got over it. "The issue was that *you* don't get over it," Tom says.

"But I digress."

"Just the thought of, you have to ride on a garbage truck," JoAnn says.

JoAnn did the proofreading, and Tom mailed the letter, and they were surprised when they heard back just a few weeks later.

Tom would like to show you the letter they got back.

THE WHITE HOUSE
WASHINGTON

Dear Tom & JoAnn —

I am in receipt of your letter, and wanted to respond personally. Your story is heartbreaking, and we will do everything we can to ensure that the process of bringing all those involved in it is completed.

In the meantime, know that we will never forget Colleen, and that I spend every waking hour in search of ways to make the future brighter for your granddaughters and my daughters.

God Bless,

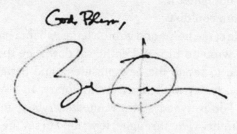

CHAPTER 5
The Idea

When I asked President Obama how he came up with the idea of reading ten letters a day, he thought a moment, then said, "Pete Rouse." He said it an offhand way, as if this was some easily recognized household name.

"Pete was almost maniacal about correspondence," he went on. "When I first got to the Senate, I was, you know, green behind the ears, and he had been there for a long time. He kind of instilled in me the sense of the power of mail.

"Pete Rouse," he said again.

I kept hearing the name in conversations about the early days of the Obama administration and the origins of its Office of Presidential Correspondence. Shailagh brought him up, and so did David Axelrod, Valerie Jarrett, and Fiona. "There are legions of people around my age who got their start in public service or politics by a conversation with Pete Rouse," Fiona said.

They all talked about him the same way—you know, *Pete!*—more or less disregarding my blank stare.

I came to learn that Pete Rouse was a guy who famously shunned publicity, who never did interviews, who worked hard to stay behind the scenes, and so even though insiders knew him as Obama's right-hand man who sat for years just two doors down from the Oval Office, to people outside the Beltway, he was a stranger.

"I'm not really good at anecdotes," Pete said when I visited him at the Perkins Coie offices in downtown Washington, where he'd worked since retiring from his White House post in 2014. "I don't remember a lot." Then he told me that although he now worked at a law firm, he was not a lawyer, and—he was quick to point out—he was most definitely *not* a lobbyist, and although people regularly asked him if he'd ever write a book about his many years in the White House and on Capitol Hill, "there is not a chance in hell I'll ever write a book."

I wondered about a person choosing to define himself by what he was not and never would be. He was in his early seventies, soft-spoken, amiable, with thick white hair, and he moved like his back hurt, which he volunteered readily that it did. We then veered effortlessly into a discussion of my brother's recent back surgery. I have no idea how we became so familiar so quickly, but within minutes we were talking like friends. Maybe this was why he didn't do interviews. He seemed to have neither guard nor guile.

I told him Obama said he was the one who'd had the idea that the president should read ten constituent letters a day.

"No," he said. "I give him credit for saying he wanted ten letters a day."

I said Obama seemed to think it all went back to him somehow.

"I don't want to sound arrogant," he said. He told me he first met Obama on the 2004 campaign trail. He had already worked in Congress for more than three decades, starting in the 1970s; he had become such a fixture in Washington that people on Capitol Hill referred to him as the "101st senator" during his long tenure as former Senate Majority Leader Tom Daschle's chief of staff. Daschle lost his seat in 2004, the same year Obama was voted into the Senate, leaving Pete, a Hill guru, out of a job. Obama asked Pete to come over to his team, become his chief of staff; Obama said he wanted to hit the ground running, and there was no one in Washington with the breadth of experience that Pete had.

"I said no," Pete told me. "I was in my late fifties. I thought I'd take retirement, do something else."

Obama asked Pete a second time. He wanted the A team. He felt the urgency of the moment, of living up to the expectations he had set when, at the 2004 Democratic National Convention in Boston, he delivered the speech that would catapult him into the national spotlight:

If there's a child on the South Side of Chicago who can't read, that matters to me, even if it's not my child.

If there's a senior citizen somewhere who can't pay for their prescription and having to choose between medicine and the rent, that makes my life poorer, even if it's not my grandparent.

If there's an Arab American family being rounded up without benefit of an attorney or due process, that threatens my civil liberties.

It is that fundamental belief—it is that fundamental belief— I am my brother's keeper, I am my sister's keeper—that makes this country work.

It's what allows us to pursue our individual dreams, yet still come together as a single American family: E pluribus unum, out of many, one.

Pete said no. Anyone listening to that speech knew that Obama was destined, one day, for a presidential run. Pete was more interested in retirement.

Obama asked a third time. "He said, 'You might have heard I'm thinking about running for president in 2008,'" Pete told me. "He said, 'That is categorically untrue. Maybe at some point in the future, but my wife would never let me do it. My kids are too young. I have no intention of doing that; I just want to get established in the Senate.'

"I thought, *This guy is extraordinarily impressive*," Pete told me.

Pete finally said yes, but only on a temporary basis. "I agreed to get him started, to set up his Senate operation, to get a good team in place, get a good strategic plan in place, get a good structure. I'll lay that foundation. I thought, *I don't have anything else to do right now. I can help set this up for a year and a half. How hard can it be?*"

Less than one year in, Obama, who had made a point to keep a low profile, focusing on local Illinois issues, found himself again in the national news. Hurricane Katrina had just hit, and after touring the devastated Gulf Coast, he made his first appearances on the Sunday morning shows, admonishing the federal government's paltry response, emphasizing not only the racial bias it revealed but also the economic one. "It was a moment I thought I might add a useful perspective to the debate," he told *Time* magazine. "If an issue of justice or equality is at stake," he said, "I will speak out on it." People clamored for more. Speaking invitations were coming in by the hundreds, and that was when Pete, a master strategist almost in spite of himself, drew up a memo:

It makes sense for you to consider now whether you want to use 2006 to position yourself to run in 2008 if "a perfect storm" of personal and political factors emerges in 2007. If making a run in 2008 is at all a possibility, no matter how remote, it makes sense to begin talking and making decisions about what you should be doing "below the radar" in 2006 to maximize your ability to get in front of this wave should it emerge and should you and your family decide it is worth riding.

It would be nine years after Pete first signed on to set up Obama's Senate office—after a presidential campaign, a presidential transition office, an inauguration (Pete turned down his seat on the inaugural platform, preferring to watch Obama get sworn in on TV at home), a three-month stint pinch-hitting as Obama's chief of staff when Rahm Emanuel left in 2010 ("I said right then, I'm not interested in chief of staff; frankly I don't want the call at three A.M. about the earthquake in Honduras. . . ."), *another* presidential campaign, *another* few years in the White House—before Pete was able to convince Obama that he really meant it, that his assistance was only on a temporary basis, and he was now going to stop, go home, and spend time with his cats.

"Pete said, 'You know, making sure that we've got a good correspondence office that constituents feel that you are hearing them and that you are responding to them, that makes up for a lot of stuff,'" Obama told me, talking about those early days with Pete in his Senate office and about how something as mundane as the mail became a part of the conversation.

"And then during the course of maybe a year and a half of campaigning," Obama said, "every once in a while people would write me a letter. Or they would slip a letter to me on the rope line. And some of them would just be amazing. And they would help shape the stories that I told during the campaign because they weren't abstract.

"You know, this is a mom who's trying to figure out, how do you go back to school and look after her kids at the same time and pay the bills? This is a dad who had lost his job and described how hard it was to feel like he was worth anything.

"And that would . . . orient me."

When Pete talked to me about the origins of the mailroom operation, he was more blunt: "I hate writing letters to friends," he said. "So if someone cares enough to sit down and write a letter, the elected official ought to pay attention to it. It's often the only direct contact that an individual citizen has with his or her elected official. My view has always been that the quality of the communication says something about how the elected official views his or her role in terms of serving the public, regardless of party affiliation or political philosophy."

It was just: Read your mail. It was basic. Like: Tie your shoes. Or perhaps: Say your prayers. It may have seemed painfully obvious. It may have been in Obama's mind all along. But Pete articulated it, and he would continue to articulate it.

"I don't want to overstate it," Pete said. "I mean, I was probably more focused on finding bin Laden than answering an individual letter from Montana. So I'm not suggesting I'm different from anybody else in that regard. But I do think I made a conscious priority to find good people to work in the presidential office of correspondence, and that it was important, and that the president and senior people understood that it was important."

After the inauguration in 2009, Obama's transition team had

arrived to find that the Bush administration had left virtually nothing in terms of guidance about how to set up an Office of Presidential Correspondence. No system in place for sorting mail, no procedure manuals, no templates, no software, no form letters you could simply spit out.

And then came the avalanche. A quarter of a million letters a week to the new president. Boxes of mail stacked to the ceiling and lining the hallways. The Obama team didn't yet have stationery.

Mike Kelleher from Obama's Senate office was the person who stepped up to tackle the mess.

Pete was surprised. He'd figured Mike would want a job like assistant secretary of commerce, something with the oomph and pizzazz befitting a guy of his pedigree. Mike had known Obama since 1999; they were rookies carving careers in politics together—Obama coming from his work as a community organizer and Mike from the Peace Corps. They ran and lost side-by-side campaigns for Congress together, and Mike went on to serve as director of economic development and outreach in Obama's Senate office.

Now Mike said he wanted to do the mail. "It's a challenge, it needs to be done, and I'm willing to do it." He rolled up his sleeves. He carved out the OPC mission statement—"To listen to the American people, to understand their stories and concerns and respond on behalf of the president." He came up with an organizational chart and started interviewing. Candidates would have to pass an elaborate screening process if they wanted to work in OPC. They would have to be willing to volunteer in the mailroom before getting hired; Mike wanted to see how they interacted with one another and with elderly and student volunteers. He looked for compassion. He told them how lucky they would be to be reading mail. They would get to know America better than anyone.

He built the staff, drew up a ten-page strategic plan for the mailroom, wrote algorithms for a mail coding system, set up a casework decision tree, assembled a library of policy response letters, and developed quality-control manuals. He put in sixteen-hour days, weekends, creating order out of the chaos and assembling an army of empathic mail-reading soldiers, including Fiona.

When I reached out to Mike to ask him about all of this, about building OPC, he said, "I didn't build it. I was there and I managed the people . . . really talented people. . . . I made a couple good decisions in hiring people."

And then he said, "Pete Rouse. Pete Rouse set the tone of what a public servant is for me."

It kept going around like that—Mike crediting Pete, Pete crediting Mike, Pete crediting Obama, Obama crediting Pete.

Say what you will about the Obama administration, but this was not a braggy bunch.

Word came that President Obama wanted to see some of the mail just the day after he took office. Mike got the call from the Oval saying the president wanted to see five letters. Then they called back with a correction. The president wanted to see fifteen letters. They called back one more time. He wanted to see ten that day, and every day.

"By the time I got to the White House and somebody informed me that we were going to get forty thousand or whatever it was pieces of mail a day," Obama told me, "I was trying to figure out, how do I in some way duplicate that experience I had during the campaign?

"Ten a day is what I figured I could do. It was a small gesture, I thought, at least to resist the bubble. It was a way for me to, every day, remember that what I was doing was not about me. It wasn't about the Washington calculus. It wasn't about the political scoreboard. It was about the people who were out there living their lives who were either looking for some help or angry about how I was screwing something up.

"And I, maybe, didn't understand when I first started the practice how meaningful it would end up being to me."

One side benefit of a president asking to read ten letters a day was that it sent a message that reverberated throughout the White House, from the lowest-ranking staffer working the scanners over in the EEOB to speechwriters, policy makers, and senior advisors in the West Wing: Mail was important. And if the mail was important, so were the people handling it. In the early days, Pete would head over to OPC himself, tell everybody in the mailroom how much he appreciated their contribution, tell them that it mattered to the president, that *they* mattered to the president.

"That stuff makes a difference," Pete told me. "Just knowing that your contribution had value and was valued."

He gave me an example, motioned toward a framed photo by the window. It was among a cluster of other photos. It was a picture of him seated at a dinner, the rest of the people in the banquet hall up on their feet giving him a standing ovation and Obama at the lectern. Pete said it was a gift from Obama when Obama had finally given in and let him retire. Obama had thrown Pete a dinner and given him the picture, with a small message at the bottom.

"You can go over and look at that if you want," Pete said.

Pete, there is a city full of people who owe their success to you. I'm one of them. Thank you, my friend.

"Stuff like that sticks with you," Pete said. He sat up straight, his hands resting gently on his knees.

There was a guitar hanging on the wall near the photo, and it looked like Obama had signed that too. I asked Pete about it, and he got up to come over to admire it. He rocked from side to side as he walked as if to avoid one ache or another.

"A Fender," he said. There was a Senate seal painted on the guitar, an Obama campaign seal, and the presidential seal. Pete said Obama had commissioned it. Another going-away present. "What's it say on here? He wrote on it. It's hard to read."

We leaned toward the guitar, tilting our heads.

"Thanks for . . ." We couldn't read what Obama had written on Pete's guitar.

"So you're a guitarist," I said to Pete.

"No," he said.

Not a guitarist. I paused to recap Pete's résumé. He was not a lawyer, not a lobbyist, not an aspiring author, not a person who lobbied to become Senator Obama's chief of staff, let alone President Obama's chief of staff, and he was not a guitarist. (His job title at Perkins Coie was "senior policy advisor.")

"I'm a Grateful Dead fan," he said, and he smiled. His face was wide, puffy, and the smile lifted all the worry off it. "My two greatest professional accomplishments," he said. "Number two is helping elect the first African American president; number one is reuniting the Grateful Dead."

During the 2008 campaign, the Grateful Dead's Bob Weir had reached out to say he was an Obama supporter. He'd wanted to know if there was anything he could do to help.

"There's one thing," Pete said to Weir. The band had split up in 1995 after lead guitarist Jerry Garcia died; surviving members went on to tour in varying configurations, but never all of them together. "Maybe just one thing . . ."

And so it was that on February 4, 2008, a reunited Grateful Dead played before a sold-out crowd at the Warfield Theatre in San Francisco and then again in October, along with the Allman Brothers Band, before a sold-out crowd at the Bryce Jordan Center in University Park, Pennsylvania, and amid the crowd at both shows, there was Pete Rouse bopping his head to the beat.

"Greatest professional accomplishment," Pete said again.

This reminded him of a related point: Writing thank-you notes to the Grateful Dead and to the Allman Brothers should not be difficult.

Pete expected Obama to gush in the thank-yous. This was *the Grateful Dead*. And this was *the Allman Brothers*.

When it came time to write them, Obama had been on a plane to Hawaii to see his grandmother, who was dying. "That's a long trip," Pete told me. He had sketched out some ideas for the thank-you notes and had sent them with Obama to do on the plane.

"I asked him, 'Please handwrite each one.'" Pete had provided a list of all the band members and some suggested lines so that Obama could personalize each note.

Pete got a call from a staffer on the campaign plane. Obama wanted to know about these thank-you notes. Why couldn't he just write one to the whole Grateful Dead and then one to the whole Allman Brothers Band? Wouldn't that be sufficient?

"Tell him I'm going to quit if he does that," Pete joked to the staffer.

As he relayed this story to me, he underscored the word "joked."

There was no way he would have ever quit on Obama. Pete wanted me to make sure that point was clear and could not be misinterpreted; he was getting antsy. He was not a person who did interviews. He was not good at anecdotes.

"To me it shows that he doesn't have the same sensitivity to this that you or I would," Pete told me. "Which is why he *did* relate to the mail." Expressing heartfelt thanks to famous legends of rock and roll was one kind of communication (pretty basic), answering mail from random folks in Idaho or New Jersey quite another. "When he was responding to individual stories, as opposed to just thanking someone for doing something for him, it became very personal to him. Then he *wanted* to do it."

We went back to the couch, and Pete winced as he sat. He said he had to fly to Chicago in the morning for a meeting, was considering canceling on account of his back. He looked at me, seemed to assess my reaction, as you do when you need a friend to give you permission to bail on something.

"Yeah, you should cancel," I said. "Just walking through the airport—"

"For a two-hour lunch and a dinner," he said. "You know?"

Oh, absolutely.

"Did the surgery help your brother?" he asked.

A hundred percent.

Somehow this led to news of my husband's successful knee replacement.

"Oh, my knees," he said.

Samples, 2010–2012

July 23, 2012

Ms. Emily Nottingham

Tucson AZ

Dear President Obama,

When my son was killed in the Tucson mass murders last year, you asked if there was anything you could do. There is. I am asking you to support some reasonable steps to protect your citizens. Reinstating the ban on assault weapons and extended magazine clips should be a simple step to make our public places more safe for citizens. Our rights of assembly are threatened. I believe that you can be a vigorous supporter of the second amendment and still support modest regulation of weapons of mass murder. If you will not oppose the NRA, then seek out the support of the NRA in this gun safety measure. My son was killed in the mass murder in Tucson. Now it has happened again and more young people have been senselessly murdered by a stranger in a public place armed with weapons designed to kill many people very quickly. Enforcement of existing laws is not a sufficient response; additional steps are necessary to restrict easy access to weapons of mass murder. The Tucson shooter was not diagnosed as mentally ill when he legally purchased these super-lethal weapons; I would not be surprised if the Aurora shooter also had no such diagnosis. We need to look at the weapons themselves.

Please consider being a leader on this issue; others will follow behind you. Thank you for thinking seriously about this and seeking a resolution.

Emily Nottingham

THE WHITE HOUSE

WASHINGTON

Emily —

Thank you for your letter. I can only imagine
the heartbreak you've gone through. I agree with
you about common sense gun control measures, and
although I confess that it is currently challenging to
get Congress to take on the issue, I will do my best to
help move public opinion.   Sincerely!

5/9/12 co 4

Contact Us - Civil Rights

Submitted: May 9, 2012 16:16
Originating Host:
Remote IP: **Back from the OVAL**
From: Laura King Ph.D.   *5/30/12*
Email Address:
Phone:
Address (Domestic)   Columbia MO
Topic: Civil Rights

Message:
I have no idea why you decided to endorse marriage equality today. But I wanted to say thank you, on behalf of myself, my partner, Lisa, and especially our 8 year old son, Sam. In the last few days, I think I had myself convinced that I would be fine if you played the political game and stayed silent on our family's right to exist. I kept telling myself that I "knew" you supported us, even if it didn't make political sense for you to say so. I am a strong supporter of you and your agenda and I had myself convinced that I wanted you to be re-elected more than I needed to hear you say you believe that my family deserves a place at the American table. It turns out I was wrong about that. After hearing about your interview today, I find myself sitting in my office crying and realizing that hearing those words from you means more to me than I ever imagined. I am overwhelmed--touched and surprised and just tremendously grateful that anyone in your position would put principle above politics, would just say the truth about what is right. I admire your courage and character and I am so glad that you are our President. I am proud of you.

My partner's parents live in North Carolina and last night's results were very hurtful to all of us-our son is their only grandchild-as if people could vote away our family. I spent the better part of this morning contemplating what it means to be a member of a tiny minority, so small and dispensable that it seems to be no problem for people to put my civil rights up for a popular vote.

I know from experience that change can only occur when courageous and compassionate straight people take action. To me, the stakes for you seemed impossibly high. I don't know why you decided to take this stand. And I hope that it does not cost you dearly. And I will do all that I can to see that it doesn't. And in the meantime, thank you so much, Mr. President.

Best,

Laura King

Laura A. King, Ph.D.

Columbia MO

February 1, 2010

Pres. Barack Obama
1600 Pensylvania Avenue NW
Washington D.C. 20500

Mr. President:

I operate a small weekly newspaper in Espanola, NM. You visited here in September 2008 when campaigning.

The Rio Grande Sun was started by my parents in 1956. I don't need to tell you the state of newspapers today. It's hard out there for an editor.

My largest expense is payroll. The next is printing. The third is health care.

I have cut other expenses or not replaced employees who have left on their own to avoid layoffs. I will go into reserves to avoid layoffs. Not many newspapers have that luxury.

I have cut pages and "tightened" the newspaper to lower printing costs.

Health care I can do nothing about. I pay all of the premium for my 13 full-time employees. I also pay their deductible and share in their costs to meet the maximum out-of-pocket expenses.

There are two employees on thyroid medication. They both require quarterly blood tests. Insurance doesn't cover the tests. I pay for them. Last year I paid $204 per month, per person. With minimal small insurance claims and no major claims, my rates went up 35 percent this year.

Instead of paying the ransom, I dropped to a plan with a higher deductible, which I will again pay. The employees will have the same coverage. My gamble is that no one will have a catastrophic event and force me to pay the $4,000 deductible. This is how I deal with health insurance.

I did some calculations regarding my old health plan of 1995 when I received my renewal notice last month. In 1995 I paid $112 per person for a great plan: low copay, no deductible, $15 prescription card. That plan today would cost me over $600 per person.

Mr. President, please keep fighting the lobbyists and business-owned right that does not want real reform in this country. Little people like me need you advocating for common sense. Health care reform must happen if we're to move forward as a country.

Sincerely;

Robert B. Trapp

Managing Editor

Sample E-Mail Viewer   Page 1 of 1

3/26/10
MK

Dear Mr President
I wrote you and email a few months ago about the health care bill and how I support of what you are doing and ask if congress could please act faster on this bill. I wrote this letter on behalf of my girlfriend Jana Smith On March 18 2010 Jana passed away. Jana had some medical problem. She could not afford to go to the doctors and was waiting to see what would happen with the health care bill. She knew Mr President that you were working on this so all American could receive this much needed health care. I Know that this cannot help My Jana now but I just wanted you to know that We support everything you were doing. Thank you Mr President. I am Retired from the Military and I help Jana through what she was going through. We were going to get married I am very lost right now but I just wanted you to know from me that I want you to keep the great work that you are doing for all American
Thank you for listen to me

SSGT Robert J Doran
U.S. Air Force (Retired)   *Reply*

==== Original Formatted Message Starts Here ====

Date: Mar 23 2010 11:30AM

<PREFIX></PREFIX>
<FIRST>Robert</FIRST>
<LAST>Doran</LAST>

<ADDR2></ADDR2>
<CITY>Gilbertsville</CITY>
<STATE>Kentucky</STATE>

<ISSUE>W_POTUS</ISSUE>

Robert Doran

Gilbertsville, KY

COPY FROM ORM

THE WHITE HOUSE

WASHINGTON

Robert —

Thank you for your letter. My heart goes out to you for the loss of Tana; but because of the support of people like her, we passed health care reform and can hopefully prevent such hardship for others. God Bless,

Also, thanks for your service to our country.

www.avery.com
1-800-GO-AVERY

AVERY® 5163™

Mr. Robert Doran

Berkley Michigan

JUN - 1 2010

(monthly Mail)

1/3/2010 6:14:28 PM
Desert Hot Springs, California

The unemployment rate in Riverside County, CA, the county in which I live, is over 30%. There are no jobs in sight. Are you going to keep even one campaign promise upon which you built your presidency? I worked for you, I contributed to you and what do I get in return: I'm out of work, I get no cost of living increase on Social Security, and you are going to pay for the new health insurance plan by cutting my Medicare.

Thank you very much.

Respectfully,

Eileen M. Garrish

THE WHITE HOUSE
WASHINGTON

Eileen —

I got your note and wanted to respond.

The day I walked into office, I inherited the worst economic crisis since the Great Depression. And after a very tough year, we have begun to turn the corner, with the economy growing again.

That may be little consolation to you and others that are out of work, and I won't be satisfied

until jobs are being created in Riverside and across the country.

Having said that, I do want to challenge the notion that I haven't kept my campaign promises, or that I have weakened Social Security or Medicare. The existing Social Security formula didn't provide a cost of living increase because prices/inflation went down this year. Nevertheless, I ordered a $250 stimulus check to seniors that made up for it. And contrary to what the Republicans have said, health care reform does not cut Medicare benefits!

Best wishes,

CAS
Sample

January 8th, 2010
Star— 2/25/10
                    MK

                    Reply:

Dear barack obama,

Hi my name is Rebecca ████.
I am 16 years old, I will be 17 in
march, I live in florida.

I am also in DCF care, which is
foster care. I have been in foster care
ever since I was 2 years old. I have
3 sisters too. The 2 younger ones names
and ages are, B████ she is 15 and
J█████ she will be 13 on January 10th 2010.
My older sister ████████ is 23 years old.

When I turned 6 years old I found a
family that wanted to adopt me and
my three sisters, so when I turned
7 years old we all was adopted by
the ██████. It was a ladie named
J████ ████ and a man named
D████ ████. Let me tell you a
little about them, well I wanted
to start a new life so I thought
D███ and J██ could be the one's
that would help me start that
new life but, I guess I thought
wrong, because D████ ended up
physically and sexually abusing me,
and J███ had physically abused me.

J████ also new about what D████
did to me and she would tell
him not to take it too far or
don't get caught.

████████████████████████████
████████████████████████████
████████████████████████████
████████████████████████████
████████████████████████████ I also
told D████ and J████ parents
and they told me that they would
never do anything like that. I
wouldn't tell my little sisters
what was going on because
they were too young at the time.
they wouldn't understand. so I
went to my older sister and
told her what was going on, so
that night she called the police
and the police came to the house
that night and took me away and
interviewed me, then I was
thrown into foster care. My
little sisters were bribed by the I████

to stay, so they did. Then D████
was arrested over night, then
released the next day, and
nothing happened to J███, so I
went on through life with
every one thinking that im a
liar. When I left the ████████
house they wouldn't allow me
to talk or see my sisters, so
I ended up getting locked
up, smoking weed, and drinking
liqour, and running away. Then
the last time I was locked up
which was when I was 16 ﹘
years old, I told my caseworker
that I need help. and that
I can't keep living this life, so
she recomended ████████████
████████ @ ████████████
My second day at ████ I ended up
attempting to runaway with another
camper. We ended up getting caught,
so they brought us back to
████████ ever sense that day I
was a whole new person.

Now it is my 6th month here
and I am a whole new person.
I am a role model\Leader now.
During my 3 month here I found
out that the something that happened
to me happened to them. They
was then put in foster home
with a nice older lady. I have
visits and weekley phone
calls with them. D███ is
locked up in prison. We don't
know how much time he
has yet, but I do know that
J██ has 2 years of probation.
So now I am back in contact
with my sisters and I am
trying to get in contact with
my biological parents, but the
only problem is that my
biological parents droped there
right towards us, so now they
are struggeling getting
visitations with me.
    I am so happy with
myself I never new I could

be who I am today. Thanks
to _____ when I finish
Highschool I want to go to
collage for social services
to be a case worker to work
with other foster kids.
   I am so happy to have
a president like you. you
have already changed alot.
I had wrote a letter to George
Bush when I was younger,
but I think one of the
people that works for him
wrote me back. I hope that
didn't happen. so can you
please write me back and
please send pictures to me.
   Thanks alot

   Sincerely, Rebecca _____
        Rebecca _____

COPY FROM ORM

THE WHITE HOUSE

WASHINGTON

Rebecca —

Thanks for the moving letter. I am inspired by your courage, and am sure you will succeed if you keep at it.

Best of luck!

Miss Rebecca

November 18, 2012

Dear President Obama -

My name is Chana Sangkagalo. I came to the United States of America from NortheasternThailand in November of 1988. I remember it being Thanksgiving.

The reason I came to America is because it is a land of opportunity. The United States is known as a country where one can begin with nothing and build it into whatever he wishes and can afford. One's destiny is not pre-determined in the United States - you have the right to become whatever and whoever you wish. You work hard for opportunities for a better life. Hard work and determination can get you much farther in this country than anywhere else in the world - as long as you are working hard enough to do so. I began my work here at Burger King in Rhode Island. Through the years and with education I was able to develop my creativity and open my very own hair salon. I am a successful small business owner in this great country. I am a United States citizen. I have much to be thankful for.

The reason that the United States needs a constant flow of immigrants is because we are the people that have the dream - the desire - the fire inside to do something to better our financial situation. We do not feel entitled to a job or education. We believe in personal responsibility and accountability.

We need new producers in the United States. It's about new blood - new life - new givers - not takers. If you look back through history you will see how new blood has produced and grown our economy.
Immigrants have one thing in common - we work like crazy. We save our money. We open stores and many other businesses. We do not sit around and complain about this - that and the other thing. We do not feel entitled. We are not takers but producers. We need producers and immigrants like myself that provide production. The reasons that so many immigrants came to America are the same reasons that each and every one of us should feel grateful for - freedom - freedom of religion - to escape poverty and oppression - a better future for our families. In short - opportunity.

So Mr Obama - I believe that you are a real person with real beliefs. You have patched many of the holes left by your predecessor and you continue to do so. I applaud your re-election. I believe in you and am excited to see what you can accomplish over the next four years.

God bless you Mr President.

Respectfully -

Chana Sangkagalo

Chana Sangkagalo
Thailand

10/14/1988
10/16/2012

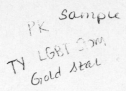

UNITED STATES NAVAL ACADEMY

Dear Mr. President and First Lady,

I want to Thank you for this milestone in my DAughter's life. Signing the bill and Repealing DADT on Sept 20, 2011 changed her life and that of many of her shipmates.

As A Parent I know that there isn't Anything that would stop you from Encouraging your daughters to Reach for their dreams. Caitlin went to I-DAY, not under the Radar and I often feared what would happen to her.

You know what she did? She and 5 others STARTED the NAvy SPECTRUM Cot the Naval AcAdemy! Nowhere near flying under the Radar. They started the Club Because of YOU!! They only had 5 attend but Now it's 2nd largest Club at the AcAdemy. She's my hero and now leaves a legacy at the Naval AcAdemy. She's #1 to become a pilot after that.

UNITED STATES NAVAL ACADEMY

I just wanted to thank you again on behalf of my daughter, the entire Navy Spectrum Club and parents around this great nation of children who are SAS. Thank you for standing up for them.

With much love and gratitude from one parent of an amazing daughter to another parent of two awesome Daughters I thank you.

Regina Bryant
Gold Star Wife
and mom
to an 'incredible Daughter!

Go Navy!

I've made Caitlin a recipe box as part of her graduation gifts. Enclosed you will find a recipe card. If you have an easy, non-fail vegetable or no-meat recipe, please fill it out and we'll include it in her surprise. Bring it to graduation or you can mail it to the address below and I'll add it to her box. You may also email it to

████████████ and I will print it out and put it in her box

I know this will be something that she will treasure for years to come.

Caitlin Bryant

c/o R. H. Bryant

████████████

Pensacola, Florida. ████

September 23, 2011

President of the United States
1600 Pennsylvania Ave. NW
Washington, DC. 20500

RE: LETTER BY FEDERAL INMATE JASON HERNANDEZ #07031-078 IN
SUPPORT OF HIS PETITION FOR COMMUTATION OF SENTENCE

Dear Mr. President:

Greetings. My name is Jason Hernandez. I am sure you have no idea
who I am, and probably wondering why on God's earth am I writing to you.
Well, to summarize it as best as I can I am a 34 year old federal inmate
who has served over 14 years on a sentence of life without parole, which
I was given for conspiracy to distribute crack cocaine and other controlled
substances. As a result therof, I have filed a Petition for Commutation
of Sentence with the Pardon Attorney in hopes you determine there is
sufficient cause to grant my request.

As you are aware there has been major support to completely eliminate
the disparity between powder cocaine and crack cocaine. But that is not
what the substance of this letter is about. I'm not going to sit here
and try to downplay the effects crack cocaine or any other drugs have on
our nation. I know first hand the distruction drugs cause on people,
families, and communities.

Nor will I attest that because I didn't kill anyone, commit rape,
or a crime against a child, that I shouldn't be in prison for an excessive
amount of time. Because the simple truth Mr. President is that I was a
drug dealer. And what I didn't know then that I've learned over the years
is that it would not be an overstatement to view my crime as equivalent,
if not more detrimental, than those just stated. I realize this because
I was selling drugs in the community I was born and raised in. I was
selling drugs to people I grew up with, most of whom were either friends
or family. Everybody I came into contact with I was destroying in one
way or another. From the addicts and the families of those addicts, and
the individuals I encouraged to sell drugs that ended up losing years of
their lives in prison; resulting in parents being without a son, wives
without a husband or kids without a father. Now I can see the cycle of
destruction that drugs have caused on my neighborhood and those across
the United States.

I acknowledge that I deserve to be in prison. For how long? I am
in no position to say. I'm sure there are people who could argue either
for or against my current sentence of life without parole. What I can
say for certain Mr. President is that I am a changed man from that boy
who ran those streets over 15-20 years ago. And if I were given a second
at life I would not let you, my family, or society down. I would do
everything I could to right what I have wronged and try to prevent kids
from making the same mistakes I did when I was young.

If you review my Petition for Commutation you will see I have dreams
Mr. President, big dreams. And not just dreams of being free, but dreams
of becoming someone who is going to make a difference in this world. But
to speak of my goals as dreams doesn't do them justice, for I can see
everything I want to accomplish and how I am going to accomplish it as
clear as day. All I need now is for you to give me a chance to turn those
dreams into reality.

I thank you for your time Mr. President, and I hope that after you
read my Petition for Commutation you come to the conclusion that I was not
a bad person growing up, but a person who made bad decisions.

Sincerly,

Jason Hernandez #07031-078
Federal Correctional Institution
Post Office Box 1500
El Reno, Oklahoma. 73036

C.O..Y.

9/10/12 wo 6

Sandy Swanson

Merion Station, PA

Reply

August 8, 2012

President Barack Obama
The White House
1600 Pennsylvania Avenue, NW
Washington DC 20500

Back from the OVAL
9/10/12

Dear President Obama,

I'm writing to tell you about the $15 my family just donated to your 2012 campaign.

It was $15.

That's really all we could give. My husband is currently a student at Temple University, in the final year of his PhD. Since starting his degree, three years ago, we've been living at several hundred percent below the poverty level (I keep forgetting which percent...does it matter?)

But we aren't complaining. Two healthy daughters– dusty, well-travelled backpacks in the basement – a house full of memories – a future full of hope. We're the lucky ones.

So - we're currently *"poor on money – rich in life"* (as we like to say). It hasn't always been like this. My husband spent most of his life doing what he loved -- playing or coaching basketball. Born in SE Iowa, he was an Academic All-American and once-upon-two-good-knees-ago, the local town hero of his small town – after bringing home the State Championship during his junior year of high school, followed by NJCAA National Championship years later as a coach. Then came a coaching stint in Europe (UK), before returning to the States to coach another small town Division I team. Basketball has been his heart-n-soul; his bread-n-butter for decades. And now, a student again. He hopes to teach one day – to pass on all he's learned coaching here&abroad. His research focus is on leadership – what makes a leader and that sort of thing. He's a big fan of yours by the way...as a player, father and president...not necessary in that order. <wink>

But this really wasn't supposed to be a letter about him.

It's about this year's campaign. It's about wanting to say that $15 means something these days and deserves a moment of pause (and some words on paper) for this girl and her family of Obama fans.

- ❖ $15 is a special pizza dinner at our local pizza stop (Poppy's in Wynnewood).
- ❖ It's 1½ tickets to see the newest film at the old-school cinema we walk our daughter's to.
- ❖ It's getter fresh fruit, instead of frozen; fresh veg, instead of canned.
- ❖ It's tickets to the Franklin Institute in the heart of Philly. (We've never been)

It's all these things to a family like ours.

I've listened with curiosity, mostly frustration, as the nation debates Citizens' United and the string of new laws that now allow the bellowing voices of private interest to drown out the sounds of tiny voices (like ours/mine). Our pebble-in-the-ocean support feels almost pointless. *"Leave the campaigns to the rich,"* I think to myself, *"get your daughters a pizza instead."*

But I refuse to allow new laws to stop us/me from being A PART of this campaign. After all, I will never be a "player" (in the political sense), but I still want to believe I can play a part.

Then, out of the blue, there you are – shooting a jumpshot on my (Facebook) wall– and asking for "players" to join you on your home court. I had to smile, and then I couldn't resist. And so, I have relinquished those $15. Please know that they count. To us. Please stay in Washington. Do, in this second term, what you were not assisted/supported to do during your first term. Get this country moving/working/hoping again. I'm hoping the next pizza will be on you.

Wishes to your brave wife and beautiful daughters from another brave wife with two beautiful daughters.

All good things,

Sandy

Sandy Swanson

p.s. if you're looking for a hard-working, All-American boy from Iowa for your pick-up game, I know a guy...my husband. His name is Steven.

Sandy
Swanson

*"Code 100"
response*

THE WHITE HOUSE
WASHINGTON

Sandy —
Your letter inspires me so much.

Thanks,

[signature]

Ms. Sandy Swanson

Merion Station, Pennsylvania

SEP 19 2012
(Priority w/Tracking)

CHAPTER 6

Bill Oliver,
June 20, 2012

UNDISCLOSED LOCATION

Some of this will have to remain vague. Bill Oliver does not want anyone to know where he or his family lives, not the town, not even the state. MS-13, the most violent street gang in the Western Hemisphere, has a presence even in this sleepy city, and if gang members want to find someone, they can.

Needless to say, this has been an education. He is not the person he once was. He just turned eighty.

The reckoning for Bill Oliver began in 2011 when he was on a trip to El Salvador. He had long since retired from teaching, had raised two kids with Sandra, his wife of nearly a half century, and they had fled the Snowbelt for the Sunbelt. He signed up to teach a few courses at the local college to keep his mind active. Taking students on a study abroad trip to Central America was about waking them up. Showing them how the other half lives. "Appreciate what you have." They were international business majors studying things like finance, predictive analytics, and best practices in marketing management strategies. Bill was a lifelong Republican who believed in things like small government, low corporate tax rates, and tight border security.

The dinner the villagers put on was cooked in a big pot boiling over an open flame. Bill wanted his students to see that. The coconut milk came out of the coconuts that they had seen the boys pull off the trees. *Real coconuts.* Before they ate, the local kids challenged Bill's students to a soccer game. Those kids had bare feet. Bill took his students aside. He said, "Now, don't be rude. Make sure you let them win." The local boys completely demolished the American college students. "Well, there you go," Bill said. "*Would you look at that? Look at that.* Look at these people; they have no shoes, they have nothing, and they appear *happy!*"

After dinner, Bill got to know a man who said he was the father of several of the boys. His wife had cooked. Bill and the father stood in the kitchen, and the floor was dirt. The roof was corrugated metal, and the father didn't have a shirt on. He was talking about his six sons, telling Bill all of their names, and he said one of them was not there. That one had just turned seventeen and his name was Quique. Key-kay. The father told Bill about MS-13, about the violence that was rapidly turning El Salvador into the murder capital of the world. He said Quique's school was across the river, a good distance from the village, and that's where the gang was. Gang members had been recruiting Quique, a lonely kid who needed friends and who made the mistake of listening to them. Soon he had found himself caught in a tragic dilemma. Gang members threatened to kill him if he didn't join, and the price of admission was that he murder someone in his own family.

Quique's only hope for survival was to flee. So the father put him on a bus with enough money, he hoped, to pay the coyote to smuggle him across the U.S. border. The father never heard from him again.

Bill is a kind and polite person, and any kind and polite person standing on a dirt floor in El Salvador under a corrugated metal roof with a grieving father would have said the same thing. "Well, if there is anything I can do . . ."

There was nothing Bill could do.

Two weeks after he got home, Bill told Sandra, he said, "Well, I made a promise to the father that I would look for his son." He can't say for sure when or how the notion of a promise kicked in. He hadn't promised anything. His students were finishing the semester, and they would soon move on to MBAs and careers in big banks. Bill was not a busy man, not the way he used to be. If he took a shot at looking for the boy, perhaps he could be the man of honor he believed himself to be.

There was no way he'd be able to find the boy.

Bill started in Texas. He started in Houston. "I'm looking for a boy," he said. Needle in a haystack. He could have stopped there, and his soul would have been at peace because, after all, he did try. He can't say for sure when the compulsion to keep going kicked in, but if he's honest, he'll say at first it was about winning. Like you're doing a crossword puzzle, and this one is not going to beat you. "I'm looking for a boy," he said. "I'm looking for a boy."

By 2012 more than 150,000 kids had been caught crossing the U.S. border, having run from countries in Central America, principally El Salvador, Honduras, and Guatemala, to escape MS-13. They get picked up, detained, and designated as "unaccompanied minors." The Office of Refugee Resettlement, part of the U.S. Department of Health and Human Services, screens the kids for gang ties and holds them in shelters while attempting to place them with relatives or sponsors as they await hearings in immigration court.

New York is where Bill found Quique. The Office of Refugee Resettlement had sent him to a relative of some sort; this part is sketchy. Bill wrote a letter to the district court that Quique had been transferred to. He got no response, so he kept writing. He wrote so many times the judge finally called him. You have to get an attorney and file motions if you want to do anything for the boy, she told him. Bill went online and learned about motions, and he wondered what, exactly, he wanted to do for the boy.

He thought about the father and the metal roof and the dirt floor. The conversation with the father that had been redrawn in Bill's mind as a promise had bloomed into a full-blown test of character. He looked around his house at the display of pots, furs, masks, and other beautiful items crafted by villagers he had met on his various travels to remote parts of the globe. People who came by could see he was a worldly man who knew the taste of food cooked in pots over open flames.

To file the motion in district court, you had to indicate certain things. "I have the means to take care of him," he wrote on the form. *I have means.*

When the motion was granted, they put Quique on a plane, and

Bill went to the airport to pick him up. He recognized Quique because he was brown. Bill is big and round with a white beard, a Santa Claus look, not by choice. Quique went to him, and they walked together to Bill's car. Bill spoke no Spanish, and Quique spoke no English. Bill didn't know if Quique was coming for a day or a month or a year, and neither did Quique. Bill took Quique to a Salvadoran restaurant to make him feel at home. They ate *pupusas,* and the waitress had enormous breasts spilling exquisitely out of her shirt, and that was the only common language, and so that's what they talked about with their eyes and their embarrassed laughter.

There's an app you can get on your phone that translates. You speak English into it, and it comes out Spanish and vice versa, so for weeks at the kitchen table, that's what they did. Bill asked Quique about his journey. In the beginning it had been exhilarating, Quique told Bill. His first time out of El Salvador. On a bus alone to Guatemala. He'd felt like a man. He felt the freedom of someone escaping death. In Mexico, with the strangers, in the back of trucks, he didn't make friends. The Rio Grande was so shallow you could walk the first part. When it got deep, he took off his clothes and held them over his head and swam, and here's where having grown up next to the ocean helped. Some of the others couldn't swim. He put out his arm to help one of them, and that's when he gave up trying to keep his clothes dry. It looked like the coast was clear, but none of them had ever been there before, and so they didn't know where to look. The coast wasn't clear. The person who grabbed him was not rough. He put Quique in a truck. The detention center was clean. You could earn points if you followed the rules. Points bought you candy, toothpaste, and time in the videogame room. He had never seen a videogame. He spent all his remaining points on candy on the last day and then gave it to the other kids because you weren't allowed to take it with you.

Bill told Quique about the promise he had made to Quique's father.

"*Mi papá está muerto,*" Quique said. *My father is dead.*

The news had come from the relative in New York. "*Tu padre está muerto.*" They said it was a heart attack.

"I'm sorry," Bill said.

Bill gave Quique his choice of bedrooms, and Quique picked the one in the corner. Bill said he would have to go to church on Sunday and eat dinner with him and Sandra, and he would have to go to school and learn English. Quique said he didn't want to go to school. At the school Bill told them; he said, "I'm going to be honest with you. He doesn't want to be here, and he's illegal." They said they would figure something out. Bill hired a tutor. Quique discovered the Food Network, and that's what he did after homework. He helped Sandra in the kitchen.

Bill and Sandra decided to adopt Quique. The lawyer said they were too old, and so was Quique. Bill could remain his sponsor until his hearing in immigration court when they decided what to do with him.

Quique got a girlfriend, Rebecca, a sunny, college-bound woman with sleek brown hair who said Quique was so much more mature than American guys. Quique made a lot of friends. He and Rebecca were in the back seat when the other car sped through the intersection. They were wearing their seatbelts. Rebecca was fine. Everybody was fine except Quique, whose bowel was severed by the seatbelt. At the hospital Bill told the ER surgeon; he said, "I'm going to be honest with you: He's illegal." The surgeon said he would figure something out. When the people at church heard about the accident, they said they would figure something out. Rebecca's parents said they would figure something out. It was a community coming together. The question of citizenship, papers, race, who belongs or who doesn't—who is deserving and who isn't—never came into it. It was people helping people, paying for the surgery, nursing Quique back to health.

Bill had no idea where immigration court was or how it worked. He bought Quique a pair of dress pants and a blue shirt. At the hearing Bill made the point that Quique had cost the American taxpayer nothing. People were helping him out. Quique was doing everything right. He had followed the rules. He was in school, and he was learning English. Bill had letters praising Quique's conduct from teachers and from church and even from the mayor, because Bill did know how to pull some strings.

The judge said there was no immunity for a kid who made an illegal crossing on account of MS-13. She said Quique had to go back to El Salvador.

"I'm sorry," Bill's attorney said. Bill told her he was going to appeal. If Quique were to go back to El Salvador, he would have to face the gang he had fled that wanted to kill him and that would almost certainly kill him now.

Bill's attorney hung her head and looked at her shoes. Everyone, she said, appeals. Everyone had the same story.

That same week, on June 15, 2012, President Obama was in the Rose Garden announcing a policy called Deferred Action for Childhood Arrivals (DACA). It allowed certain immigrants to escape deportation and obtain work permits.

Bill was desperate. He was not an Obama supporter. He was the opposite. But he felt like a changed man. Would that make a difference to the president?

Bill reflected on what, exactly, about him had changed. The entire saga could be summed up in one sentence: Bill had gotten to know a person who was in America illegally, and he had grown to love him.

Bill needed his letter to sound important. Just saying "Help!" seemed undignified.

June 20, 2012

**President
Barack Obama
1600 Pennsylvania Avenue NW
Washington D.C.
20500**

Dear Mr. President:
 I have always been a strong Republican. I have disagreed with you on many issues, especially immigration issues.

I believe myself to be an objective person, and because of that I could not understand your tremendous focus on immigration. I disagreed with almost everything you identified.

However my objectiveness "kicked-in;" I decided to personally incorporate some of the immigration beliefs you espoused over and over, identifying your determination in "making things right." Honestly, I didn't believe a difference could be made!

As a retired university provost and chief operating officer, I continue to do adjunct work as a professor ▓▓▓▓▓▓▓▓▓▓▓▓ **I take International Business majors to Central America on a regular basis.**

My last trip, while exposing students to a different culture, a life of poverty for many families, I had the opportunity to interact with one family in particular. This is a family of six boys, father, mother, plus another relative. Father's monthly income is about$140.00. They live without the any of the comforts we know, such as electricity and running water. Their "home" has dirt flooring, and corrugated metal walls and roofing. Cooking is done over an open fire and washing clothes in a wash tub.

His letter went on another page and a half, single-spaced; he told Quique's story, and at the end he wrote:

Now what? What can we do? . . .

How can I help the young man of which I speak, and others like him?

He signed it, "William C. Oliver, Ph.D."

At the White House, the OPC machine was in motion, just as it was always in motion. Like probably every other person who wrote a letter to the president, Bill had no idea that interns and staffers with pencils were busily making their marks.

Sample/Immigration Hardship

Bill had no idea that Obama, too, was making his marks.

"Reply," Obama wrote, on the top, in blue ink. And then along the right side he scribbled: "Can we find out from Cecilia what the best options for this young man would be—does he qualify for deferred action?"

. . . .

Bill was surprised when he got a personal note back from the president on a white card, handwritten. It's here somewhere. If he finds it, he'll show you. Frankly, the personal note didn't mean nearly as much to him as the phone call he got from a White House staffer who instructed him to call a certain number at a certain time; the person he reached was with U.S. Citizenship and Immigration Services, and she asked Bill questions about Quique's situation.

Among other requirements, to qualify for deferred action, you had to be younger than thirty-one on June 15, 2012, and you had to have come to the United States when you were younger than sixteen, and you had to have lived in the United States since June 15, 2007. The Pew Research Center estimated that as of 2014, up to 1.1 million people were eligible.

Quique wasn't one of them. He was too old, and he hadn't been in the United States nearly long enough. DACA was of no help to Quique.

"I'm sorry to hear that," Bill said.

Bill told Quique to make sure his shirt and dress pants were clean and ironed for whenever the appeal hearing came up, and he called his attorney for an update.

She said something happened. She said Quique's case had been abruptly closed. "Prosecution discretion," she said.

Bill would prefer not to disclose the details of Quique's immigration status, especially given the current climate, but the news is good: "He has the lowest status you can get for someone to stay in this country legally, but he's here legally."

Bill would never know if the ruling had anything to do with his letter to the president; he wondered whom he would even ask. Did it matter? Quique would not have to go back to El Salvador. Quique had a new life. America had given him a second chance. It turned out that finding Quique was about more than finding Quique. For Bill, it was a journey to a whole new kind of patriotism.

Bill took Quique shopping for an engagement ring. Quique and Rebecca got married, and on their honeymoon they watched dolphins swim, and they got back in time to go to church, where Bill was leading the singing.

Bill bought Quique's mom a refrigerator and a microwave, the first in the village.

CHAPTER 7

Fiona Picks the 10LADs

Fiona's office was on the fourth floor of the EEOB, well off the main drag—through a narrow corridor, down a ramp, behind a heavy wooden door. It was a quiet space with a large window too high to reveal anything but a solid cornflower-blue sky, and when I found her there, on a Thursday afternoon, she was perched at the edge of a couch with letters strewn all around her—letters draped like doilies on the couch, letters in piles on the coffee table at her knees, letters on the floor, letters on her lap; the net effect was of the old lady who lived in a shoe with so many children she didn't know what to do.

"It's like a crowd all talking about different things at once," she said. Every day at about four she sat down to do this, cull through the day's samples—about two hundred of them between the letters the hard-mail team set aside and the emails forwarded to her from the email team—and pick which ten the president should read. And no, she didn't want help. "I have to read," she said, bouncing a stack of pages up and down and into order. She was the kind of person who wore her professionalism earnestly: a well-practiced posture, a sensible maroon dress, practical flats. You could imagine her becoming dean of a liberal-arts college one day.

She told me she had never had designs on the kind of life that involved serving a president, although she had grown up in a family loud with conversation about the way government works—her father is the presidential historian Richard Reeves, and her mother, who is no longer living, worked for the United Nations and once ran for the state senate in California. Her mom was the type to decide on a lark that it might be fun for the family to go on a thirty-day trip around the world, and that's what they once did, hopping among sixteen countries, resting on the bank of the Nile, where they studied the clouds. Fiona went to boarding schools, the first of which, on a farm in upstate New York, she still regards as home. "My dad would visit about one weekend a month, and that was different than a lot of other kids, so I felt like my parents were a big part of my life." High school was in England, in the Malvern countryside, and when she came back to the United States to go to Duke, she majored in public policy and African American studies. "I remember my mom really discouraged political science. She said there's no science to politics—it's such a sham. So I was naïve to the process, and I was naïve to the country; I hadn't seen much of it. If President Obama hadn't run for office, I and lots of other people my age wouldn't have dipped a toe in public service."

It was Obama's 2006 book, *The Audacity of Hope,* that first drew her in. Not exactly a self-help book, by not exactly a guru, but something in that direction, especially for the young, the well educated, the dutiful seeking duty.

At the core of the American experience are a set of ideals that continue to stir our collective conscience; a common set of values that bind us together despite our differences; a running thread of hope that makes our improbable experiment in democracy work. These values and ideals find expression not just in the marble slabs of monuments or in the recitation of history books. They remain alive in the hearts and minds of most Americans—and can inspire us to pride, duty, and sacrifice.

As soon as she graduated college, in 2007, she applied for a job on Obama's campaign staff. She eventually landed an interview with Pete Rouse.

She had no idea who he was. "I'm embarrassed by the approach I took. I didn't understand how important he was to Obama. If I'd been more savvy, I would have worked a little harder at seeming smarter or more informed. But I think he must have had so many conversations with folks like me that I like to imagine he doesn't remember how ridiculous I was."

(He doesn't.) He hired her, sent her to New Hampshire to knock on doors.

In almost every successful social movement of the last century, from Gandhi's campaign against British rule to the Solidarity movement in Poland to the antiapartheid movement in South Africa, democracy was the result of a local awakening.

Fiona had the audiobook on a continuous loop on her iTunes. Obama in his own voice, day after day through her earphones. "Of course there's this beautiful cadence, and I would say it to myself again and again while walking down these driveways," she told me. "So he'd say things like 'I ask you to believe in this campaign; I ask you to believe in yourself; I ask you to believe again in the dream that we call America.'

"That middle part about believing in yourself—we all felt that that was the message we were conveying to voters. We didn't realize—folks involved in his campaign and later working in his administration—he was giving that to us.

"It was that idea of courage by necessity being a real gift that he instilled."

She was in Manchester for the 2008 primary, working from the basement in the home of a family who had opened their spare rooms to the team. Obama had won the Iowa caucuses less than a week earlier, and in an ensuing debate, Hillary Clinton had tried to turn his soaring rhetorical skills into a liability. "Making change is not about what you believe; it's not about a speech you make," she had said. "We don't need to be raising false hopes."

"The truth is actually words do inspire," Obama shot back. "Words do help people get involved. . . . Don't discount that power, because when the American people are determined that something is going to happen, then it happens. And if they are disaffected and cynical and fearful and told that it can't be done, then it doesn't. I'm running for president because I want to tell them, yes, we can."

By the eve of the New Hampshire primary, Obama was surging in the state's polls, up by as many as thirteen points. "And it was this feeling of 'The biggest day of my life is tomorrow,'" Fiona told me. "All my high-school girlfriends had come up. None of them were comfortable knocking on doors, but they did a shift. Some of my parents' friends came. My mom reached out and said her friend had told her that my skin wasn't looking well and I needed to take better care of myself. Yeah, thanks, Mom. But you felt like you had been away from friends and family working on this thing that you knew was important, and then really briefly, on election day, you become the center."

Fiona was alone in the Manchester home, cleaning up the kitchen, when the results started coming in. She had the radio on. What she would remember most was the guy on the radio saying how interesting it would be to hear a speaker as powerful as Obama give a speech after a loss.

He lost.

"Yes, we can," Obama said, that night, turning those words into a campaign slogan as he accepted defeat in New Hampshire.

It was a creed written into the founding documents that declared the destiny of a nation: Yes, we can.

It was whispered by slaves and abolitionists as they blazed a trail towards freedom through the darkest of nights: Yes, we can.

It was sung by immigrants as they struck out from distant shores and pioneers who pushed westward against an unforgiving wilderness: Yes, we can.

It was the call of workers who organized, women who reached for the ballot, a president who chose the moon as our new frontier, and a king who took us to the mountaintop and pointed the way to the promised land: Yes, we can, to justice and equality.

Yes, we can, to opportunity and prosperity. Yes, we can heal this nation. Yes, we can repair this world. Yes, we can.

People like Fiona—crowds of already-devoted pollsters and organizers standing out in the cold—listened to those words, felt them
in their toes; his words supercharged them. They would commit to
working even harder. They would give the next ten months of their
lives over to him, and when he was elected president, they moved to
Washington, many of them without jobs but knowing they were part
of a movement.

"And I remember feeling maybe the landlord wouldn't put me
on the lease because there was no proof that I was going to stay,"
Fiona told me. "The city was so dense with people who worked on
the Obama campaign. There were a lot of hang sessions around
town."

That was when Fiona met Mike Kelleher, who interviewed her
for a job in the fledgling correspondence office. It was not a great
interview. She didn't make eye contact. She was painfully shy. She
didn't look happy. But Mike saw something. Perhaps it was whatever
Pete saw when he hired her to knock on doors. A combination of
earnestness, some apparent well of empathy, and the unflappable
dedication to the president and his message that so many young
Obama devotees had. Courage by necessity. He taught them to believe in themselves.

Cascading emotional chaos—that's how people would remember those early days in OPC. Fiona's first job was as an "analyst,"
which meant she sat in a cubicle reading constituent mail with a
team of other former Obama organizers. They were as overwhelmed
by the volume—boxes of mail lining the hallways, *millions* of emails
in the inbox—as they were by the content. People telling their stories. Intimate, sad stories. People needing healthcare, people losing
businesses, people bankrupted because they couldn't pay student
loans, people saying "Help!" Here was the new guy who said he
could fix things. It was the getting-to-know-you phase. People told
him their problems. They told him to quit smoking. They told him,
wow, a black guy in the White House. They told him to get bin
Laden. They told him to create jobs. "Let's see if you're as smart as
we hope you are." There were threats to the president and first
family—about a hundred a day of those alone. In OPC they had to
assign one person full-time to deal with nothing but threats. Tea
Party protesters flooded the mailroom with tea bags. People sent

their credit card bills, showing jumps in interest rates. People sent mortgage foreclosure statements. "HELP!" "DO SOMETHING!" "YOU PROMISED!"

The campaign workers had believed themselves responsible for opening a conduit between the vulnerable and the influential—the powerless and the most powerful man in the world—and now, in the mailroom, they were expected to make good on it.

Youth was the main thing that Annmarie Emmet, a volunteer and a retiree, told me she noticed about the new crop of people coming in to work in OPC under Obama. She had been reading mail, three days a week, since 2001, through most of Bush's two terms in office, and would go on to keep reading through all of Obama's. "I've never been ashamed to say I worked for either administration," she told me.

"When this new group came in, they were maybe twenty years younger than Bush's," she said. "They were very devoted. They were single-minded in making Obama look good."

The tone of the incoming mail was dramatically different, she said. "It was cozier, maybe because of the younger children, watching these girls grow up. With Bush they appreciated the family, but they didn't know it much."

The closeness, she figured, accounted for the personal nature of the letters people wrote to the new president. "With Bush it would be more like 'Why aren't you helping these people as a group or doing more for that group?' as opposed to personal struggles. I would say they felt a more personal connection with the Obamas. Kind of like: 'I'm like you were; I need your help.'

"And then from the beginning the LGBTQ people flocked to him. You never saw that in the Bush administration."

January 2009

Dear Mr. President,

(Because the person I love can be dishonorably discharged for loving me back, even though he is honorably serving his country right now

in Iraq, I have to send this letter anonymously. It pains me to have to do so.)

My partner is currently serving in Iraq, and is in a situation where he is under fire on a daily basis. He's a good soldier, and our country needs him to continue doing the excellent job that he has been recognized for.

The day he deployed, I dropped him off far from his base's main gate, and he walked alone in the dark and the rain to report for duty. Where the rest of his buddies were surrounded by spouses and children at mobilization ceremonies, he stood by himself.

The phone trees don't have my name on them, and base support services don't apply—even though we've been together for 16 years and are raising a beautiful child together. Our communication is self-censored, and we are cruelly unable to nurture each other at the exact moment we both need it the most.

If something were to happen to him, no one from his unit will call me. If, like so many good soldiers before him, he gives that last full measure of devotion, no one will come knock on my door. No one will present me with a flag. It is, and would be, as if the most important thing in his life—his family—never existed.

I am not sure if I can adequately convey the mixture of fear, pride, heartache and hope I feel, all jumbled together, on a daily basis.

Fiona began her career reading letters like that—scanning, coding, sampling—and she gradually took on more responsibility. Mike Kelleher moved on from OPC in 2010, passing the directorship over to Elizabeth Olson, whom both Mike and Fiona would regard as essential in maintaining the stability of the operation, a noble shepherd. Fiona was next, taking the role of director of OPC in 2013. The shy young woman who had interviewed terribly, who could not make eye contact, was now a force.

.   .   .

"It's a funny channel," Fiona told me that day in her office when she sat on the couch surrounded by letters and worked on figuring out which ten she should give to the president. "Sometimes I think of it as a tray passing under a door."

Curating the 10LADs was a job she regarded as sacrosanct. It was her daily conversation with the president, each package an array of voices she believed most accurately rendered America's mood: *Here's what America is feeling, Mr. President.*

"Well, this one is lovely," she said, holding one letter with her fingertips. "He's a welder. He really paints the scene. A log cabin. A faithful dog. His wife volunteering. 'If you ever need something welded . . .'" She smiled, read it again, considering. "It's largely a support letter, so that's why I'm not sure it will make it." The president needed to hear from more than just supporters, and she was mindful of the mix.

"This one is definitely staying," she said, reaching for another letter. It had pages stapled to it. "She encloses a letter her dad once sent to Roosevelt. I think the president really eats up that historical perspective.

"Oh, and then this one just slays me," she said about another, declining further comment and laying it on her "yes" pile on the couch.

"Then this person is alleging that the Small Business Administration was very present in the disaster recovery immediately in the wake of a flood, but then when the cameras pulled out, so did the resources. I think that's an interesting voice to put before the president, because it's hard for that kind of information to reach him."

Getting a couple hundred letters down to twenty was one kind of challenge, but the real work was getting from twenty to ten. She had to be ruthless. A linear system like subject folders might seem the simplest method: Sort them all by topic, and then give the president one letter about energy, one about healthcare, one about immigration, and so on. "But then letters in each folder would be sort of in competition with each other instead of with the broad group," she said.

I suppose the point was obvious, but it took me a moment to compute the implications. It had to do with fairness and an underlying assumption that the letters represented people, not problems.

"Anyway, a disorderly pile is more honest," she said.

When she had the day's pile down to fifteen, she read through them again, one then the next. Her fingers were long, and her nails were painted shiny red, and she held the pages gently, laying each one down slowly, as if she didn't want to hurt it. "Well, this one has to make it. . . . And then this one—it's hard to follow, but I think even the fact that it's hard to follow is part of the story. . . . And then this. We're getting so many of these long-term legacy reflections. I don't know. . . ." She looked for stories. Not pro-this or anti-that, not screeds, not opinions about what someone heard on NPR. The president needed to hear the stories—that's what he couldn't get himself. "He can't walk down a street and see what it normally looks like," she said. She thought of the letters as a periscope looking outside the bubble, as a way for him to see as he used to see, before Secret Service protection and armored vehicles and a press pool and the world watching.

I asked her if she had a soft spot, a kind of letter or a subject that she might more readily want to put through.

"Inmate mail," she said without hesitation. "Ever since the beginning. It's one of the most extraordinary relationships in letter writing, I suppose because letter writing is more a part of prison culture than the rest of society."

She told me about one of the earliest inmate letters she got. A guy had written in from a prison out west, and he made mosaics. "From candy wrappers," she said. "And he had done a portrait of the president. It was on thick watercolor stock." He had glued tiny pieces of candy wrappers in varying colors to make a convincing likeness. "It was just beautiful," she said, and from the way she averted her eyes, I could tell this story was not going to end well. She said this was back in the early days, when she had just started at OPC. "It was just a support letter explaining that he was excited about this presidency and he wanted to offer this. I remember he also included this detail that for part of his work, he would've liked to have Twix wrappers to capture the color that he was going for. But that there had been an inventory change in the vending machines in his prison, so he had used Rolo wrappers, which he felt didn't convey quite the stroke that he was going for, but it was the best he could do."

She smiled, took a swig from the purple water bottle beside her. She said she had wanted to save that letter and the inmate's gift. "I wondered if I was just allowed to tack it up in my cubicle or something," she said. "But back then you couldn't do things like that— especially not with inmate mail."

There were protocols. Inmate mail didn't get saved. It didn't go to the president. "You would scan it to see if it was a pardon request," she said, "or if the person alleged he was being abused. Those got forwarded as casework. The rest basically went in a box to be shredded."

She took another sip. "It was a policy that had been in place for years and years, and we were just the new guys, you know?"

When Fiona first became director of OPC, one of the first things she did was challenge the policy about inmate mail. Where had it come from? Who had started it? Was it even written down? She credited a plucky intern for encouraging her to look into it. "Well, that doesn't make any sense," the intern had said when she was learning the rules. Surely a president who got his start as a community organizer doling out food to the homeless would want to hear what people stuck in prison had to say.

One day, Fiona wondered what would happen if she simply added a letter from an inmate into a batch of 10LADs. What would Obama do? What would senior staffers do?

Nothing, it turned out. No one said a word about it. So she did it again. And again.

"Well, this is now something we do," Fiona told the staff, and that was how the policy was changed, Fiona-style. Inmate mail got its own code in the hard-mail room, and people were encouraged to sample it along with all the other types of mail.

It was a private triumph, a mailroom coup. "Because there was this feeling like only we knew about it," she said. All those people writing in about sentencing disparities and criminal-justice reform. Not a particularly hot topic in the news. But now the letters made their way to Obama. In 2014, when the administration rolled out a Justice Department program offering executive relief to federal prisoners serving long sentences for nonviolent drug crimes, it surprised no one in the mailroom. The president, they were happy to see, was paying attention to the mail.

There was a similar trajectory with issues around same-sex marriage and repealing the military's "Don't Ask, Don't Tell" policy. Conversations about these things happened in the mail whether or not they happened anywhere else at the White House. Fiona, and Elizabeth before her, and Mike before her made sure to include those voices in the 10LADs. In that way, little by little, voice by voice, the mail could drive actual policy decisions.

The guy who wrote in anonymously in 2009 wrote again in 2014, after "Don't Ask, Don't Tell" was repealed. This time he used his name.

July 4, 2014

Dear Mr. President,

On August 3rd my husband, David Lono Brunstad, will be promoted to Senior Master Sergeant, and I'll be there to hand him his new shirt with the extra stripe on it. I know this is a pretty common occurrence for many military families, but it has special significance for mine—not that long ago our relationship had to remain a secret because of Don't Ask, Don't Tell.

David's deployment to Iraq in 2009 under this misguided policy was [a] dark and lonely time for the both of us. It was common for me not to hear from him for four or five days at a time, and for most families the old axiom "no news is good news" applied. Same-sex partners knew, however, that we weren't on anyone's contact list should something bad happen, so the pressure would just build and build until finally I heard his sweet voice on the other end of the line.

I knew he was under fire on a pretty regular basis and there were times that I struggled with keeping it together at home all by myself. On those days, Mr. President, it was your commitment to end this discriminatory policy that kept me going. I believed you—I trusted you—and I knew that, no matter how bad it got, that there was a light at the end of the tunnel.

My husband will deploy next June, but this time his pack will be a little lighter without the worry of whether or not his family will be taken care of. Sir, I doubt that I will ever be able to thank you in person, so I just need you to know that this military family will always be grateful for all you have done for us.

With Sincere Gratitude,
Darin Konrad Brunstad
Vancouver, Washington

"So we have one, two, three, four," Fiona counted. She was closing in on the finalists. "Nine, ten, and then this one is eleven, so we have to remove one." She read, shook her head. "Okay, okay, I guess." She draped the discard on the far end of the couch. She looked over at it, then reached out to give it a little pat.

She gathered the final ten and began shuffling them, pulling one out, putting it behind another and another in front. I wondered about all the shuffling. "Oh, the order is critical," she said. It was like putting a book of poems together, or a playlist. "The order in which you see stories affects the way you perceive each one," she said. "We sometimes use the term 'sucker punch' in this office, which is brutal, but . . ."

"Ballsy" was the word Yena used to describe Fiona. She did not hesitate to give the president mail brutally critical of his administration, or mail that was disturbing, or mail that was heartbreaking, and when she put the letters in order, it was for maximum impact. She could put three gun-violence pleas back to back. She could set the president up with a letter from someone gushing about the Affordable Care Act and then another from someone on the margin whose life had been made worse because of it. "It's not 'You failed,'" she said. "It's more 'Solutions don't solve things for everyone.'"

She grabbed a pencil. "Sometimes on Friday, particularly on Friday, we'll end with one that's like 'Hey, I like the way you tie your tie.'" She called that a chaser. It could be a comment about the dog or about the president riding his bike, or it could be just "Hey, are you a pancakes or waffles man?"

Dear Mr. President,

I think this country needs more spunk. With all the attack, the Zika virus and the wars, this country is a very sad place. Please do something fun. Wear a tie-dye shirt and shorts to something important. Go on a water-skiing trip in the caribbean. Take your family to disney world. Do something fun and outgoing. Also, please say something that will make everyone calm. You do not know how many polotics worries I have. . . .

Sincerely,
Lily
8 years old

"Okay, this is it," Fiona said, gathering the pages on her lap, smoothing them the way you would pet a cat.

"So I'll open with this one. 'This letter has been in my mind and heart for so many years.'

"And then this person who volunteered on the campaign and has been disappointed with the Affordable Care Act . . . a real personal story.

"Then this notebook paper from a social worker in Texas that talks about trying to make a difference and against a lot.

"And then this letter about a DOJ correction that didn't extend to DHS.

"Right behind the prison comment, I'll have the son with the felony background.

"Then right behind that is this one that's tougher to read but a haunting message from this vet who is haunted by what he's seen.

"And then this reflection on support being temporary after natural disasters.

"And this is one, frankly, I don't have an intuitive place for where it should fit in the batch, but I think I'll have this in here. Dakota Access Pipeline.

"And then the grandson, Jake. His quote: 'I hope Clinton wins.' This little African American boy with two white parents. I'll end with that. That's a powerful line to give the president.

"So that's the order."

She flipped around her pencil and went at the letters with her eraser, removing any and all codes. The president should definitely not see codes. "If a letter takes a turn that is surprising in the text—say, on page three something surprising happens in her life, but the way we've assigned what category it falls into kind of spoils the surprise—then the writer doesn't get to bring the president through her experience in the same way." That was why everybody in the hard-mail room had to use pencil.

Before I left her office that day, I asked Fiona about the candy wrapper mosaic that the inmate made. What ever happened to it? Had it been spared from the shredder?

"It only exists in my memory," she said. "And that just eats at me."

CHAPTER 8

Marnie Hazelton,
April 5, 2011

FREEPORT, NEW YORK

She wore a tan jacket and a loose-fitting tangerine blouse. Did she look okay? How about the necklace? Too much? One thing about standing under those insanely hot lights, with gobs of makeup caked on her face, there, in that distinctly American *Who Wants to Be a Millionaire* moment, was that it was very, very hard to think about anything besides *Holy crap, I'm on TV.*

> *[Applause]*
> I'm well. How are you?
> I'm very well. Yes, I mentioned in the introduction that you've had some hard times, got laid off as an educator, even though you are an acclaimed educator, obviously, but you got a letter from the president that gave you confidence.
> Yes.
> And you brought it with you, I noticed, today. So can you read that to us? He really wrote this to you, right?
> Yes. Yes, he did.
> You're not a crazy woman.
> *[Laughter]*
> No, no, no. I had just wanted him to—

It's the official stationery!
Yes. The official White House stationery.
Oooh. Very nice.

She had the letter on the desk in front of her, and she kept her fingertips touching it. It was handwritten in Obama's distinctive swirl (he doesn't cross all his Ts, she had noted) on a white card. The letter had nothing to do with appearing on a game show; it was a private thing, something in her recent past she had happened to mention when they were trying to flesh out her story, make her more TV worthy. They said, "Bring the letter!" Would she read it in front of a live studio audience? (She made a photocopy. There was no way she was going to take the real letter out of her home.)

> Uh. It says, "Marnie." Uh. "Thank you for your dedication to education. I know that things seem discouraging now, but demand for educators and persons with your skills will grow as the economy and state budgets rebound. In the meantime, I'm rooting for you! Barack Obama."
> *[Applause]*
> That is very cool! That is something you keep forever. For sure. Wow. Well, you hold on to that, and keep positive thoughts going about the future in terms of jobs—and the immediate future right here, because you are now going for one hundred thousand dollars. You have forty thousand six hundred dollars in your bank. It is time to play . . . Classic Millionaire!

"I'm rooting for you."
Coming from the president of the United States, those would be powerful words for any one of millions of unemployed people hit by the economic downturn, but for Marnie they were magical. They could transform her. She'd start getting depressed, frustrated, hopeless, and then just thinking, *I'm rooting for you* would turn her back into Marnie again.
Marnie Hazelton!
Marnie Hazelton was not just some unemployed single mom in her forties in a tan jacket and a tangerine blouse trying to win some cash.

. . .

"Get it together, girl," she had told herself back in the day, when she was a young woman just out of college trying to make it as a rapper. (She was selling mixtapes on the street.) "Get it together." It was her dad's voice, her mom's, her grandparents'; backward and backward, all the ancestors telling her the same thing.

Her dad: one of the first black students to integrate Baltimore Polytechnic high school. Her mom: a week in prison after being arrested for trying to integrate a movie theater in Baltimore, then the Peace Corps. A grandfather in World War II, two great-grandfathers in World War I. A great-great-great-grandmother who arrived in the hull of a ship and was sold as a slave. "Get it together, girl." You were part of a continuum. You weren't random. You were the end of a long line of courage and fight, and you had to keep it going. "A life of service," her parents preached. That was her destiny.

"One out of four students in New York cannot read," the ad in the newspaper had said. "What are you going to do about it?" She applied, got the fellowship; in September 2000 she stood for the first time in front of her class of fifth graders at PS 309 in Brooklyn, New York's Bedford-Stuyvesant neighborhood, one of the lowest-performing schools in the state. The fifth graders could neither read nor write. The level of poverty. The stories of violence. "I didn't come from this," she told the students. She did not hold back. She said, My mom went to college, and my dad worked for a large corporation, and I'm telling you there's more to life than what you see at home. (Some of them didn't have homes.) She wanted them to know there was a whole world out there. She showed them photos of her and 50 Cent, Eminem, Public Enemy, from her fangirl days. She showed them maps of all the places she'd seen, said they could see them, too, one day. She taught them their opinions mattered. What did they think of President Bush financing mosquito nets to help all those people in Darfur dying of malaria? They said, "It's great!" She told them, she said, Well, don't tell me. Tell *him*. They wrote to President Bush. He wrote back! With a photo of his dog, Barney! It was a teachable moment. She had become giddy with the idea of teachable moments.

One year later, in 2001, she was in the middle of an English lesson when the first tower of the World Trade Center got hit. They could see it out the window. Then the second tower. Gray smoke turned to black smoke; they could hear people in the street screaming. She told the kids, she said, Everybody stay in your seats; just please stay in your seats, and then the principal came on the loudspeaker telling everyone to remain calm, and teachers ran into the halls asking one another what the hell was going on.

That fellowship in Bed-Stuy was supposed to be for only two years, but she extended it for three more. She had found where she belonged, in the classroom, serving scared kids desperate for heroes.

She rooted for Obama to become president long before any of her friends believed a black man could become president.

In 2011, she listened intently to his second State of the Union address; he was talking to her:

> The biggest impact on a child's success comes from the man or woman at the front of the classroom. In South Korea, teachers are known as "nation builders." Here in America, it's time we treated the people who educate our children with the same level of respect. . . .
>
> . . . To every young person listening tonight who's contemplating their career choice: If you want to make a difference in the life of our nation; if you want to make a difference in the life of a child—become a teacher. Your country needs you.

A nation builder. A patriot. That's what she was.

After Bed-Stuy, in 2005, she accepted a job in another district, the Roosevelt Union Free School District on Long Island—a whole different set of needs, a district so poor and so deeply in debt that the state had to take control of it and put it on a watch list for "fiscal and academic concern." She brought ambition to that school. She won teaching awards, got promoted to an administrative role, to coordinator for elementary education.

It's hard to say exactly how it all unraveled, but after a few years, she could tell something was up. She even went down to the human resources office one day. "Guys, is there something I need to know? Is there something you need to tell me?"

"Nope, everything is fine!"

She came home that same day to a letter waiting for her in the mailbox. "The position has been eliminated . . . budget cuts."

In the mail. *Are you kidding me?* Budget cuts. In the mail.

All right, Marnie, just to recap, you have banked forty thousand six hundred dollars. You are just four questions away from a million dollars, but you have no lifelines left. Here's your question for one hundred thousand dollars—

No lifelines left. This was so pathetic. And let's not even go into how she had to go out and shop for this jacket and this shirt because she had nothing to wear on TV. Did she look fat? Did her eye just twitch? *Holy crap, I'm on TV.* You can't imagine how hard it is to *think* in a situation like that. Put it this way: She'd had to use a lifeline on the question before this one. It was about "Rub-a-Dub-Dub, Three Men in a Tub." Seriously. Here she was, a nation builder, a patriot (she was also by this point two years into a doctorate in educational leadership and policy), and she was stumped by a nursery rhyme.

It was the butcher, the baker, and the what? *The what?* "I think I'll ask the audience, Meredith." *Ninety percent* of the audience (most of whom were probably not two years into a doctorate in educational leadership and policy) knew that, no, there was no *cobbler* in the nursery rhyme.

Four questions away from a million dollars. No lifelines left.

She was at the end of her rope.

She needed the money. She needed to make rent. She was an unemployed single mom in a tangerine blouse, a nation builder with no nation to build.

The night when she got the news *in the mail* about budget cuts, about her position being eliminated—that was probably the lowest point in her life. She needed to do something. She decided what she needed to do was write a letter of complaint to the president. That was who she needed to tell. It takes a certain amount of fury. Sorrow.

The world caving in. Everything you believe in. An entire identity you had carved for yourself. It takes a couple swigs of vodka. Calling your mom, crying your eyes out.

She poured another drink. She called her mom again. She called friends. Crying. Another drink. Look, she's not going to deny she had a lot to drink. "Dear Mr. President."

This was about more than soothing her own ego. This was about soothing cries that went back centuries. The great-grandfathers who had served. The courage and the fight. A great-great-great-grandmother.

April 5, 2011

Dear Mr. President,

My parents represent the very best of America. . . .

My father went on to serve . . .

My mother answered John F. Kennedy's call to serve. . . .

My parents' maternal grandfathers fought together in World War I. . . . My maternal grandfather and great-uncle both fought in World War II. . . .

I followed in my mother's footsteps to become a teacher. . . .

"A nation builder."

Mr. President, I have committed myself to educating America's future and helping them give back to the world when some of them went home at night to homeless shelters. I spent this past February in the Langa Township in South Africa with my five-year-old son, giving school suppl[i]es to students in the township schools.

Mr. President . . . I am sure you receive thousands of letters with the woes of the unemployed and there is very little you can do on an individual basis. But I felt compelled to reach out to you. . . .

I lost my job because the stimulus money to schools has ended and New York Governor Andrew Cuomo took an ax to school aid. My question to you is, if I have dedicated the last eleven years of my life to nation building and educating America's children, how do I now go about providing for my family . . . when the education job market is flooded with thousands of teachers dismissed due to budget cuts?

Carpe diem,
Marnie Hazelton

She was stunned when she got a letter back from the president. She stared at that thing. The official White House stationery. His handwriting is more like drawing. He doesn't cross all his *T*s. She stared at that thing for what felt like hours.

"I'm rooting for you."

No lifelines left. Four questions away from a million dollars. The lights. The makeup. Were her bangs too long? Look, she'd be fine if she didn't win a million dollars. *Fine.* She was thinking a hundred thousand dollars. Walk out with a hundred thousand dollars. A game show. Whatever it takes. Solve the problem. All the résumés she sent out. All the interviews. Nothing. Countless interviews. Nothing happening. Nobody calling back.

Here's your question for one hundred thousand dollars.
[Tense music, blue laser lights beaming in an upward circular motion]
Canada's Simon Fraser University made headlines in 2009 by introducing what educational innovation?

An educational innovation! Well, surely she'd know this one, as an educator two years into a PhD. It was a multiple-choice question, and there were four choices:

A. A major in "everything"
B. A library with no books

C. An all-female football team
D. A grade worse than "F"

Think. A game show is built on the principle that the contestant can disregard these lights and this makeup and *think*. (Or maybe it's not.) On game shows they want you to think out loud so the audience can feel a part of things.

> If I think about innovation, I'm thinking, "Library with no books." Football team, an all-female football team is not innovative. A major in everything . . . Innovation versus motivation . . . I wouldn't say motivation for . . . a grade worse than F.
> Well, here's the deal. You do have forty thousand six hundred dollars. You could walk with that, if you choose to, um, but if you get this right, it's worth a hundred thousand dollars. If you were to miss it, you go down to twenty-five thousand dollars.
> I came here with nothing.
> Heh heh.
> *[Tense drum music]*
> All right, Meredith, like I said yesterday, I came to win; I'll go with my gut feeling, and . . . I'm going to say a library with no books, *B*, my final answer.
> *[Blue laser lights beaming in a downward circular motion]*
> It made sense to me, but it was *D*, a grade worse than F.
> *[Sorrowful sounds from audience]*

Meredith explained that the correct answer had something to do with a grade for kids who got caught cheating. Something. Something. Something. Her heart. Her stomach. The thud you feel, in your gut. Letting everyone down. Her mom. Her kid. The ancestors. No lifelines. No million dollars. No $100,000. No $40,600. She would be sent home with a consolation prize, $25,000.

> All right, well, I had a wonderful time. I had a wonderful time.
> The grade is "FD." It stands for "failed for academic dishonesty."
> Oh, a grade worse than F. Okay.

But you know what? As the president said, we are all rooting for you.

[Applause]

Okay.

Meredith leaned in for a kiss, and Marnie obliged and then sauntered off the stage, carrying the letter she had read to the audience, the blue laser lights going around and around.

She got home and took off that stupid jacket and that stupid tangerine shirt and poured some wine and climbed into bed. It took her a moment or two to get it together. To grasp hold of reality. *Wait, I just got handed a check for twenty-five thousand dollars.* It took her a few beats to embrace how lucky a person would be if the clouds suddenly coughed up that kind of cash. But of course she did grasp it.

"I'm rooting for you."

I am Marnie Hazelton!

In the months that followed, she went to more job interviews, and for good luck she carried Obama's letter (the photocopy) with her. She kept it in her purse. It became her talisman. She would pull it out at lunch and after dinner and before breakfast.

Thirteen months after she got laid off, she got a call from the Roosevelt Union Free School District.

They wanted her back. They needed her. *They needed Marnie Hazelton.*

Reinvigorated, reinvented, when she got back into the classroom, she showed her students the note she got from President Obama; it was a teachable moment. She told the kids, she said, "I'm rooting for you." At parent-teacher nights she told the parents she was rooting for them. She told the bigwigs on the school board, teachers, and coaches; she told business leaders in the community (who needed to get it together and *help* that school); she told everybody, "I'm rooting for you!"

She got promoted, she got her PhD, she got promoted a few more times, and then one day in early 2016 she was named superintendent of the Roosevelt Union Free School District.

Superintendent of the school district that had once laid her off.

No longer will you find it on the New York State watch list for fiscal and academic concern. The "Roosevelt Renaissance from

Good to Great!" has begun, with the goal of a 100 percent graduation
rate by 2020, and Marnie Hazelton, nation builder, is in charge.

THE WHITE HOUSE

WASHINGTON

Marnie —

Thanks for your dedication to education. I know
that things seem discouraging now, but demand for
educators and persons with your skills will
grow as the economy and state budgets rebound.
In the meantime, I'm rooting for you!

July 16, 2016

Dear Mr. President,

. . . The sincerest thanks I can convey to you is a quote by the late
Maya Angelou:

"I've learned that people will forget what you said, people will forget
what you did, but people will never forget how you made them feel."

Carpe diem,
Marnie Hazelton

Samples, 2013-2014

Contact Us - Other

Submitted: April 20, 2013 02:10
Originating Host:
Remote IP:
From: Susan Patterson
Email Address:
Phone:
Address (Domestic):
Topic:

Message:
Dear Mr. President,
I've written and complained about a lot of your policies. I got a response to my opinion on gun control. The response I received I think changed my mind. My concern, one of them, was that mental health seemed over looked. If you do, all you said in the letter, I will support your gun control bills. I also would like to say, I felt very good about the speech you gave last night after the second Boston bomber was captured. I still HATE Obama care, the entire thing. But, the gun stuff could work.
Thank you for the response letter, Susan Patterson

From: Erv and Ross Uecker-Walker

Submitted: 11/17/2014 6:35 PM EST

Email:

Phone:

Address: Milwaukee, Wisconsin

Message: We offer our sincere thanks to President Obama and his Administration for their consistent support of civil rights for the LGBT Community and especially for marriage equality. As a result of your efforts, after being in a committed relationship for 57 years, we will be able to be legally married on November 30th at our church, Pilgrim United Church of Christ, Grafton, Wisconsin. It is particularly significant as November 30th is our 57th anniversary. We never thought it would happen. Thank you for the bottom of our hearts.

From: Ms. Melina S

Submitted: 7/15/2013 5:16 PM EDT

Email:

Phone:

Address:

Message: Dear Mr. Presdient,

Today I went to my Kaiser pharmacy to refill my birth control prescription. Automatically I gave my Kaiser ID card and credit card. The pharmacy said to me 'no co-pay' and gave me back my credit card. I slid it back over the counter to the pharmacist and said, 'It's 30 dollars'. She slid it back and said 'you don't have to pay co-pay'. I asked 'why? Since when?' I was puzzled and sure this was a new employee and she was doing something wrong. She said 'it's the new health care provision'. When she said that, it clicked. I have been hearing about it. I knew about it. But here it was in action, and I could not believe it. I kid you not, I felt'emotional'right away. I felt something. Like an injustice, was turned. Like a wrong was, made right. Like when you hear an apology, you know you deserved' I suppose can't describe it very well in an e-mail. But I felt something so strong, that I had to write you right away and say THANK YOU. Thank you for standing up for women. THANK YOU FOR STANDING UP FOR WOMEN! I know it's a small thing' but it's so big to little old me. What it means, and what it stands for; there is a hope. Things can change. Women do have a friend in politics. And I appreciate you so much for doing the right thing. Really, truly' thank you so much!

Sincerely and respectfully,

Melina S

The President
The White House
1600 Pennsylvania Avenue NW
Washington, DC 20500

✓ #043 485
MAY 20 2013

*LOS support
sample* 7/12/13
$f.1$

Dear Mr. Obama,

"We are true to our creed when a little girl born into the bleakest poverty knows that she has the same chance to succeed as anybody else, because she is an American, she is free, and she is equal, not just in the eyes of God but also in our own."

Do you recognize this? You said this in your presidential inauguration in January, right around my eighteenth birthday. I wanted you to know how much this impacted me, it made me want to succeed more than ever. I don't want to tell you my whole life's story, but I do want you to know that I was one of those little girls. I was born into horrible poverty, and my parents didn't think that I had much of a chance at a future because of our financial circumstances. I proved them wrong. Every statistic said that I didn't have good chances of getting into a good college. I proved them wrong. I met your wife once, she came to my high school,   and I was one of the lucky few that got to shake her hand. I thought that was the coolest thing that had ever happened to me in my entire life, and it made me realize that I had just as much of a chance getting into a good college as anyone else. I worked harder after that, and when senior year came around I started doubting my future as a college student, through becoming homeless and finding out that I am a lesbian, I got through all of it and here I am. A soon-to- be high school graduate going to   in the fall, and I am telling you all of this so that you know that you had a hand in helping me get where I am today. I heard your inaugural address at school and when you said what you said, I started crying, because I had never had anybody in my entire life tell me that I could succeed just as much as anyone else just because I am an American. People told me that I was crazy, that someone else wrote that speech for you, but I didn't care, I chose to believe your words and I'm happy I did. I just wanted to thank you for saying that, and I wanted to thank your wife for helping me realize that I am equal to everyone else, regardless of how much money I have.

A Hopeful Future College Student,

P.S.: I'm glad you got re-elected☺

From: Matthew Tyrone Pointer
South Gate, California
December 23, 2013

My name is Matthew Tyrone Pointer and I am a varsity basketball player for South Gate high school, located in South Gate, California

This is my first year at South Gate high school. I recently transferred from our town rivals, The South East Jaguars. The reason I transferred was because of basketball. It keeps my grades up and in the long run I know it'll make me a better person as I grow.

The basketball program is great here, we go to many gyms located in many different cities and sometimes even in different counties. I can say the most amazing school/gym I visited was Beverly hills high school, when my team and I were walking around the campus looking for the gym, we all happen to notice this one classroom. The reason for that was because the classroom was filled with ipads, for the students of course. All of us basketball players coming from South Gate high school, were very shocked and just amazed. While we were stuck on talking about how we wished we had the supplies these Beverly Hills students have, a Beverly Hills student walked by and looked at us, we were all in our South Gate attire so that led up to him asking us where South Gate was located, we all replied "by South Central, on Firestone and State St." the student had no idea what we had just said but we all understood why. He just proceeded to wherever he was going.

Well now to express the way I feel on being treated unfairly with equal access of school resources/supplies. Schools like Beverly Hills high school and Redondo Union have great electronic resources and pretty neat school supplies, that us lower class schools like South East, South Gate, and Huntington Park don't have.

I dont know if its because we're a minority as a community or maybe because of our location, but I really feel that school supplies such as computers, classrooms, even pencil and paper should be equally distributed to all schools no matter the district or location. What makes those schools like Beverly Hills and Redondo union better than us? Is it the students? I hope you get the point I'm trying to make Mr.Obama, I just want equality within every community and imm only talking about school wise. To some kids, school is the only thing that can help them make it out of where their stuck in. You want change? , well give us a chance and we'll do our part by doing our job in school.

I dont really care if I get a response back after writing this letter, as long as somebody hears me out and understands im trying to do better for our community.

THE WHITE HOUSE

WASHINGTON

February 11, 2015

Mr. Matthew Tyrone Pointer
Los Angeles, California

Dear Matthew:

I've been meaning to write since I read the letter you sent
some time ago. Playing basketball in high school taught me about
who I was and what I could do, and I'm glad it's played a positive
role in your life as well.

You're right—education is the key to success, and whether
students live in Beverly Hills or South Gate, they all should have a
world-class education with access to the resources they need to reach
for their dreams. Your generation deserves a system worthy of your
potential, and every day I'm fighting to make that vision a reality.

Thank you for your message—your passion to lift up your
community is admirable. Keep up the hard work, both on and off the
court, and know I expect big things from you.

Sincerely,

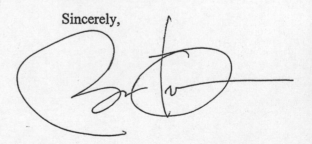

7/8/13
x/4

VI
Sample Firearms

Back from the OVAL
7/9/13

Reply

Dear Mr. President,

My name is ▮▮▮▮▮ and I'm from ▮▮▮▮▮ ▮▮▮▮▮ a suburb ▮▮▮▮▮ ▮▮▮▮▮ of Boston. I'm a retired Union Ironworker ▮▮▮▮▮

Enclosed please find my still valid NRA card. I will not be renewing my membership after today's' disappointing Senate vote.

Reasonable people expect reasonable action to be taken by their elected officials. That did not happen today. Evidently the NRA's influence is too intimidating for many people. I no longer feel properly represented by the NRA and I would be very surprised if there weren't a lot more who share my opinion.

If you tell the citizens of this country of my actions, I think you'd wind up with a mailbox full of NRA cards. Background checks are the very least we can do in light of Sandy Hook ,Aurora, and Arizona, to name a few. Reasonable people can accept reasonable laws.

Thank you for your time,

Back from the OVAL
10/18/13

A message from: John Mier

Submitted via www.whitehouse.gov/contact

Submitted: 10/16/2013 11:34 AM
Email:
Phone:
Address:

Reply — and save for me.

Leetsdale, Pennsylvania

Message:

Dear President Obama,

My wife and I are signed up for medical insurance due to begin on January 1, 2014 which we bought off of the Healthcare.gov marketplace.

Yes, the website really stank for the first week but it just stank for the next week. Now, it still smells BUT: instead of paying $1600 per month for a group insurance plan of just me and my wife (we are both self-employed and it was the only way we could get coverage) we will have a plan that will only cost us $692 a month - a savings of $900 per month. Once this program gets underway, I would expect the cost to go even lower. And by next year, the website will work like a champ.

You and your team envisioned, put together, and got through a balky Congress this plan. Despite all the histrionics and lies from the Cruz Control, it will be good for America.

Thanks for doing it and thanks for not caving into the idiots.

Best regards to your wonderful wife, Michelle, and to your fine young daughters Talia and Sasha. They have a father to be proud of.

Very Sincerely,

John M. Mier

p.s. In one of the greater acts of hypocritical gall, there are GOP congressmen who want to investigate why the ACA website didn't work very well in those states where Republican governors would cooperate with the program. But they are losers and in '14, not all of them will be coming back for their government job.

Case Number:

THE WHITE HOUSE
WASHINGTON

John —

Thanks for the letter. The website really was a screw up, but I'm glad to hear the actual program is saving you money!

Best wishes,

10/19/14
7/1
Sample/Ind/Support/younger/PW

Jordan Garey

Independence Ky

Dear Mr. President,

I am 7 years old. My name is Jordan. I want to tell you that I am getting adopted on Oct 8, 2014. I have been a foster kid for 6 years, and I have finally found my forever family. I have two dads named Jeremy and Matt that are keeping me forever. I know you can't come to my adoption, but I wanted to tell you thank you for everything that you are doing to keep me safe.

Thank you, Jordan Garey

Jordan Garey

P.S. I wish I could spend the night sometime in your big house.

Mr. Daniel F. Jurain
New York, NY

President Barrack Obama
The White House
1600 Pennsylvania Ave, NW
Washington, D.C. 20500

20500

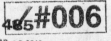

485 #006

MAR 20 2013

NEW YORK NY 100
08 MAR 2013 PM 10 L

sample/LGBT prob-LGBT
6/25/13
f6

New York, NY

March 6. 2013

President Barrack Obama
The White House
1600 Pennsylvania Avenue NW
Washington, DC 20500.

Dear President Obama,

Martin Luther King, Jr. once said, "Our lives begin to end the day we become silent about things that matter." That statement kept going through my mind as I listened to your inauguration speech. It was a moment that was so surreal ..., I never thought I would hear these words in my life from a president:

"We, the people, declare today that the most evident of truths – that all of us are created equal – is the star that guides us still; just as it guided our forebears through Seneca Falls, an Selma, and Stonewall."

My Facebook page got hit like crazy. Family and friends keep calling me on the phone to ask if I heard it. I did, and at first I didn't believe my ears. I thought you must been talking about slavery in Stonewall, Mississippi. I mean after all it was also Martin Luther King, Jr. Day. Then it dawned on me. You were talking about the Stonewall Inn. My Stonewall Inn. My eyes fill up when I thought back to the first night at the Stonewall Riots when I was a 20 year old gay kid at the bar the night of the raid.

You see Mr. President; I was there for the first 2 nights of the riots. It was like a war zone. I saw garbage cans burning in the streets; bricks being thrown in the air and young silly little gay kids like myself being beaten by police officers and the tactical police force till they bleed. All this violence because we wanted to dance alone and be unseen from a society that did not want us. I was so unaware at the time that I was being denied my right as an American, but I that I was also being denied my basic human right. It is kind of funny when you think about it; my grandfather came to America as an Irish immigrant. He got a job as a laborer assembling the new Stature of Liberty in the New York Harbor. The same one with the mounted plaque that reads "Give me your tired, your poor, your huddled masses yearning to breathe free." I yearn to breathe free Mr. President.

As gay man back then in 1969 I could not serve openly in the military. I could not get a license to practice law or be a hairstylist; if I was trapped doing something "Lewd". I was dammed by almost all religions. The American Psychiatric Association told me that I was mentality ill. I was not allowed to get married, and had to keep my love of another man hidden. I could not adopt children. I was not allowed to receive a legal drink in any bar in New York City with out them loosing their license for serving a "sexual deviant." It was a life that was bleak and filled with one word "NO" and to top it off that night in June 1969, they were now going to tell me I couldn't dance … not even hidden in back of a dark bar.

You made me proud sir when you mentioned that significant part of my life, but it is a battle that is not over yet, and we still have a big fight on our hands. I still have not gotten to dance that dance I started 44 years ago. The big joyous "I Am A Completely Free Gay American Dance" yet, and I so badly want to dance that dance before I meet my maker … not just have spent my life listening to the music.

Thank you for making that dance floor a little bit more accessible and starting to play the music.

Sincerely yours,

Daniel (Danny) Garvin
Stonewall Inn Veteran

THE WHITE HOUSE

WASHINGTON

November 29, 2013

Mr. Daniel Garvin

New York, New York

Dear Daniel:

Thank you for the powerful letter you sent this spring—I read it with interest.

At Stonewall, people joined together and declared they had seen enough injustice. While being beaten down, they stood up and challenged not only how the world saw them, but also how they saw themselves. History shows that once that spirit takes hold, little can stand in its way—so the riots gave way to protests, the protests gave way to a movement, and the movement gave way to a transformation that continues today.

You are right that the dance is unfinished. But as long as I hold this Office, I will keep fighting to open the floor for everyone.

Sincerely,

Barack Obama

Contact Us - Economy

Submitted: August 28, 2013 01:40
Originating Host:
Remote IP:
From: Tom Hoefner
Email Address:
Phone:
Address (Domestic):
Topic:

Back from the OVAL
9/12/13

Reply

Message:
Dear Mr. President,

My wife and I live in Brooklyn. I have a Master's Degree from an Ivy League school. She has one from a CUNY. I haven't been able to find full-time work since 2008. I have six figures of student loans I can't pay, most of which I've defaulted on and are now with private collections agencies. We worry about paying bills from week to week. Yesterday I went over the limit on my Target credit card and had to wait with my 6 year old at customer service figuring out how I could pay for our very modest selection of carefully chosen groceries. I have looked for steady work for five years in my field, education, presumably a stable field that is proving not to be. I send resumes out into the void, never to hear from them again.

I am 34. I will likely never own a home. I will likely never have a retirement pension. My generation was always told that if we worked hard and did well in school and stayed out of trouble we'd have secure futures. We were lied to, or at the very least misled.

We do not have pay-cable channels. We have cell phones, but no landline. We have never taken a vacation.

We get by, day to day. Barely. We will never achieve the American Dream, if it ever existed. We will be silent victims, never suffering enough to be pitied but never succeeding enough to pay off our debts, to be able to live as we were promised.

The system is broken. The middle class is dead. We are its silent victims.

Sincerely,
Tom Hoefner

P.S. - I don't expect a response to this. I'm used to getting form letters as a response, or no response at all. This is just one more thing I needed to shout into the empty void.

THE WHITE HOUSE
WASHINGTON

Tom —

I got your letter. I know things are tough out there right now, and I won't try to pretend that I've got a guaranteed solution to your immediate situation. But the economy is slowly getting better, and we are working every day to push through Congress measures that might help - like student loan forgiveness or mitigation.

I guess what I'm saying is that your President is

thinking about you. And your six year old is undoubtedly lucky to have a dad that cares.

From: Mr. Bob Melton

Submitted: 12/18/2014 11:27 PM EST

Email:

Phone:

Address: Morganton, North Carolina

Message: Dear Mr. President,
I thought you would like to know that because of the ACA I went to see a Doctor for the first time in 12 years. I am having pain and the ACA enabled me to at least get examined and now treated. I'm 61 years old and in pretty good shape (At least I think so} but without your help would have had NO insurance. At all. Thank You again Mr. President. You remind me of President Roosevelt. A man was weeping on the street when FDR died. A reporter asked,"Did you know him, you are so upset?" The man replied,"No, I didn't know him. He knew me". I feel that same connection to you Mr. President.

THE WHITE HOUSE

WASHINGTON

December 13, 2016

Mr. Bob Melton
Morganton, North Carolina

Dear Bob:

I wanted to take a moment to extend my appreciation for the note you sent a few years ago about the difference the Affordable Care Act has made in your life—as you know from my staff's outreach to you, your message moved me and my team deeply.

Over the course of my Presidency, I've seen in letters like yours the courage, determination, and open-heartedness of our people. "The faith of America" of which President Roosevelt spoke still echoes in every corner of our land—shaped and carried forward by generations. I am confident that it will continue to guide us as long as engaged citizens like you keep speaking out for the ideals that bind us as a Nation and as a people.

Again, thank you. You have my very best wishes and my gratitude for your steadfast support.

Sincerely,

Dear Mr. President,

My name is Gavin Nore. I am a 15 year old young man from Fort Dodge, Iowa. I first met you when I was eight years old. Back in 2007, you gave a speech about your campaign. Once you were done, people were allowed to ask you questions. I got the chance to meet you and I asked, "Would you continue stem cell research?" You told me, you would continue the research. When I turned 14, I was diagnosed with Hodgkins Lymphoma on February 14, 2013. I beat the battle. During the summer of 2013, I was cancer free. Then, in August of last year, I was re-diagnosed. I had to have a stem cell transplant. I beat the battle once again. I would like to thank you very much for continuing the research. If the research hadent continued, I wouldn't be here today. Once again, thank you very much Mr. President!

Sincerely,
Gavin Nore

CHAPTER 9

Barack Obama

THE WHITE HOUSE

I asked Obama if he read the letters in the sequence in which Fiona so carefully arranged them.

"I actually do!" he said. "I'll go through them one at a time. Yeah, I know. You've been rifling through my mail—"

It was a cool autumn afternoon, the trees outside appropriately dropping their leaves, marking the end of a season and, soon, the end of an era. The first African American president. Two terms. Closing.

Obama's Oval Office was decorated with more restraint than many of his predecessors'. He kept a wooden bowl of fresh apples on the coffee table; George Bush usually had an abundant bouquet of roses there. Obama had added striped wallpaper in muted gold tones, and he'd replaced Bush's formal white damask couches with quiet tan ones in soft brushed corduroy. (Clinton had bold, bright stripes. Bush, Sr., had the whole place done up in baby blue and cream.) Red curtains added a pop to Obama's Oval Office; overall the effect was a tailored mid-century modern look.

Soon all that would change to reflect the tastes and the mood of a new leader.

I asked Obama if he typically read the letters there, in the Oval Office—or someplace else? Did he have tea? A brandy, perhaps?

"Usually my habit is to have dinner with my family," he said, "and then I head into the Treaty Room. And I'll have a stack of work. So I'm sitting in my chair, and I've got policy briefings, and I've got decision memos, and I've got, you know, some intelligence report, so it will take me a couple of hours to plow through that. And I usually save the letters for last. And they're in a purple folder. And typically the letter is stapled to the envelope that it came in. Sometimes the packet is sort of bulky and unwieldy, because somebody sent some object along with the letter. The most common would be drawings from kids, or pictures of a family, or some document that shows their interaction with some bank or some bureaucrat that wasn't particularly helpful to them. Every once in a while you'll get some personal artifact that somebody sent, like copies of letters from their dad when he was fighting in World War II or some, you know, personal object that really meant something to them that they wanted me to have."

I don't know why I was surprised by how slowly the president talked. You hear him in public and he sounds so . . . pensive. One on one, he seems even more so, perhaps given your own urge to . . . help, maybe, speed things up? But there is no interrupting; he's in command, plodding forward, each thought a complete sentence with, that is, commas—each word seeming to have come out only after a good amount of consideration. The image I got listening to Obama that day as he sat in the Oval Office courteously contemplating the seemingly mundane matter of his daily mail habit, was that of a conscientious old man putting together a jigsaw puzzle. Some swirly seascape where there is blue, but then there is *blue,* and then there is "blue" and . . . blue! You couldn't argue with it; he's getting it right, and the picture is coming together.

"There have been recurring letters," he went on, "and in that category, I would say, are veterans looking for help, young people with heavy student loan debt trying to figure out whether they qualify for some relief, military personnel or military families who are struggling in some fashion with either a decision or a lack of help from the Department of Defense.

"If there was a letter that particularly moved me, jolted me, saddened me, I got in the habit of asking people to circulate it. So that everyone could take a look at it."

He talked about scribbling notes on letters, asking questions of staff. "Somebody would explain, 'This is what it's like to deal with the federal government on this issue.' Or 'This is how this law has affected me,' regardless of what the theory was." He wanted to know why and what could be done to improve the situation. "And those staff probably didn't always enjoy getting those notes," he said. "But they understood that if I wrote on this letter, I wanted an answer, and I wanted an explanation—that they had to come up with one. Sometimes, you know, you'd hear back from the staff, and they'd say, 'Well, you know, this is why we're doing it this way.' And I'd say, 'Well, that doesn't make any sense. And let's try to change the policy.'

"That would be an interesting exercise, to track the number of initiatives—most of them small, most of them not ones that would get a headline—that we ended up modifying or sparked, at least, a discussion about how we were doing business. It would not be a negligible number.

"And then there have been times where you've seen the reactions to a response," he said. "Probably the most powerful example was we typically have wounded warriors and veterans come in for tours at the White House, and I'll greet them. I remember once meeting a beautiful family, relatively young mom, dad, couple of little kids, and as I came up to shake their hands, the mom started tearing up. And she gave me a big hug, and she said, 'You know, the reason we're here is because of you.' And I said, 'Why is that?' And she said, 'Well, my husband here, who had served, you know, he had pretty severe PTSD, and I was worried that he might not make it, and you had the VA call us directly, and that's what prompted him to get treatment.' You know, and that's when you're reminded that there's something about this office that, when people get a response, they feel that their lives and concerns are important. And that can change in some small way, and maybe in occasionally big ways, how they view their lives."

I asked him how he decides which letters to answer personally. He said that part was easy: "The ones that I usually respond to right then and there are ones that involve somebody having a very personal issue where my sense of what they need is just an affirmation of some sort." I thought of Shelley Muniz from Columbia, California, who had written in 2009 to tell Obama about her teenage son

Micah who had died of leukemia and about the enormous health-care bills facing her grieving family. "It is for families like yours that I am fighting so hard for healthcare reform," Obama wrote to her.

"There have been times I've gotten a letter from, say, a senior, and they'll just go through their budget," he told me. "You know, literally here's what I'm spending per month, and here's what my Social Security check is. You know, 'It's really hard to make it.'

"Sometimes people share letters with me about some sort of transformation they've gone through. There have been a number of letters where somebody talks about how they were raised in a family that was suspicious of people of a different race, or background. The growth that they or a loved one went through in seeing themselves in other people in a way they wouldn't have expected.

"And then there are occasions where the letter is particularly, uh, pointed at what an idiot I am—I feel obliged to respond then and there.

"My correspondence office has always been very clear that if all I'm getting is letters from people saying I'm doing a good job," he told me, "I'm not getting half of the population.

"But, you know, I will tell you that the letters I remember so often are not the ones in the heat of battle that speak directly to an issue that we're in the middle of a fight on, because oftentimes those are fairly predictable. The letters, I think, that matter the most to me are the ones that . . . make a connection, that speak to people's lives and their values and what's important to them."

I resisted the impulse to ask him if he had a favorite letter. I felt it might be like saying, "Hey, who's your favorite American?" And I was more interested to find out which letters, if any, might pop up for him all on their own. Thousands of letters, over an eight-year period, coming to him in the back of his briefing book—would any specific ones come to mind as he looked back on all this?

That day there were three. Three that came up in our casual conversation about the mail and his presidency and the degree to which one influenced the other.

"I remember a father who said, 'I'm very conservative and gener-ally have a very negative view of immigration, but then my son be-friended a young man who, it turned out, was undocumented,'" Obama said, describing the first.

I'd read several letters from conservatives who found themselves changing their minds about immigration, like Bill Oliver's letter about Quique, but I think this one, from Ronn Ohl of Sanford, North Carolina, who wrote to talk about a DREAMer he'd gotten to know, was the one that Obama was referring to that day:

Ronn Ohl

Sanford NC

Back from the OVAL
7/30/12

17 June 2012

TO: President Obama
     1600 Pennsylvania Avenue, NW
     Washington, DC 20500

Mister President,

Thank you for your leadership in signing the executive order to permit children of illegal aliens to be able to live and work in this country without being deported. You took action where Congress was unable to do the same with the Dream Act. You took bold measures in doing so, even though it was most likely for political purposes. This may be the initial step to resolving the illegal immigration problem and hopefully the next Congress is able to build from this initiative.

I am a descendant of an illegal immigrant into this country. My great-great grandfather was an Irish stow away on a cargo ship of walnuts from England in the late 1800s. I have served in the military for 21 years. I now reside in a community that has a predominate populace of Hispanics. One of my son's friends since middle school is an illegal alien. My son recently graduated from college with a MPA. This friend came to in the United States when he was 4 years old with his parents looking for a better life. That was 21 years ago. He graduated from high school and played varsity soccer. However, he radically found out that he was unable to do other things legally as his other friends. He could not receive a driver's license, could not apply for college, and he could not find legitimate work.

Again, I strongly agree with your decision. I talked to my son's friend this past Christmas about this topic and he thought it would be years before anything would happen to keep him in this country and not being afraid of being deported. For his entire life all he knew was living in the United States as an American. Now he tries to find odd jobs and always on the alert. The illegal immigrants find a way to make a living without being caught and deported. However, many unscrupulous employers and landlords take advantage of this thus abusing and stealing from them.

As I stated in the initial paragraph, I thought this was probably a political tactic. This is the only issue that I agree on your part for the past 3 1/2 years. I am a Tea Party conservative. I believe in fiscal responsibility with balancing the federal budget. I also believe in limited federal government with certain responsibilities passed to the state governments, such as health care. I do not concur with your notion that the elite rich should pay a little more of their fair share of taxes. That would in line with a rich person paying $4 for a Big Mac sandwich while the poor person is only expected to pay $3.50 for the same. Where is the Liberty and Justice in that?

Respectfully,

RONN OHL

CC: My personal U.S. Congress Representative

Ronn Ohl

Obama sometimes stewed over letters that were critical of him or his administration. This one was particularly confounding. Why was this "Tea Party conservative" so skeptical about the president doing the very thing he was writing to say he thought was commendable?

THE WHITE HOUSE
WASHINGTON

Ron —

Thanks for the letter. Your cynicism about my motives may be a bit misplaced; I know, and similarly care for, a lot of young people like your son's friend.

I won't try to persuade you about the rest of my agenda, but who knows — maybe we have more common ground than you might think.

Best wishes,

I told Obama I was surprised by how much thought he seemed to put into some of these responses. I mean, one guy in North Carolina doesn't trust the president's motives. Was that really so surprising? And he's going to try to change the guy's mind in a note?

"When you're president, so often you're talking in shorthand," he said. "Almost always you're being reported in shorthand. You can get into habits. You forget that on the other side of any issue is a complex person, or people, or communities that are trying to sort through a whole bunch of stuff that they're dealing with."

So when those sorts of letters landed on his desk, he took special note. "Sometimes I felt as if I was being a little unfair, because I'd sometimes devote more effort and attention to those letters. Because I really wanted them to know that, you know, this isn't just the comments on the Internet. That that's not the function of this. The function is: We're going to engage."

. . .

The second letter Obama mentioned to me that day was one that had stirred up a fuss.

"A letter I received from a woman in Minnesota," he offered. "I actually used her and her family as an example of what was best about America in a State of the Union speech. And if you read the letter, it was just describing, you know, 'Here's what I'm going through.' And 'I'm not looking for a handout or a guarantee for success; I just wish there was something that would maybe make this a little bit easier.' "

It wasn't a particularly exciting letter. It wasn't cute. It wasn't emotional. There were no photos or drawings attached. Even the author of it, Rebekah Erler, told me, when I reached out to her, that she thought it was unremarkable. "I wrote it in like fifteen minutes," she said. "I just wanted him to know what was going on out here."

March 1, 2014

President and Mrs. Obama,

I am writing to you as a voter, a politically involved woman, a wife, and a mother. I want to tell you a little bit about our family. My husband worked in Construction trades from the time he finished high school and I was a college educated administrative professional when we met. . . . If only we had known what was about to happen to the housing and construction market. I was pregnant with our first child.

. . . We decided that in order to survive, we would relocate from my home town of Seattle back to his home town in the midwest and into his parents['] basement with our 6 month old son.

. . . My husband was hired to work as a freight conductor in the railroad industry—a great job with great benefits, but a miserable lifestyle. We had our second son, and I went to a local community college to retrain for a new career as an accountant. I was simultaneously home alone with two kids under 2 years old. I took out very

reasonable student loans. We did everything right. Last October we bought our first house. My husband was able to leave the railroad and return to the remodeling industry. Now he is home for dinner every night, and gets a full night of sleep. It's amazing what you take for granted. It's amazing what you can bounce back from when you have to.

The reason I'm writing to tell you all this is simple. I did what the economy, and you and the country is calling for people to do—go out, retrain, reenter the workforce in a great job with upward mobility.

The cost of our groceries has skyrocketed while we feverishly cut coupons and meal plan. . . . We pay $1900 a month to send our kids to the local preschools while we work. My student loan payments will start in a few months. . . .

The truth is—in America, where two people have done everything they can to succeed and fight back from the brink of financial ruin—through job loss, and retraining, and kids, and credit card debts that are set up to keep you impoverished forever, and the discipline to stop spending any money on yourselves or take a vacation in 5 years—it's virtually impossible to live a simple middle class life. We drive our 10 and 15 year old cars that are too small for our family because they are paid off. When my dad was diagnosed with cancer, he had to pay for the plane tickets for my kids and I to visit because at 35 years old, I can't afford to fly my family to visit their grandfather.

My husband and I can barely afford the basics. Our big splurge is cable TV so we can follow our beloved Minnesota Wild during the hockey season (and watch Team USA in the Olympics!). We don't go out with friends or shop for clothes or toys or anything except at Christmas time or birthdays.

We don't feel like victims of our life—we have a really good life, and we are proud. We have a garden in the back, and we run around

outside in parks and every other free and wonderful thing the Min-
neapolis area has to offer. We are a strong, tight-knit family who has
made it through some very, very hard times in our short 7 years.

I teared up when you were elected President. I took my son to the
voting booth with me in 2012 so when he grows up he can say he
went with me to vote for Barack Obama. . . .

I am just writing to remind you that the silent ones out here, the
ones who are just working as hard as we can to make it, the ones
who voted for you—are out here.

We need childcare to be reasonably priced, or subsidized. Two thou-
sand dollars a month for preschool is an astronomical price to pay
to have your child be safe and taught well while you go to work. . . .
We need food to be affordable. Our wages have not increased in
the last 10 years but the cost of living has multiplied many times
over.

I'm pretty sure this is a silly thing to do—to write a letter to the
President. But on some level—I know that staying silent about what
you see and what needs changing never makes any difference. So
I'm writing you to let you know what it's like for us out here in the
middle of the country. And I hope you will listen.

Thank You, and Best Regards,
Rebekah Erler
Minneapolis, MN

"Everyone was saying the recession is over," Rebekah told me when
I asked her what compelled her to write in 2014. "And I'm like,
'What? No it's not.' And I'm like, 'Surely Obama gets it.' I knew he
wouldn't think that we were just, like, irresponsible. I just thought
that he had been one of us not that long ago. He had student loans.
A regular family. You know, there's that old thing that people would
say Bush didn't know what a gallon of milk cost. Obama struck me
as someone who knew what a gallon of milk cost."

Like almost every other letter writer I talked to, Rebekah hadn't expected the president to read her letter, much less respond to it. But she did get a response, about three months after she sent it. It was a phone call from the White House. "They said, 'The president wants to have lunch with you. He's coming to Minnesota.' I'm like, 'What?'"

Within days, on a Thursday in June 2014, Rebekah was sitting at Matt's Bar in Minneapolis ordering a "Jucy Lucy" (a burger with cheese in the middle), and Obama ordered the same. She was too nervous to eat. He thanked her for her letter. He told her it reminded him of something his mother would have written. He invited her to come with him to a town hall meeting afterward up at Minnehaha Park, and so she rode with him in the motorcade, sat next to him and across from Valerie Jarrett, and they asked her if she'd be able to maybe introduce him the next day, at an economic policy speech he was scheduled to deliver over at Lake Harriet, and so she did that too, brought her family, and when it was over, they all hugged, and Obama said, "Hey, if you're ever in Washington—" and then he was gone.

"And my husband was like, 'What the heck just happened?'"

People in the media were predictably and perhaps appropriately skeptical. The White House featured photos and videos of the visit on its website; they billed it as "a day in the life" of Rebekah. The midterms were coming up, and Obama's approval rating was sitting at just 41 percent. So maybe it was a political stunt. Or maybe, as even staffers readily admitted may have been the case, Obama was just yearning for the old days, when campaigning meant you got to hang out with people outside the bubble and eat burgers.

"People said, 'Oh, he used you,'" Rebekah told me. "'You were a prop.' But I never once felt that way. It just wasn't like that. Even now people ask me, 'What was your impression of him?' And I always tell them he's exactly who I hoped he was when I voted for him. He made me feel like someone was steering the ship. That if we just hung on, we'll be okay. It was like, we've got somebody at the top who cares. And that matters for something."

At Christmastime Rebekah heard from the White House again. Would she and her family like to come to the State of the Union address? When she arrived, she was introduced to people, speechwriters, cabinet members, policy makers of all kinds. She met Fiona. Fiona introduced her to the intern who had been sitting in the hard-mail room the day Rebekah's letter came in. It was among the stack of hundreds he had read that day; it was just one he had sampled, hoping he was doing it right. "I was like, 'Wow, look what you did,'" Rebekah told me. "He was twenty-three or something, and look what he did." She met then–Secretary of Labor Tom Perez. "And he said, 'The president gave every member of the cabinet your letter and said, "Remember who we're working for."'"

At the State of the Union address, she sat between Michelle Obama and Jill Biden. The speech was built around her letter. Obama told Rebekah's story, and he quoted the letter, returning to it like a refrain in the middle and once more at the end.

> I want our actions to tell every child in every neighborhood, your life matters. . . .
> I want them to grow up in a country where a young mom can sit down and write a letter to her president with a story that sums up these past six years: "It's amazing what you can bounce back from when you have to. . . . We are a strong, tight-knit family who's made it through some very, very hard times."
> My fellow Americans, we, too, are a strong, tight-knit family. We, too, have made it through some hard times. Fifteen years into this new century, we have picked ourselves up, dusted ourselves off, and begun again the work of remaking America. We have laid a new foundation. A brighter future is ours to write. Let's begin this new chapter together—and let's start the work right now.
> Thank you. God bless you. God bless this country we love.

There was one more letter Obama brought up that day in the Oval Office when I spoke to him about the mail. It was one that had just crossed his desk, and so it was fresh on his mind. "Somebody just recently wrote me a letter about when they were growing up their mom always used the *N* word and was derogatory about African Americans," he said.

Save PDF 10/3/16
Light Version 8:10

Back from the OVAL
10/4/16

From: Mrs. Joelle Graves

Submitted: 9/29/2016 1:25 PM EDT

Email:

Phone:

Address: Medford, Oregon (Valid)

*Reply — nice story!
personally*

Message: Dear President Obama,
I needed you to hear this story before your last day in the White House. And today's date
reminded me to tell you. My mother-in-law (Peggy) was an Indiana girl; adored Chicago; grew
up in the suburbs; had a job in a dress shop; met her husband to be and moved to California -
the promised land - in the late 40's. Peggy and my father-in-law were life long Republicans.
They were surprisingly prejudiced. They used the N word often! At one point I had to actually
ask them to refrain from saying such harsh things about African Americans in front of their
grandchildren. When my girls were old enough, they asked them that themselves. Fast forward
to today's date seven years ago - the day we buried my mother-in-law at the age of 94. She had
outlived everyone in her family. I took family leave from my work the last 30 days of care to
provide 12 hours a day of care to save the $7,000 a month it was costing for round the clock
care for her. We were out of money, but didn't want her to know. As I sat with her each of those
30 days, chatting about her life - one day I asked her what was her proudest accomplishment.
She looked at me with a twinkle in her eye and replied, "The day I voted for a black man to be
President of the United States!" She and I both knew that was BIG. She went on to say that she
would go to her grave knowing that finally she had cast a vote that would matter. That she was
part of history. That she was ashamed of the using the N word her entire life. That she never
thought she'd vote for a black man from Chicago! That is was the first time she had voted
Democrat. And that she cried tears of joy during your inauguration. She made me promise to
work hard to be sure you were elected a second term. So when that time arrived my youngest
daughter and I canvassed for you. And we canvassed Peggy's neighborhood. When I
encountered a nay sayer, I told them this story and just asked them to think about it before
casting their vote! She would be so proud of your two terms in office. Somewhere in heaven
she is all dressed up, ready to vote democrat! If only she were here today, right? I just wanted
you to know.
Sincerely,
Joelle Graves

"There are those kinds of letters, I think, that shape your attitudes,"
Obama told me that day. "The individuality and the specificity carries a power that is different than any rational argument that is made
or policy presentation that is made. It carries with it a force that's
different."

I asked him what he thought letters like Joelle's said about the
relationship he'd formed, over the past eight years, with the people
he was elected to serve.

"It says the American people are full of goodness and wisdom,
and you just have to be paying attention," he said. "And sometimes
that's hard to do when you're inside this bubble, but this was a little
portal through which I could remind myself of that every day.

"The letters are beautiful, aren't they?"

CHAPTER 10

Marjorie McKinney, August 21, 2013

BOONE, NORTH CAROLINA

Marg was in Albany when the incident happened. It might seem like a tiny thing. A run-of-the-mill, everyday thing. But Marg couldn't shake the memory of it, carrying it the way another person carries grief, a feeling of heaviness inside, unmovable and flat.

How do you describe it? Okay. Imagine it's getting dark outside. Cold. Gray. The dreariest dusk, everybody aching to get home for some mashed potatoes and TV. Marg was at the New York State Museum there, doing some work for her husband, Ken, a geologist at the university back home in Boone, North Carolina. Marg helped Ken his whole career; it had been a willing partnership ever since the 1950s when they met in paleontology class. They decided he would get the PhD; she would stay home with the kids. She loved it. They traveled the world together hunting fossils, debating plate tectonics and all the exhilarating implications.

Then Ken had developed muscular dystrophy, and then came the wheelchair, so now Marg, who was in her early seventies, did most of the traveling alone. She's a short woman, compact, with a paper-thin complexion, wire-rimmed glasses, and shaggy white hair she lets fly around naturally. That day she had traveled to Albany to pick up some images of fossils that Ken had requested, and she was headed to her car. (This was 2011, when Ken was still alive. He has since passed.) The plaza outside the museum was huge, a broad quadrangle, acres of concrete reaching toward the horizon, nothing to cut the wind, and the weird thing was not a single person was out there except Marg and one shadowy figure in the distance. Weird because it was a weekday, rush hour, and people should've been storming out of those buildings headed home to their mashed potatoes, shouldn't they?

The person in the distance was a guy, definitely a guy; he was way across the plaza on that parallel sidewalk there. Suddenly he started walking toward Marg. He quickened his pace, came closer. She felt uncomfortable with the way he seemed to be zeroing in on her like that. He looked young. He was black. He was wearing a hoodie. In one swift move, he flipped the hood up and over his head, concealing his face.

I should run, Marg thought. It was more instinct than thought. Her short legs wouldn't take her very far very fast. He kept getting closer. *At what point do I run?* There were no nearby buildings to duck into. She started walking faster, toward the stairwell that led to the parking lot. He did too. She felt hot. She felt a pulse in her toes and on the tips of her ears, a pounding all over saying, "Run like hell."

They both reached the stairwell at the same time. He looked up at her. "Bad wind, isn't it?" he said. Then he told her there was a pedestrian walkway underneath that linked the museum to the parking lot, in case she didn't know. Next time if it's cold out, she might want to take that, he said.

And that was it. He was gone.

It might seem like a tiny thing. A run-of-the-mill, everyday thing. But for Marg it marked a break in who she believed herself to be.

"Why was I afraid of this very pleasant young man? It was just all because I saw he was a black man. I had no reason to be afraid of him. And that just knocked me flat. It wasn't anything I ever expected to feel. It was a turning point in my life, because I realized then, you know, that I was racist. And I had to find a way to get rid of that."

Now, a big part of the problem for Marg was she thought she *had* gotten rid of it. She had made the decision long ago to get rid of it.

For people who grew up in the Deep South, in Birmingham, Alabama, it was a steep climb to work on something like that. It was a decision you had to make, yes or no, if you wanted to learn how to free yourself of racist thinking that had been more or less ingrained in you.

Marg was six when she discovered the white robe and the pointed hood hanging in the neighbor's den on the back of the door. She was playing hide-and-seek with her sister. "What are you doing in here?" the mom said. "You are forbidden to enter this room." She knew what it was. She always wondered who was under those things. He was the town barber. He was so jolly. He and her dad were pals. There were things you didn't talk about.

The black neighborhood was across the street from her school. It was like a separate village you didn't go into. And they didn't come into yours. The buses would come and take the black kids miles away to another school. The public buses had a wooden placard behind the white section. If you were white and got on the bus and there was no place to sit, you pushed the placard back, and those people had to move. And if their section got full, one of them had to get off the bus.

It was normal. It was just the way the world was divided: two types of people. That's why you needed two types of everything: seats, stores, schools, theaters, ball teams. Nobody said anything about it being wrong. She heard about Martin Luther King, Jr., when she was in high school—some of the stuff about the Montgomery bus boycott; she did hear about some of that. At home, when she brought it up, she was told to leave the dinner table and never mention it again. Nothing they should be involved in. It was up to somebody else to get involved.

The first time she ever talked to a black person was when she was in grad school, at the University of North Carolina at Chapel Hill, in the early 1960s. "Well, hello," she said. She had no idea what to expect. "My name is Marg." It was just a normal conversation like she would have with anybody, and that was the thing that jolted her. He was acting like a regular person.

She had a friend, an exchange student from Germany who was considerably older, and at lunch one day, she told him she didn't understand some of the sit-ins and other civil rights demonstrations that students were starting to organize at segregated restaurants and businesses in town. "Black people are satisfied with their lives," she said. "Why stir up a fuss?"

"Where are you hearing this?" her friend said.

"That's how it is back home in Birmingham," she said.

Except of course that's not how it really was back home in Birmingham. That was a polite white girl's dinner table version, where you were told to leave if you brought anything up. In fact, in the 1950s and 1960s, racial segregation was legally required in Birmingham, where just 10 percent of the city's black population was registered to vote, and the unemployment rate for blacks was two and a half times higher than it was for whites; there were no black police officers, firefighters, store clerks, or bus drivers. "Probably the most segregated city in the United States," Martin Luther King, Jr., said about Birmingham.

So there was Marg in grad school, her friend from Germany trying to wake her up from her stupor, explaining racism and bigotry and hate, telling her about his country and his life and about the Hitler Youth. First it had just been a group of little kids. Then other youth groups had to join, church groups, sports leagues. Hitler consolidated them; he outlawed all other youth groups except for the Hitler Youth. It grew to eight million kids. You had to read Nazi books and sing Nazi songs. You could be refused a diploma and a job if you didn't join. Your parents would be hunted down. Two kinds of people, pure or impure, an army enforcing the divide.

Marg would stay friends with the guy from Germany. She would continue to thank him for everything he had explained to her in the lunchroom that day and for setting her life on a new course. "You needed it," he'd say.

In 1963, police dogs were unleashed on black protesters in Birmingham, and then police turned on the fire hoses. King was thrown in jail, and from his cell he wrote an open letter to America. "Injustice anywhere is a threat to justice everywhere," he said.

Marg got involved in the civil rights movement. Throughout her life she tried to see beyond race. Even when she and Ken planned their family. Four kids, they said. One by birth, the rest adopted. So many kids needing love. Two of them were biracial.

So imagine. With all that behind her, all that evolving, a whole life with Ken and the kids. And then she's in Albany, and it's cold and dark, and she finds this pit of ugliness sitting inside her like some dormant worm wriggling to life.

What are you supposed to do with that?

In the background, on the news, the Trayvon Martin tragedy was unfolding. This was now 2012. Trayvon Martin, a seventeen-year-old kid coming back from a run to the store on a February night in Sanford, Florida. He was wearing a black hoodie. George Zimmerman, part of a watch group for the gated community, thought Trayvon Martin looked suspicious, so Zimmerman went after him and after an altercation shot him dead.

Marg heard about it on the radio, at home in Boone, in the house she and Ken had built together, on seventeen acres overlooking the Blue Ridge Mountains. The kids were grown, and Ken was gone, and so it was just her, two goats, a donkey named Rosie who liked Cheetos. Marg was following the Trayvon Martin saga on the radio, thinking about a divided America. She felt complicit. She wondered about Zimmerman. Did he have the same piece in him that she had discovered in herself? Was that what made him do it? Was he surprised to find it, as she was?

Zimmerman walked free for six weeks before he was charged with second-degree murder, provoking protests in Florida and across the country. The trial lasted a month, and when the not-guilty verdict was announced, people took to the streets and social media. "Black lives matter!" became the cry of a new movement.

On July 19, 2013, six days after the Zimmerman verdict, President Obama gave an impromptu speech in the White House press room. "Trayvon Martin could have been me, thirty-five years ago," he said. "I think it's important to recognize that the African American community is looking at this issue through a set of experiences and a history that doesn't go away."

Marg thought it was a gracious speech. She thought Obama was trying to explain the insidious nature of racism by making it personal.

"What I identified with was the complexity of it. I felt that Obama was trying to say, 'You can't just say that this man cold-bloodedly decided to kill Trayvon Martin. There were things going on with him, and with his thinking.'"

That was the way Marg heard it. Things going on in him, like the things she discovered going on in her.

Other people heard it differently. On the radio, conservative commentators and callers were sharply critical of Obama's words. The Zimmerman shooting wasn't about race, they said. It was a scuffle that had ended in tragedy. Nothing more. Obama shouldn't be making it about race, they said. He shouldn't use this tragedy as a way to appease critics decrying him for not doing more during his presidency to address race relations in America.

What is the matter with you people? Marg thought. Of course this was about race. And why wasn't anyone talking about all the other things Obama had to say in that speech that day?

"I think it's going to be important for all of us to do some soul-searching," he had said. "There has been talk about should we convene a conversation on race. I haven't seen that be particularly productive when politicians try to organize conversations. They end up being stilted and politicized, and folks are locked into the positions they already have. On the other hand, in families and churches and workplaces, there's the possibility that people are a little bit more honest, and at least you ask yourself your own questions about, Am I wringing as much bias out of myself as I can? Am I judging people as much as I can based on not the color of their skin, but the content of their character? That would, I think, be an appropriate exercise in the wake of this tragedy."

Marg went to her computer and began typing. She wanted President Obama to know someone was listening. She had never thought of writing to a president before. But this guy needed it. Soon enough she found herself confessing about what had happened in Albany. "I wanted him to know that I had a reason to feel the way I did. I wanted to claim it for myself too. Because I wasn't doing this intellectually; I was doing it from my experience. It was something that was real to me."

"Dear President Obama," she wrote. "As years went by, I thought I had done a pretty good job of shedding the racism in me. . . . Then, came a cold evening in Albany, NY." She told him about the cold and the darkness. "As I pulled a scarf around my neck to cut the wind, I saw the man pull his hoodie up." She told him about the fear that overcame her and how she didn't understand it. "Into my mind popped the notion that he was a black man, had hidden his face (I had, too). . . . I was embarrassed to think that, but it was there."

She thanked the president for his speech about Trayvon Martin, and she said she owed that young man in Albany an apology. "I hope that others who heard your words will be more aware of the fear that lurks within many of us," she said. "It's unreasoned, but there."

Gws Trayvon martin
& Sample
8/21/13
f & 8

Marjorie McKinney

Boone, NC

Back from the OVAL
8 / 22 / 13

Reply

President Barak Obama
The White House
1600 Pennsylvania Avenue, NW
Washington, DC 20500

Dear President Obama,

Thank you for your recent statements after the Zimmerman trial about your own memories of being a young black male. I am a "white" American, born and raised in Birmingham, Alabama where I lived until I moved to North Carolina as a grad student. When I left Alabama, I had the opportunity to know many different people and was impelled to examine the racism in me. I didn't know it existed. I didn't even think about it before.

As years went by, I thought I had done a pretty good job of shedding the racism in me. I had African-American friends, two of my children are bi-racial, I was involved in civil rights issues. Then, came a cold evening in Albany, NY.

I was in Albany for a short visit and was walking in the area between the museum and government buildings. It's a huge plaza with an underground pedestrian area that links the buildings. I had used that to walk to the museum but decided to walk back outside. It was getting dark. The only other person on the plaza was a young black man who was walking parallel to me on the other side. As I pulled a scarf around my neck to cut the wind, I saw the man pull his hoodie up as he changed direction and began walking quickly toward me. Much to my horror, I became afraid and tried to figure why. Into my mind popped the notion that he was a black man, had hidden his face (I had, too), and had suddenly changed direction when he seemed to have looked up and seen me. I was embarrassed to think that, but it was there. I decided to wait and see what happened, fearful all the time. I changed my direction a bit and he seemed to as well. He continued to come directly toward me. As he came near, he looked up and said "Bad wind, isn't it?" and showed me the nearest entry into the pedestrian underground. He was cold as I was and his change of direction was to go into the building close to where I walked. I wish I could have apologized to that fellow. That experience stays with me.

I hope that others who heard your words will be more aware of the fear that lurks within many of us. It's unreasoned, but there. I hope to never forget my walk in Albany and the young man I encountered that cold day. Your candid comments last week meant a lot to me. Thank you.

Sincerely,

Marjorie McKinney

THE WHITE HOUSE
WASHINGTON

Marjorie —

Thanks for your thoughtful letter. Your story is an example of what makes me optimistic about this country!

It was a surprise and a pleasure hearing back from the president. Marg had never expected anything like that. She put the letter in a frame and hung it beside her favorite chair, the blue one with the wooden arms, so she could sit by it. And so that's what she did. She sat by it and did some soul-searching, just as the president had recommended in his speech.

She decided she needed to get out more. Soul-searching, she discovered, goes only so far.

"Convene a conversation on race . . . families and churches and workplaces." Marg thought about some of the other things the president had recommended in his speech. She drove over to Raleigh, attended one of the Moral Mondays civil disobedience protests that were gaining attention there. They were organized by religious leaders like the Rev. Dr. William Barber II, head of the North Carolina chapter of the National Association for the Advancement of Colored People (NAACP). For Marg it was uplifting to be among all those people marching, saying that black lives matter, saying that we have to protect voting rights for all.

She wondered why they didn't do Moral Mondays marches in Boone. (She didn't want to have to keep driving over to Raleigh.) So she got some people together. "Convene a conversation on race." Part of the reason they didn't have Moral Mondays in Boone, she found out, was there was no officially chartered local NAACP chapter in Boone—or anywhere in all of Watauga County, for that matter.

That's when Marg started collecting signatures. "We need a chapter."

On February 15, 2014, three years after her encounter with the kid in Albany, seven months after she'd heard Obama's impromptu speech about Trayvon Martin, the Watauga NAACP branch was officially chartered.

They held meetings. They invited speakers from Appalachian State University. They started seminars, an Unlearning Racism discussion group, a three-part UNpacking (our own) HATE series. They started the Coffee with a Cop series down at the Hospitality House. Hey, cops, they said, come on out and talk to the community that's so scared of you.

Somebody in one of the meetings got the idea about kickball. It's a few years going, the Community Unity Picnic, and of all the things that Marg, now seventy-five, and the newly established Watauga NAACP branch do, that's probably her favorite. They added a dunking pool. Everybody getting dunked—it's so hilarious. Black people, white people, Hispanic people, cops, kids, old people. Everybody likes kickball and getting dunked.

Marg circulates and makes sure people aren't sitting by themselves and also that everyone knows where the food is.

CHAPTER 11

Red Dot

"So I walked over to him, um, barefoot, stepping over all the glass and everything that he had shot. And he was still yelling, and he was still holding the shotgun, and I went to him, and—he was larger than me. My dad was a large man. And immensely strong—I never appreciated how strong he was until that day. But he just started crying and yelling that no one appreciated him and that everybody had forgotten him. And that everybody just shits on him. And that nobody cared. And so I put my arms around him to try to console him, and I guess he took that as a sign of aggression. And he started shooting, and I was trying to restrain him while he was shooting, and he just kept shooting and kept shooting, and at that point—I don't remember screaming. The only reason I know I was screaming is because my brother told me I was. I saw my brother run out of the house. I kind of emotionally shut down. My dad started crying, like sobbing uncontrollably. And I'd never seen my dad cry. As a marine, he put on this façade that he was so strong and that nothing could harm him. I'd never seen him cry. And so his phone was in his pocket, and it started ringing. I took it from him and answered it. It was our neighbor. He said the police were coming. I didn't want my dad to hear because I knew it would just make him even more angry.

So I hung up the phone, and I guided my dad to his room, and on his bed I saw he had laid out every single weapon that he had owned and all the ammunition that he had for those weapons. And I knew what he had planned to do. It was Christmas Eve.

"I was trying to console him and talking very soothingly and re-assuring him everything would be okay and nobody was upset with him. I guided him to the front steps, and I got him on the porch. I was trying to push him to go down the steps into the front yard. And it was raining. I saw all of these people surrounding our house. I finally got him into the front yard. And my dad always kept a knife on him, which a lot of marines do. And so they saw the knife, and they told him to drop it. And, um, he wouldn't. So I tried to get it. And he dropped it, and then he tried to lunge for it. So then I tried to push it away, and we were both on the ground at this point when it was raining. And it was muddy. And it was cold. And I'm here, like, with the last amount of strength that I have physically trying to hold him to the ground, yelling for everyone to help me.

"I don't know how many people came to pick him up.

"At the hospital I cried in the hallway on a stretcher until I could no longer cry.

"On Christmas Day my mom, my brother, and I were cleaning up the glass and all the remnants of, um, the fish tank and everything that he had shot up. He shot the flag that was awarded to him when he retired and all of his medals and everything—all the memorabilia associated with the Marine Corps. We cleaned up as much as we could, and then I went upstairs, and I wrote the letter. That's when I wrote the letter. The VA doctors had failed him; his so-called friends had failed him; the Marine Corps had failed him. I didn't know where else to turn. And so I thought, *If the last person that I can think of is the president, and if that's my last resource, then I'm going to give it every single ounce of energy that I have.*"

At the White House, Ashley DeLeon's 2014 letter about the events that occurred at home with her father on Christmas Eve ended up in a pile just like all the others in the OPC hard-mail room. On a cold January afternoon, a staffer named Garrett picked it up. He read through it quickly, as he had done with the letter before it and the letter before that. A few paragraphs in, he slowed down. He rolled his chair back, started from the beginning again, and got to the end. "I need to take a break," he said to an intern nearby.

He took the letter with him on a walk and ended up at the desk of Lacey Higley, whose office was just across the hall from the hard-mail room. "I've been wandering around the hallway," he said.

"Are you okay?" Lacey said.

Lacey was by then used to identifying the various looks people had when they came to her desk. She was the person in charge of Red Dots. A Red Dot was an emergency. Suicide, self-harm, eating disorders, rape, domestic violence, addiction—the flow, as many as four hundred in one day, varied. The rule was that every Red Dot had to be processed within twenty-four hours, assigned to an agency or organization like the Substance Abuse and Mental Health Services Administration or the National Suicide Prevention Lifeline. This rule made more sense with email than it did with hard mail; weeks had already gone by since Christmas, the day Ashley put her letter in the mail.

"We have to figure out what to do," Garrett said, handing Ashley's letter to Lacey.

Lacey began reading Ashley's letter, then slowed down. She started from the beginning again and got to the end. She said she needed a walk, and so she did a lap around the first floor of the EEOB, and Garrett joined her, the two of them talking about what they had read.

Ashley DeLeon
Jacksonville, NC

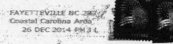

The White House
1600 Pennsylvania Avenue NW
Washington, DC 20500

485
JAN 08 201 ✓#031

December 25, 2014

Dear Mr. President,

My father was a United States Marine for 22 years before retiring as a MSgt. As part of the infantry, he deployed on six occasions. Each deployment my father came back less and less like himself. He missed many moments of my life: birthdays, holidays, award ceremonies. He used to love to hunt, to fish, to spend time with my mother, little brother and I. But after he retired, my father was forgotten. You see, when my dad retired he no longer had the brotherhood of fellow marines; no one thanked him for his service; no one called to check on his well being. He was diagnosed with severe PTSD and was medically disabled.

So he drank. And drank. My father's alcoholism stole the man that I had known for 21 years of my life. He could easily spend $100 a night on alcohol. He would drink all night, come back at 6 am, sleep all day, and repeat the cycle.

I am a junior at the University of North Carolina Wilmington. My father never called me to ask how I was, how my classes were, or if I had a good day at work. Everyday I would look in the mirror and see the remnants of him in my facial features. But the man that I resembled so much, the man who constituted half of me, wasn't one that I knew any longer.

Christmas Eve was a rainy day in Jacksonville,
NC Mr. President. I was taking a shower
upstairs when I heard the first two shots.
I knew it was him. As I jumped out of the
shower and ran down the stairs in nothing
but a towel I could see my father pacing
in the living room with a shotgun in his
hand and tears in his eyes. He yelled at
me, his little girl, "Get the f*** out of
my house! GET OUT!" And in that moment
I knew that I had two choices: to run and
leave my little brother upstairs + my dad
with a loaded weapon. Or to stay. I chose
the latter. You see, I chose to stay in that room
and fight over that gun because I knew that
my dad was still in there somewhere. He
had to be. As I struggled with my father,
he shot. And shot. The small girl who
grew up waving the American flag at her
daddy's homecomings yelled "NOOOO"
from the bottom of her gut. Glass shattered.
The dogs barked. And in my peripheral
vision I saw my brother run out of the
house.
   I didn't care if I died Mr. President.
I'm 21 years old and I would sacrifice
myself without a second thought to save
the man who raised me from taking his own
life. Because when his country turned
their back on him, I was still there. The
light has long been gone from his eyes,
but he is still my father. I am still his

little girl. A little piece of me died that day.
I will never be the same. This time of year
is one to celebrate with family and to be
thankful for the blessings provided to us.
Instead I spent Christmas Day sweeping up
glass and looking at my home riddled with
bullet holes. Like a war zone.
    I'm writing to ask for your help. Not for my
family Mr. President. My family died that
night. I'm asking you to help the others.
The little girls and boys who have yet to
see their mothers and fathers souls
die away. They need help. Get them help.
Don't forget about them. They need you.
Just like Sasha and Malia need you.
They do.

        With hope,
        Ashley De Leon

One thing everyone in OPC learned quickly was that they needed
one another. They needed to talk this stuff out. The content of the
letters, the constant pleas, the emotions jumping and bouncing off
the page. It was impossible to explain to people outside of OPC what
it was like to sit all day in the intensity of the material, and that's why
so many OPC staffers lived with one another, roommates commuting together, eating dinner together, watching Netflix together. Lacey
lived with Vinnie and Steve, then Mitchell, then Heidi. In the office
she shared a wall with Yena, and throughout the day they would
knock on it, give the signal: *Come over here and read this one, please. I
can't deal.*

    Lacey was taller than most of her friends, lanky and unadorned;
she moved with a stiffness that suggested her height was a burden.
She was just twenty-three, and if you asked her to describe herself,
she would say she was timid. Perhaps the last person you'd imagine

being able to handle a portfolio as emotionally challenging as Red Dots. She had started at OPC as an intern while still in college. Walking to the EEOB that first day, she had felt like a bird falling too soon out of the nest. She got lost, called her dad in tears. "Help me." She believed she was too anxious to make it in the real world, her voice too thin, her throat too tight, air not moving. She would never make it in the real world. She thought there was something wrong with her, and surely one of the people at the White House would discover she had no business being among them. She had no background in government; she would not be able to participate in conversations about policy or policy making; unlike the others she had not worked on Obama's campaign—or anyone's campaign. She was a nobody who would never belong.

"One voice can change a room." If she had a favorite speech of Obama's, it was that one, an old one, inspired by a woman with a gold tooth. The woman with the gold tooth was in Greenwood, South Carolina, at a rally for Obama in 2007. The rally was a bust, no one there but a small gathering of local folks needing something to do. Obama was looking out at the emptiness. "Fired up, ready to go!" the woman with the gold tooth abruptly shouted. And as if on cue, the people around her repeated her words, began to chant, and in an instant the rally went from dismal to glorious.

"It shows you what one voice can do. That one voice can change a room," Obama said at a campaign rally over a year later, recounting the story. "And if a voice can change a room, it can change a city. And if it can change a city, it can change a state. And if it can change a state, it can change a nation. And if it can change a nation, it can change the world."

If you asked Lacey about her evolution from scared intern to the warrior who could handle hundreds of Red Dots every day, she would say it had to do with Obama and those words. One voice. One letter. One intern. Everybody matters.

"You will cry," she would tell each class of new interns that came under her charge, now that she was the person manning the Red Dot desk. "It's normal. You will see me cry at least twice while you're here. This work is intense. This work is hard. If you need to go home, you can go home."

. . .

When she finished her walk with Garrett that day, Lacey ran Ashley's letter through the scanner and forwarded the scan to the VA's crisis unit. She wondered about the idea of sampling the letter; what would happen if the president had a chance to read Ashley's story? It was not something people did. Red Dots were special cases that required emergency assistance, and taking the time to run them by the president could only bog down the effort, so they were never sampled. That bothered Lacey. She had herself recently begun treatment for depression and anxiety, and she knew all too well the damaging effects of the stigma surrounding mental health issues. Perhaps she was in a unique position to help raise the voices of people who were so often suffering in silence.

She saw Fiona in the hall. "The president needs to see this," Lacey said, handing Fiona Ashley's letter. *"He needs to see this."*

Everyone in OPC had one letter that defined his or her work, and for Lacey it would be Ashley's. She made a photocopy of it and taped it to the wall above her desk. She took a pink highlighter and marked the last paragraph.

> *I'm writing to ask for your help. Not for my family, Mr. President. My family died that night. I'm asking you to help the others. The little girls and boys who have yet to see their mother's and father's souls die away. They need help. Get them help. Don't forget about them. They need you. Just like Sasha and Malia need you. They do.*

"I hold on to it as my guidepost for what I'm doing and why I'm here," she would later say.

That afternoon, Fiona included Ashley's letter in the stack of 10LADs that went to the president.

The letter didn't come back in the next batch marked, "Back from the OVAL." It didn't come back in the batch after that either. Some letters the president sat on.

It would be more than a week before Obama had a response ready for Ashley.

THE WHITE HOUSE
WASHINGTON

Ashley —

I was so moved by your letter. As a father, I can only imagine how heartbreaking the situation must be, and I'm inspired by the strength and perspective you possess at such a young age.

I am asking the VA to reach out to your

family to provide any support that you need. And please know that beneath the pain, your father still loves his daughter, and is surely proud of her.

Sincerely,

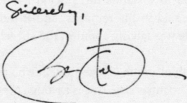

"I received a manila envelope from the White House. And inside was a note—it was a small note, and it was handwritten by the president. I was completely taken aback. I didn't expect anyone to read it, much less respond to it. And it basically said to stay strong.

"They called me, and they put me in contact with the VA, and they were trying to get my dad resources that could help with his addictions and with his depression. But by that time I wasn't in contact with my father because I didn't feel safe around him to be honest. He went to FOCUS, a marine rehabilitation program, I believe.

"My mom tried so hard to try to get us to be closer again. That's my biggest regret—that I believed so much in the future, that I would have time to heal."

The conversation about Ashley and her dad didn't end with the president's response, or with the assistance from the VA to get him into a rehab program, or, for that matter, with Lacey's decision to hang the letter over her desk. Every letter that came into OPC was in essence a potential conversation starter that could zig and zag and meander throughout the White House and Congress and to people watching on TV.

When people in the West Wing talked about "the letter underground," this is part of what they meant. This whole thing was just supposed to be about the president getting ten letters a day, but it grew into something else; letters informed policy proposals and speeches, and they affected people personally.

Just seven weeks after Ashley sent her letter, on February 12, 2015, in the East Room, Obama signed the Clay Hunt SAV Act into law. "And SAV stands for Suicide Prevention for American Veterans," he said in his remarks, and it didn't take long to figure out whom he was talking about in the speech.

> I think of the college student who recently wrote me a letter on Christmas Day. This is as tough a letter as I've received since I've been president. She talked about her father, who's a retired marine, and told me about how her dad used to love to hunt and fish and spend time with her and her little brother. But gripped with post-traumatic stress, he became less and less like himself and withdrew from the family. And yet, despite these struggles, she wrote, "I knew that my dad was still in there somewhere. . . . He is still my father. And I am still his little girl." And she was writing, she said, to ask for help—help her father find his way back—"not for my family, Mr. President," she said. "I'm asking you to help the others"—other families like hers. And she said, "Don't forget about them."
>
> And that's really what today is about: Don't forget. . . . If you are hurting, know this: You are not forgotten. You are not alone.

You are never alone. We are here for you. America is here for you—all of us. And we will not stop doing everything in our power to get you the care and support you need to stay strong and keep serving this country we love. We need you. We need you. You make our country better.

So I thank all of you. God bless our troops, our veterans, our military families. God bless the United States of America.

"I was sitting on campus, I remember, by myself. I was streaming the video. And it was more towards the end of the remarks. They had asked my permission. I agreed, if they omitted my identification. I didn't know how my letter was going to be interpreted or if it was going to be misconstrued in some way. I just had all these thoughts racing through my mind. And then I heard it, and I started crying because he said that it was one of the hardest letters that he's had to read.

"We have this idea that the president is so much larger than us and that he's this other type of person. But he's exactly like we are.

"And so for him to read my letter and for me to see his reaction—that he was able to use it on a platform to help other people, that was powerful for me.

"My mom said that when my dad was watching the remarks, he cried. And he kept repeating that he was sorry."

Lacey hadn't heard the speech, so she didn't know why her Black-Berry was buzzing the way it was—emails from coworkers using exclamation points. People knew how important Ashley's letter was to Lacey. It was the first of many Red Dots to make it to the president's desk, and here was the president talking about it as he signed a bill into law. Lacey read Obama's remarks. She was so easily moved to tears; that part of her had not changed. Maybe this was as good as it gets for a letter, she thought. A person suffering, making a call for action, and the president hearing—and acting.

She would later decide to pursue a career helping veterans.

·   ·   ·

Months passed, and still Ashley had not talked to her father. She needed distance. She buried herself in schoolwork, began to feel strong for taking charge of her life.

"And then in May, I was intending on taking summer classes, so I was living on campus. I was getting ready for work, and I got the call around six A.M. And it was from our neighbor. And it was from my mom's phone, which I thought was odd. So I knew immediately something was wrong. He said, 'You have to come to Greenville. There's been an accident.'

"When I got to the ICU, they had someone come talk to me. And they were like, 'We're doing everything we can.' I asked all the questions I could. I'm the type of person that likes to know everything as soon as possible, and I like to have control of situations. And my dad was the exact same way. And so this, for me, was torture, because I didn't have control of anything. And they said they were doing everything they could do but that they didn't know. That's what they kept telling us—that they didn't know if he would make it. They didn't know if he would be normal if he did make it. They didn't know.

"He was in the first room on the left. And as I entered the double doors, I saw him. But it wasn't him. It was a completely different thing. It wasn't a person. I collapsed. I started yelling, 'No!' Just like I did when he was shooting. And I just kept yelling no. And they said that the main problem was that when my dad was on the motorcycle, he hit, um, an SUV at an intersection going fifty miles per hour. And when he inhaled, he inhaled all of the fumes. So that was burning his lungs. And they said you can't fix that. They said that there wasn't anything that anyone could do to fix that.

"They said, 'No, ma'am, we can't save him. You have to tell us what you want us to do.'

"I went through denial that it wasn't happening, that he was deployed and that he was coming back. Just like he was when I was little. That if I waited long enough, he would come back."

Samples, 2015

Ms. Alisa Bowman

Submitted via whitehouse.gov
6/27/2015 2:33 PM

Dear President Obama,

I've been voting Democrat since age 18, and I voted for you three times (including in the primary against Clinton). Throughout your Presidency, I've rooted for you and cheered for you and celebrated you. But last week, when you said "Shame on you" to Jennicet Gutierrez, I felt chilled and disappointed. You are a living example of civil rights progress. I've always seen you as someone who gets the plight of marginalized and discriminated against people. In that moment, I realized that I was wrong. You don't seem to get it. Jennicet was not heckling you. She was merely trying to get your attention -- on an important issue that affects a nearly invisible class of people. I understand she may have done it in a rude way, but you are in a position of great power and she is in a position of being marginalized. You've so many times demonstrated your ability to be the big person -- the mature person, the right person, the intelligent person. In this case, you stumbled, and I forgive you for it. But please, make it right. I am not trans, but I am raising a transgender child. This world terrifies me -- how it brutalizes, openly discriminates against, and shames trans people. Gay marriage was a big step, but only one step. You are in a position to take many more steps before your last day in office. Please invite Jennicet to the White House and hear her out. Please look into the injustices happening to trans women-- especially trans women of color. Please ask the attorney general to do the same. Please listen to their voices rather than shaming them. That is all I ask.

THE WHITE HOUSE
WASHINGTON

Alisa —

Thanks for the letter, and the support.

I've got to disagree with you on my handling of the heckler awhile back. This wasn't a public event; she had been invited. We fully support the trans community agenda, which is why they were so well represented at the event. Rather than start shouting, all she needed to do was talk to the numerous White

House staff who were there and already working with the LGBT community on a wide range of issues.

So... there's a need sometimes to shout to be heard. I'm an old community organizer, and have organized disruptive actions myself.

That wasn't the time.

But I really appreciate your thoughtfulness and compassion.

14 simple/ TT Prayers

1 . . . 7/9/15
      fr 1

President Barak Obama
The White House
1600 Pennsylvania Avenue NW
Washington, DC 20500

Back from the OVAL
7/10/15

(Reply)

Dear Mr. President:

I am writing to tell you how my heart went out to you the other day when you announce
that you have to make too many announcements about violent episodes in this country
At that moment, I felt a deep kinship with you, albeit a rather sad one. You see I am th
pastor of a small church in Newbern, Virginia. Each time one of these horrors occurs I
know that on Sunday morning my little flock will be expecting their pastor to have
something meaningful to say to them – something that will help them make some
semblance of sense out of it all and offer them some comfort and hope. Frankly, Mr.
President, I have grown bone weary at this repeated responsibility and I have only
twenty souls in my care. Your congregation is so much larger.

I hope it is helpful to you to know there is a pastor in southwestern Virginia who
understands something of what you are going through and is keeping you in her
prayers.

Shalom, Mr. President,

Christine G Reisman

Rev. Christine G. Reisman,
Newbern Christian Church

Christiansburg, VA

DF
Sample

July 1, 2015

President Barack Obama
The White House
1600 Pennsylvania Avenue NW
Washington, DC 20500

Dear Mr. President,

As we approach Independence Day, and after I heard you sing Amazing Grace at my fellow Pastor's funeral, I wanted to share with you my story.

I grew up in a white, military, Christian, right wing family. I have always towed the republican line. I have never voted for a democrat in my life. I worked against your election and reelection, not that the republican candidates were so great, I just knew that democrats were "bad for America". But inside I was facing a struggle, a struggle I'd been dealing with since I was 6 years old.

I grew up, married a wonderful woman, helped create two awesome kids and have lived my life as a conservative Baptist minister. In December, my struggle nearly brought me to the point of ending my life and on December 7, 2014, I finally admitted to myself that I was gay AND that God made me that way. I shared this with my wife and it has been rough these 6 months. I am also looking for another job as this information would be grounds for dismissal in my church if it were discovered.

I write all this to tell you, thank you for being my President. After December 7th my outward perspective reflected the man within and your presidency changed in my eyes. You have done a remarkable job in spite of incredible opposition. From health care, immigration, marriage equality to normalization of relations with Cuba, your presidency will go down as historic. You have brought social justice to so many.

I see our flag in a new light now. To me it always stood for American power in the world, but today for me it stands for liberty and equality for everyone, no more second class citizens.

Thank you for being the first President of ALL the people. I am so proud of you, Mr. President. You have been so good for America and in fulfilling the vision for a truly free republic for everyone.

From the depths of my heart, thank you, Sir.

Cordially,

REINVENTING
ReEntry

Sue Ellen Allen, Founder

Scottsdale, AZ

May 11, 2015

President Barack Obama
The White House
1600 Pennsylvania Ave
NW Washington, DC 20500

Dear President Obama:

You get a lot of mail. I hope this reaches your file, particularly in the light of the deep-seated rage that is exploding in our country. I'm sad, I'm privileged, and I care.

10 reasons why I'm privileged
1. White
2. College educated
3. Mother & Father who believed in me.
4. Taught in very underprivileged schools.
5. Worked in corporate America.
6. Served time in prison late in life with advanced breast cancer. Found my life purpose there.
7. Upon release six years ago, co-founded a 501(c)3 organization to bring educational programs into women's prison. Our success rate is an unprecedented 6%.
8. After AHA moment, founded a new nonprofit with a mission to educate and reshape society's perception of former inmates because Nothing will change unless the perception changes.
9. Am a Tigger in an Eyore world. I never give up.
10. Am aware that I'm privileged.

3 reasons why I'm not privileged
1. I'm old. Definitely a woman of a certain age.
2. I'm poor. I don't look or feel poor but legally I live below the official poverty line.
3. I'm a felon. I will have a prison number **forever**.

You know the recidivism rate. Imagine if Mayo Clinic or Apple with their budgets had a business plan with a 60% failure rate (through death or product returns). That business plan would be unacceptable. So why is our prison business plan with a 60% failure rate acceptable in our country?

School failures; dropout rates; marginalized, disenfranchised. Add to that the complete distrust of our police force. We have a problem. **Remember, I'm privileged.** I was taught to believe the police were my friends, lawyers never lied, and judges were fair and honest. **I was wrong.**

Mission: To educate and reshape our society's perception of former inmates so they may successfully reintegrate and be given a fair chance for employment, housing, education and entrepreneurial opportunities.

If you had told me what I would see and experience in prison, I would have said, "Not in our country. We don't treat people that way." **I was wrong.** Seven years in prison for securities fraud gave me my life purpose. The treatment inside is draconian; the preparation for re-entry is laughable.

Now that I'm out and have created two useful organizations, the judgement and treatment continue in myriad humiliating ways (like a decent place to live for starters). **Remember, I'm privileged.** How much harder is it for a poor Black or Latino man or woman?

How about a task force? Not one full of law enforcement, prison officials and academics. Consider former inmates who have from 5 to 30 years experience inside, mothers willing to chase their sons down the street during a riot, people sent down because they are mentally ill, women and men who are making a difference because of and despite their records. Real prison experts at the table. There are many of us who would be honored to serve. Then add some of the "officials."

The primary reason for this letter is to once again encourage you to visit a prison, not a sanitized Presidential visit (OK, that might not be possible), but a real one, talking to inmates and seeing their cells, eating real prison food. This would be a powerful message to the 2.3 million incarcerated Americans. Most attorneys and judges have never been inside a prison except in the sanitized visitation room. No president has ever visited. You have no idea of the horror inside.

President Obama, you are my president. I admire your approach, your intellectual style, your dignity and your sense of humor. Believe it or not, I've only been disappointed about your approach to racism. I think you should be tougher. The conservatives won't like it, but they don't like anything you do so why worry? The progressives would love it and there are a lot of us just waiting for this part of your leadership. This task force of former felons would be a great start, especially if someone listens. Currently, we are invisible and voiceless. Please see us and be our voice.

Sincerely,

Sue Ellen Allen
Founder

PS: I know your staff seems to chose letters for your folder that are handwritten but I wrote with a golf pencil for a long time and swore I'd never do that again.

Submitted via www.whitehouse.gov/contact
Case Number:
IP Address:

From: Yolanda

Submitted: 10/16/2015 4:08 AM EDT

Email:

Phone:

Address:

Message: Dear Mr. President and First Lady Obama,
This is Yolanda   and it is with a grateful heart that I write this letter to you. I wrote previously a couple of years ago, telling you about my status as a veteran who is disabled and was living out of my car and constantly having nightmares from sexual trauma that occurred while I was in the Navy. You and your cabinet made a national declaration to all states to work on ending homelessness. I let you know about my silent prayer of wanting to be a productive member of society, able to live, pay rent, and contribute. I did not want to die on the side of the road like a piece of trash.

It is with grateful tears that I am able to tell you that today, I signed a lease to Veterans Village   for a 1 bedroom apartment. I am able to pay for it with my OWN money. The application process was rigorous and I was fearful that I would not be able to obtain one as there were 2000 other applicants whom I am sure had more money than me. It was my last hope. I had no other game plan left, I thought my car would be my grave.

Today, I cried tears of joys. I was so proud to be able to give them the money order for rent. It made me feel good that I have a budget and that I am making a productive move. It is all thanks to you, your administration, your staff, and your followers. I am not a number, I am not a piece of dirt that people spit on, I am not forgotten, and I am not unworthy of anything.

God bless you Mr. President and First Lady. I wish I could give you a hug or shake your hand. Something to express these tears of joy that will not stop flowing. I am literally 10 minutes away from my church where I do a lot of volunteer work with the youth and young adults. I am living!!! I am being productive!!!! I NOW have a place to live, a place I can call HOME. How can I express this gratitude that keeps me smiling and my eyes glistening? I Love you and all that work with you!!! Please communicate with them, that I do not take this lightly, I will live up to this graceful gift that has been given to me.THANK YOU!!!! I will make a photobook of my apartment and send it to you so that you can see what all your work as the President and First Lady has done. I will tell all who will listen. I pray God blesses you, your family, your administration, your staff and all whom honor is due.

Sincerely, Yolanda

6/30/15
fr 8

From: Mary Susan Sanders

Submitted: 6/27/2015 12:02 PM EDT

Email:

Phone:

Address: Kansas City, Missouri

Reply personally — and copy.

Message: Mr. President, I was deeply touched by your Eulogy in Charleston. After wiping the tears from my face, I got my paint brush and paint and went to the lawn jockey on my deck. It represented my heritage: a white, privileged woman from Nashville, Tennessee. I had great uncles who fought for the Confederacy during the Civil War. Now I live in Kansas City. I always told myself this black lawn jockey, like the Conferate flag, was a relic of history. But your words : "that Confederate flag represents more than one history", finally resonated. I began to cry. With all the pain in that Church, with all those families grieving, I made a decision. I went to that lawn jockey and painted him Caucasian. I never want to be the cause, directly or indirectly, to anyone's suffering. Thank you, Mr. President. I believe you are one of the Greatest Presidents our USA has ever had.
Because I'm also gay, I now feel I am a bonafide American.
Respectfully submitted,
Mary Susan Sanders

THE WHITE HOUSE

WASHINGTON

Mary Susan —

Thanks for your letter. It's good hearted people like you that always make me optimistic about this country.

Dear Mr. President

Two boys that are in our neighborhood said that girls can not change the world. I hope you can give us some advice to change the world, or to help us standup to the two boys.

Believe in Yourself

Girls can change the world

from,
Delaney, Carrigan and Bree

THE WHITE HOUSE
WASHINGTON

December 8, 2015

Dear Delaney:

Thanks for writing to me with your friends to let me know what was going on in your neighborhood. Don't listen to those boys—girls can change the world, and your letter gave me the sense that you are a strong group of young ladies who will always speak up when things don't seem right.

In the years ahead, remember nothing is beyond your reach as long as you set your sights high and stay involved in issues that matter to you. Know that our Nation is one where everyone can pursue their dreams and that with hard work, you can accomplish anything you can imagine. I'm confident all three of you have bright futures ahead—and if any boys tell you otherwise, let them know their President said they better start recognizing that girls change the world every day.

Your friend,

for encouragement

GPCL

Gretchen Elhassani

Wilmington, Delaware

5/1/2015

Dear Sir:

So many things happening in the world, and I feel selfish encased in my own skin, in my own dreams and aspirations. This isn't a political letter. It isn't a fan letter. It's just a letter, maybe a diary, something that I didn't want to put on the internet, and I didn't want to say to anyone I know. Maybe I choose you because I know you'll never read this, but I can put a stamp on it and drop it in the mailbox, and relieve myself of the burden of carrying these feelings around inside.

I am a writer. Not a successful writer, a struggling writer. See there, that was a sentence fragment.

I wrote a screenplay and entered it into a contest and I did not win. So I am sad. That's it. Thank you for reading.

Gretchen Elhassani

Registered Democrat
Non profit secretary
Mother

THE WHITE HOUSE

WASHINGTON

July 10, 2015

Ms. Gretchen Elhassani
Wilmington, Delaware

Dear Gretchen:

I am glad you trusted me with your letter, and I want you to
know it was read.

I write a lot, too, and it seems we both know the challenges
and disappointments it can bring. You shouldn't be afraid of those,
though, and you don't have to worry about whether or not what you
write will be considered good. I hope you'll keep working at your
writing and reaching for your goals—that's the resolve that pushes
America forward.

I appreciate the courage it took to send your note. Don't give
up—have faith in yourself and hold on to the dreams that have
brought you this far.

Sincerely,

Adam Apo

Chicago, IL

Mr. President,

As the year nears its close, I realize my list of chores would not be complete without first offering you my humblest gratitude for the great honor and cherished experience you gave to me a few months ago. I am a gay teacher and librarian in a Catholic high school in Chicago; and in early September, I wrote you the first letter I had ever written to a President. I asked that as you meet the Holy Father, Pope Francis, in September, that you keep in mind my fellow gay brothers and sisters and the legal, cultural, and moral equality we continue to fight for in our daily lives. I wrote about hardships and discrimination I have faced as a gay man and as a teacher in a Chicago Catholic high school.

A few days after I sent this letter, I received a call from Max Sgro in your Office of Presidential Correspondence; and I was honored to hear that you had read my letter and that I was invited to the South Lawn for Pope Francis' arrival ceremony. I cried during the call. The privilege of such an occasion was unmatched in my life. And despite many travel complications, Max worked diligently to see to my arrival. He even went so far as to meet me outside the White House perimeter in the early morning hours of the event to hand me my ticket personally. His hospitality was remarkable, and the experience of a member of the federal government working directly for me during those moments humbled me and breathed new air into my love for my country. Furthermore, that night he led me in a tour of the West Wing. In one of the hallways I saw a photograph of the North Portico illuminated in rainbow colors following the *Obergefell v. Hodges* decision. This was an emotional moment I will cherish forever. As a boy in Hawaii, I never thought I'd have the strength to embrace my identity, yet there I stood, personally invited to the White House, having walked the halls of the administration that fought to secure my legal right to marry. I was filled with overwhelming pride for my President, my country, and myself.

Unfortunately, I was asked by my school to withhold the news of my letter entirely. This terrific example of how an ordinary citizen, by the written word, can excel his cause to the highest office in the land, and earn the momentary ear of the President of the United States—will never reach the students who need to hear it. It was snuffed because I am gay, and because it was presumed that people in my community are not yet ready to accept that one of their teachers is gay. And while I've successfully kept my name off the growing list of gay teachers fired from schools, it does not come without pain. It makes me weary, but I have hope. And I remember the surprise and gratitude I felt when standing in the West Wing and I saw that photograph proudly hung.

Thank you, Mr. President, for all that you do, all that you've done, and all that you will do to change our history and arc it toward a greater equality for all.

With highest regards,

Adam Apo

PS: I can't wait to see your Presidential Library in Chicago! Looking for a librarian?

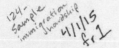

March 14, 2015

Dear President Obama,

The year was 2000, we had a small apple orchard in Eastern WA, a bright eyed 4 year old came into my house. Her family was picking apples outside and I was going to read to her in my house. She looked around and asked "what do you do with all these rooms." I told her just my husband and I lived here, but my daughter would come visit and she could have a room. I fell in love with that little 4 year old and have followed her life since that day. Attending her Cincenera and high school graduation and other milestones in her life.

Yesterday she called me sobbing that her dad had been taken away. His crime, he was trying to work. Now please understand I have known this family of 4 plus their extended family since 2000. All I can tell you about them is they came to work from Mexico. Her father said, I came to make a better life for my children. Some have graduated from colleges and hold respectable jobs. Her father's immigration papers have been a problem. Her mom has always worked and just excitedly told me her "papers" will be finalized by July.

I am aware you have worked so hard with congress to get a bill passed to assist persons living in our country without proper papers, but this has been difficult for congress to complete.

I feel such sadness, like I have lost one of my sons, but the grief this family, mom, sister, brother are feeling is immeasurable. I ask that you could please do anything in your power to assist the people of our country who are here undocumented who are just looking to make a better life and work become legal citizens.

Most sincerely,

Sheryl L Cousineau

Sheryl Cousineau

Kennewick, WA

THE WHITE HOUSE
WASHINGTON

September 15, 2015

Mrs. Sheryl Cousineau
Kennewick, Washington

Dear Sheryl:

Thank you for taking the time to write me a letter. This country's immigration system has been broken for a very long time, and stories like yours underscore the hardships created by this system. It's clear you care deeply about fixing it.

America is not a nation that kicks out hardworking people who strive to earn a piece of the American dream. We're a nation that finds a way to welcome them and to harness their talents so we can make the future brighter for everybody—that's the legacy we need to leave to the next generation.

Again, thank you for writing. In the months ahead, I will keep your letter in mind as I continue to do everything in my power to ensure America remains a place where all of us have the chance to live up to our fullest potential, and where we celebrate the diverse contributions of immigrants across our great Nation.

Sincerely,

November /21/ 2015

President Barack Obama

I am a Syrian girl, I am 17. I want to start by my life in Syria.

Before the War, my life was perfect. I used to make a small party with my friends every Friday. I lived in Idleb, in a small Town is called Taftanaz.

My school was good. I liked my friends and my teachers. I was a little child, That made my life perfect.

When the war started, the Syrian army attacked our town. Its tanks destroyed my school and some of my house. I heard much of the sounds of bombing

Because of that, we crossed into Turkey. We found a house and we rented it. There, a Syrian man established a school for all Syrian children.

It was very nice choice. I met a lot of girls from other cities of Syria. I learnt many things. My little sister sufferes from autism, we requested to come here because we could not find choices to go to the Turkesh Collages. Fortunnately, your organization accepted our request and we did come.

America is nice country. People here respect us. The school is good. Your curreculm is easy. I like it. I want to be a dotctor in the future

The helpings you give us are good. My language is not full yet, but I'm learning. I don't have any idea about your universities. I need that in order to forget everything I saw in Syria. I am thankful, I thank you from my heart because everything is nice. My teachers at school here are helpful. They are trying to help me as they can. That makes me better. I edored math. I like the American Pizza and pickle. Very nice food. The most important thing is that I'm free and living in peace with my family.

Best wishes

Heba Hallak

THE WHITE HOUSE

WASHINGTON

May 9, 2016

Heba Hallak
Short Hills, New Jersey

Dear Heba:

Your letter reached my desk, and I wanted to thank you for writing to share your story with me.

I know it must have been difficult to leave your life behind in Syria and make new friends here, but I am glad to hear you are enjoying school—and the pizza—in the United States. Despite all you have been through, I want you to know that America will always be a place where brave young women like you and your sister can come to learn, thrive, and find a sense of belonging.

The optimism and determination of families like yours are what help set our country apart. I trust you'll keep working hard in school and reaching for your dreams—as long as you do, I'm confident there are no limits to what you can achieve.

Sincerely,

Submitted via www.whitehouse.gov/contact
Case Number:

From: Mr. Dane Jorgensen

Submitted: 10/11/2015 12:52 AM EDT

Email:

Phone:

Address: Salt Lake City, Utah

Message: Mr. President, thank you.

In 2008, I couldn't afford to go to college. I tried to get student loans and was rejected. Later, because of actions taken by you, in 2009, I was eligible for and received a Pell grant and a student loan which allowed me to attend college. With federal student aid I could afford to attend college, and in May of 2015, I graduated with my bachelor's degree in Accounting. Before 2009 I had spent two years trying save enough money to attend school but, the cost of attending was always beyond the reach of my savings. Mr. President, I don't know you but; when your actions made it possible for me to pursue a college education; it felt like you knew me. It felt as if you knew how desperately I wanted to be able to afford a college education and YOU, Mr. President, decided I deserved a chance. I now earn a good wage working as an accountant at a property management firm. God bless you Mr. Obama. I will always regard you as my President because; you were the President who believed in me.

Your friend,

Dane Jorgensen

CHAPTER 12

Friends of the Mail

And why should the president be the only one reading ten letters a day? What about everyone else in the West Wing? Surely Obama's advisors and senior staff could benefit from seeing this material. "We're all kind of obsessed with this idea that this is where government is at," Yena told me. "This is the juice." Advancing the mail's reach would become an overarching OPC mission. Fiona and her team began to see it as their obligation to the letter writers, and their obligation to policy makers, and, if you got them talking about it long enough, their obligation to America: Be a megaphone for these voices. Open all the channels, full blast.

"Basically, I just started spamming people," Fiona told me. She developed a distribution list, kept adding to it. Letters to the president, dozens of them, just popping into people's inboxes. Why not? And not just 10LADs but also others from the sample piles. "We send out batches of letters we think are striking," she said. At first she worried about being an annoyance, but then she got bold. "I hope people read them; that's why I spam them. But I mean, they don't *have* to read them."

They did. Soon, people started asking why they *weren't* on the distribution list. "I remember Valerie Jarrett's assistant reached out and said that Valerie wanted to be added," Fiona said. "She had been perceived as so senior that we were not spamming her." They put her on the list. Soon the people in OPC came to know which people in the West Wing were particularly tuned in to the letters. The OPC staff came to regard these people as special agents, ambassadors, and they had a name for them: Friends of the Mail.

Shailagh, of course, was a Friend of the Mail. She told me that the constant flow of letters into the West Wing was part of the regular morning conversation among senior staff. "We'd receive them by email, and then different people would distribute specific letters that caught their eye. The chief of staff, Denis McDonough, would often distribute letters at our senior staff meetings. Just flagging things that were interesting to him or that he found especially poignant. Everybody had a different definition of what they thought was a great letter. For me, a great letter was one that would make me feel confused about issues and expand my understanding of the implications of what we were doing."

Dear Mr. President,

I have never had more conflicting emotions about a public figure. I was deeply discouraged when I heard about the ICE raids. But, you . . . have also fought hard to change the criminal justice system. There are many people in my social network that were unjustly criminalized because of their drug addictions. However, the consequences that drug convictions have on immigrants . . . remain inhumane under your administration.

. . . I have been very disappointed in you. I have also never been more proud of a president before you. . . .

Lisa K. Okamoto
South Pasadena, CA

Valerie Jarrett, Obama's longest serving senior advisor, became a Friend of the Mail. For her, the letters were a kind of nourishment. "When you're having a really bad day in Washington, there's nothing like picking up a letter from a citizen," she told me. Sometimes she would be so moved by a letter she would pick up the phone and call the person. "I want to just emphasize: Washington is so impersonal," she said. "Imagine your worst impression of what it would be like and then magnify that. It's removed. It's *physically* removed. You get caught up in the sausage making." She believed that the administration's emphasis on continued contact with constituents was a reflection of Obama's own struggles with that separation. "He did not enjoy the isolation. He spoke about it often. That human interaction—he craved it.

"What I remember is an overarching request that the president gave to us to ensure that we had regular interaction with the American people," she said. "And it began with what his wife did the day after Inauguration Day, when she opened up the White House to the American people and said, 'Please, come in. This is your house. This is the people's house.'"

And so picking up the phone and calling a letter writer seemed to her like a perfectly natural thing to do, like checking in with a neighbor. "I'd ask people what motivated them to write, and more times than not, they would say they wrote out of a feeling of frustration or desperation or inspiration, love."

Love, frustration, desperation—that was the stuff you couldn't get if you were caught up in the sausage making. The letters were access. The letters were emotion, context, and narrative.

I reached out to other Friends of the Mail and found ideas like that emerging and reemerging, going back to the earliest days of the administration and the days of the campaign. David Axelrod, who served for years as Obama's senior advisor and chief strategist on both his presidential campaigns, said the letters were Obama's lifeline from the start. "They were more than a kind of ceremonial nod to, you know, to the grassroots," he said. "Remember, you have a guy here who four years before—a little more than four years before—was a state senator. Basically representing some communities on the South Side of Chicago. And his habit was to travel that district and interact with people. And so to go from that experience in four years to being the president of the United States is, you know—it only accentuates the loss of contact.

"I was impressed by how faithful he was to the practice," he said, about the 10LADs ritual. "I saw him go back to his residence with—I mean, ultimately it was carried over there because it was such a load for him to put on the elevator. It always impressed me that he made the time for the letters.

"But, I mean, look, you serve in the White House. Everyone who's worked there and everyone who's sat in that Oval Office has served the people. So I don't mean to make invidious comparisons and suggest that somehow he was more virtuous than others. But the regularized communication he had with people seemed to me to be pretty extraordinary."

One thing I noticed about all of the Friends of the Mail I reached out to was they were delighted to learn that people in OPC thought of them as Friends of the Mail—"Oh, it's so true!"—and they readily volunteered names of others I should know about. There were recognizable names like Illinois senator Dick Durbin, White House press secretary Robert Gibbs, and speechwriter Jon Favreau, as well as plenty of people I'd never heard of, and the names kept multiplying—two more here, six more there, and then each of *those* people had more names. It got so I started wondering, *Is anybody over there in the West Wing not a Friend of the Mail?*

Probably not, Chris Lu told me. He served as deputy secretary of labor for the administration and White House cabinet secretary; before that he was in the trenches with Pete Rouse on the transition team and in Obama's senate office. Chris talked about getting "steeped in the ethos of how we do mail in Obama world" as a kind of credentialing. "It's one of the things that was really kind of ingrained in us," he said. If you didn't appreciate the mail, you wouldn't have lasted. In Obama world, letters were part of the deal.

"The president would say, 'Send this to Secretary Vilsack, and I want to know what his response is,'" he told me. "And believe me, those letters went. I would send it to, in this case, to the Department of Agriculture. And they understood. A fire was lit under those agencies to respond.

"I think it's all part of the broader spirit of transparency," he said. "The idea is that government works best when people can participate in that government. And look, obviously when you're in a country of three hundred million, it's hard to do that. But people express their views not only by voting; people express their views by writing letters."

Like so many others, Chris Lu told me that Obama carried letters around with him. If not the actual paper they were written on, which he sometimes would, then the stories they told. It was, he said, simply the way Obama thought. Stories were how he bracketed ideas. Stories had protagonists. The protagonists were the *point*. The letters would provide an ongoing supply of material. A ready inventory of parables.

Speechwriter Cody Keenan (Friend of the Mail) said the letters were constant fodder for speeches. "The president will just call me upstairs and say, you know, 'Read this letter; this is awesome; let's work this into something,'" he told me. "I remember when we were embroiled in a debate with Congress about extending unemployment insurance. And we got this letter from a woman named Misty DeMars in Chicago. She was just like your totally average American, and she and her husband had just bought a house. She got laid off because of budget cuts, and she was like, 'We are the face of the unemployment crisis.' Whereas the Republicans then were casting it as, like, you know, these greedy minorities trying to game the system. POTUS was like, 'Boom! Misty DeMars. This is exactly what we're talking about.'" Cody built the 2014 State of the Union address around her story.

> Misty DeMars is a mother of two young boys. She'd been steadily employed since she was a teenager. She put herself through college. She'd never collected unemployment benefits. In May, she and her husband used their life savings to buy their first home. A week later, budget cuts claimed the job she loved. Last month, when their unemployment insurance was cut off, she sat down and wrote me a letter—the kind I get every day. "We are the face of the unemployment crisis," she wrote. "I am not dependent on the government. . . . Our country depends on people like us who build careers, contribute to society . . . care about our neighbors. . . . I am confident that in time I will find a job. . . . I will pay my taxes, and we will raise our children in their own home in the community we love. Please give us this chance."

Misty attended the State of the Union address, sat next to Michelle Obama, and clapped on cue. The tradition of "stacking the First Lady's box" with constituents had started under President Reagan. Over the years, presidents would use the practice as a way of illustrating certain policy issues or to honor heroes. For Obama's team, stacking the First Lady's box was a simple matter of digging into the mail.

"If there was a way to make every letter he got for eight years a piece of data somehow," Cody said, "put all that data together, that would tell a pretty great story. Whether it was love finally recognized. Or despair and fear turned around. Or hopes unfulfilled. Or fear unaddressed. Or prayers answered. I mean, if there was some way to quantify that into trend lines, it would tell a pretty big story of America."

He said the letters helped inform Obama's attitudes about ending his two terms in office. "You know, he'll close a speech by saying, 'My faith in America is stronger than ever,'" Cody told me. "And people say: 'How can you say that when the country looks poised to elect some demagogue?' But it is true. And I think it has to do with these letters. He sees the unvarnished, unedited dramas of the American people every day—in a way that most people don't. We all go to our curated Twitter feeds and to our Fox or MSNBC corners and kind of wrap ourselves in our own worldviews, with people who think exactly like we do. And we assume the worst in the other side. But he sees the mail. You know? Fiona's good about giving him a really representative sample. Some are like, 'You're an asshole, and I can't wait till you lose.' But most are at least kind, even in their disagreement. One of the letters he told me to put in the convention speech this year was—there was a conservative, from, I think, Texas, who basically wrote to say: I disagree with you on absolutely everything, I'm opposed to almost everything you stand for, but I appreciate that you've been a good dad. He loves that letter."

Dear Mr. President,

As the father of three daughters, I am touched to see President Obama with his girls. Politically it would be hard to find someone further apart, I am a rabidly pro-gun libertarian, but I appreciate the sacrifices you make to serve our country and the stress on your family. I am always happy to see you as a father. I just saw your visit to central park and wanted to take the small chan[c]e you['d] see this message. Long after your term as president is done, your job as a father will continue and all accounts suggest you are doing a great job. It is also encouraging that if the leader of the United States can take the time to walk in the park with his family, the rest of us should take the time to do the same.

God bless you.
Dr. Joshua Racca
Flower Mound, TX

"I've always looked at the letters as hopeful," Cody added finally. "It's even—no matter how painful or upset your letter might be, there's still something hopeful about sitting down and thinking that maybe somebody will see this. There's a hope that the system will work. Even if you're sitting down to write, 'Dear Shit-for-Brains,' there's a chance that someone might read it, you know?

"There was one letter, one of the best ever, was just this guy who was broke, and screwed, and completely out of luck, and then he got a job as a dishwasher and said it's the best thing to ever happen to him. And he completely credited Barack Obama for it, even though I can't think of anything we did to help him get a job as a dishwasher."

Hey Mr. President Barack Obama

I just want to write to you from Richmond, Virginia and let you know my life is getting better. A few years ago I didn't have a job and my whole family was scrambling to make ends meet. I prayed daily that something would happen positive for this young man on the brink of a nervous breakdown.

I was at home watching television and the phone rang. I was sure it was a bill collector. Turns out it was a hotel in need of a dishwasher. I was so happy. To make a long story short I got the job and I have been there for two (2) years now. I [at]tribute my job finding to the

Obama Administrations relentless work to turning the economy around. I am a witness and now instead of visiting the food closet at our local church, me and my family can donate three (3) or four (4) cans a week so someone else experiencing hard times can eat. Thank you Mr. Obama!

[Name withheld]

And why did that guy think to write to Obama? That was the question that Shailagh would continually get stuck on. "You know, just going back to this notion of, like, Who are you going to tell this story to? *Well, I think I'll write to the president of the United States.* I mean, that's a powerful insight into how people view leadership and kind of still idealize it, even though they may pretend not to."

For Shailagh the letters became a resource for study, a sociology project, a history lesson. "I started looking back through letters chronologically, to get a different version of the presidency," she told me. "Establishing the public trajectory of the presidency as opposed to the legislative one or the policy calendar. This was the outside looking in."

One of the things she found was confirmation that these voices provided a kind of emotional nudge to decision-makers.

"It's apparent through these letters alone," she said, "even despite the political risk of doing a partisan healthcare bill, for example, why we stuck to that and saw it through, even at a pretty heavy political cost in the midterm elections. The raw terms that were revealed, time and time again, in letter after letter after letter, of people up against these incredible headwinds," Shailagh said, "and the one thing we could do for them was create at least a foundation of healthcare coverage where they were going to get . . . *something.* It's a totally different perspective on decisions like that. You think, *Oh, that was naïve of Obama to try to pass that healthcare bill with just Democratic votes. Didn't he realize he was going to lose Congress over that?* Well, if you're reading ten people a day, eight people a day, dealing with health-insurance problems and huge COBRA payments after having lost their jobs—it's a totally different perspective on it."

Senior staff could have, after all, opted to synthesize the voices coming out of the mailroom. They could have made charts indicating trends. "Imagine if Obama received them and we digested them for him," Shailagh said. "Just summaries of the letters, for instance. Any of these letters you could condense into a couple sentences, get the point across, without the texture and the voice and the color. And he would certainly be able to track what people were concerned about, you know? But you wouldn't have those Bobby Ingram voices; the depth; the personal, plaintive cries; and the stories as vignettes. All those things would be lost."

The human side of the story, the ideas you can't squeeze into a briefing memo or translate into bar graphs or dots on a chart. The voices of letter writers were a constant chorus in the background, pop songs you couldn't get out of your head, the tunes that defined a culture.

"I think it's the absence of that," Shailagh said, "that produces a different outcome."

CHAPTER 13

Shane Darby, February 2, 2016

KILLEN, ALABAMA

Shane Darby does not remember anything about what he wrote to the president or when he wrote it. If you're telling him it was February 2, 2016, well, he'll have to believe you, but that is surprising. That would have been just three days after everything happened. So whatever he put in the email must have been pretty terrible. Just, like, anger. That is the only thing he remembers. But why he would have written to President Obama about it, he has no idea. He's almost embarrassed to look now.

Please don't bother Stephanie with this. It has destroyed her. The person she was on the day before January 30, 2016, will never be seen again. She's doing well, given what happened.

Stephanie is sitting over by the corner hutch, listening. Not really moving, as she tends not to these days. Shane is a big guy. Thick goatee, wire-frame glasses, dressed in a black T-shirt with Mickey Mouse on it.

They bought this house two months after the funeral. It was a way of keeping Stephanie distracted. Looking at houses. The idea of decorating. And just getting away from Crissy's room and all the memories. Her door squeaked. You would not believe. He used to say good night, then shut the door super slow, let the squeak go on and on, until Crissy would say, *"Dad!"* Every night. And if she was in a crappy teenage mood (which she hardly ever was), she couldn't maintain it if the squeak went on. Every time. *"Dad!"* She was so funny. Nothing embarrassed her. Imagine a teenager choosing to go to dinner with her family over her friends. And, like, excited to go on vacation with them. A teenager loving her parents the way she did. Father's Day, taking him to see the Superman movie, showing up dressed all in Superman gear, including socks. Those socks had capes sticking out the back. Little red capes. He was like, "I can't believe you."

Crissy and Stephanie—they were like twins. They might as well have been twins. Same sense of humor. Best friends. Texting all the time. Crissy was *happy*. Honestly, there were no signs. Not one. Of course then you get into: Was he paying attention? Could he have seen something if he was paying closer attention? That is basically what every parent who has ever suffered through something like this thinks. That is where you are stuck and will be stuck for the rest of your life.

So.

It's crazy he wrote to Obama. First of all, he's a Republican. But not political. Well, he tried getting into politics; like in 2000 he paid attention to George Bush and Al Gore arguing, but after a while he quit. Nothing people in Washington, D.C., did had any effect on his life. It was better to just leave it be. So why he would have gone to the computer and typed an email to the president of the United States—it makes no sense. He doesn't even hardly use the computer. He's an iPad and iPhone guy.

Stephanie would like to put the dog to bed now. He's a golden-doodle. Yeah, pretty chill. Stephanie guides the dog to the crate, goes back to her spot by the hutch.

This house is spotless, the way Stephanie keeps it. It's like a museum. Nothing moves. He does his part. She chose the pink for the under-chair rail part. All the white wood in the kitchen. Everything is spotless, and the lawn outside is carpet smooth, and the bushes they put in are the kind that hardly grow, so you don't have to do anything.

Shane manages a paint store. Stephanie is a mail carrier. Cassie is the youngest daughter. The Cassie part is a whole thing he would like to redo. She was seven at the time. In the back seat, just sitting there. Stephanie out in the parking lot with the phone, collapsing. Him throwing up. Cassie sitting there watching this. Seven years old.

One thing that happens when someone in your family dies is people bring you food. He used to think that was the dumbest thing. Like, a roast beef is going to help? Turns out it does. Like, deeply helpful. All of that outpouring. Plus him and Stephanie had stopped eating. Stopped going to work. Mostly he just sat in his room.

The military doesn't tell you anything. There's a number you call where they're supposed to tell you things. But that guy was a robot. "No information at this time." Same thing, over and over, to the point where you're like, *"Can't somebody go bust her door down?"*

Maybe they already had and they weren't allowed to say. Maybe. The whole way they handled it—

That sound? Okay, believe it or not, it's the clock, like a cuckoo clock, but not. Just listen. It's playing "Hey Jude." The batteries are low, so it doesn't play the whole thing. At Christmas they switch it, and it plays Christmas carols. They're big on Christmas. You can see in this picture they're all dressed like elves. Even Crissy. Imagine a teenager wanting to do something like that. She was bubbly. She had that long blond hair. You see her military portrait, and it's unrecognizable.

An eighteen-year-old should make her own decisions. That's why he didn't go with her to the recruiter. But *the military?* Crissy? The girl in tie-dyed shorts and mismatched socks and Vans? She always had to have her Vans, even on those rare occasions you could get her to wear a dress. It did seem out of the blue, her wanting to be military. He thought she would be more suited to something where you use your people skills to cheer people up. When she was seventeen, she got a job at Shoney's. You know how they have that big dancing bear in the parking lot waving to people? She was the bear. Which is funny considering all her life she was terrified of anybody in costume. Like at Disney she would not go near Mickey or Minnie.

When Stephanie was Crissy's age, she did serve for a short time with the marines. So that may have been a part of it. But even that. Stephanie busted up her ankle, and they let her go or however the military does that. She didn't last long, and it's not like she was the type of person walking around like, "Oh, I hope my girls will grow up to be soldiers!" Nothing like that.

The air force recruiter must have been pretty convincing is all he can think. Germany was one place Crissy came home excited about going to. Paris. Japan. She was excited about the military sending her out to see the world. She always did like Epcot. Where you walk from country to country? That could have factored in too.

Special enforcement was her job. Military police. She worked the gates at Lackland Air Force Base. She said it was boring. He told her, "That's what it is being an adult; you have to do a lot of boring things." He was trying to instill values.

Lackland is fourteen hours away from Killen. So she couldn't just drive home. She would facetime Stephanie at least once a day. Usually a lot more. That one time she facetimed to show her mom a flame. Just a big flame on the stove. They were like, "Crissy, throw some baking soda on it!" But she left the iPad there in front of the flame, not saying anything. Maybe she thought it was funny. She didn't know how to cook.

So.

The first time she got DNA'd he didn't know what it meant. She was home on leave, and she said it casual. DNA means Do Not Arm. It means they take your weapons away for like a week because you said something that made them think you wanted to hurt yourself or someone else. She made it sound stupid, like they were being so ridiculous, like she was a kid getting caught chewing gum. So he didn't think much of it.

By the way, those figurines next to Stephanie are all Disney. All the princesses. There are more on the mantel. Then this candleholder is decorated with flowers from the funeral. That's a service you can get, making candleholders with flowers from the funeral. Yeah, he didn't know they did that either.

There was a relationship Crissy got in. Long distance. Crissy was air force, and the girl was army, and there's a thing—if you're married, they station you close together. So they got married. They didn't have a wedding. It was just quick. They got an apartment right outside Lackland. Him and Stephanie had different opinions on the relationship. But, look, this was Crissy. She could have loved a tree, and it wouldn't make no matter.

The second time she got DNA'd he probably should have thought more of it. Look, he had no experience with the military. They would give her somebody to talk to if it was serious, wouldn't they? She was fourteen hours away. They owned her. Here's where the anger comes out. He tries to keep it in. You would think they would want to protect their investment. Because that's what she was to them. An investment. But you don't have to protect your investment when you've got a busload of soldiers coming the next night. And the next night and the next. You don't have to care about any one person. If you're the commander at Lackland, you sit behind your desk watching them roll in, knowing they can be replaced.

The last Christmas Crissy ever had was in 2015. She saved up all her vacation so she could come home and go with them to Disney. His parents, Stephanie's parents, cousins—eighteen of them total. The fireworks over the castle were probably the biggest thing. They did the Bippity Boppity Boo breakfast. Crissy bit into the strawberry pancakes, and he looked over at her. "Crissy, are you *crying*?"

"It's just so . . . good," she said.

After that trip to Disney, she did not want to go back to the military. She said she wanted out. She was willing to accept dishonorable discharge in order to get out. Him and Stephanie were trying to keep her in. Stephanie has a ton of guilt over that. Being nineteen, you try to get them to follow through with their commitments to set them up for their future. But he should have just run off and brought her home. Let them do whatever court case they had to do with her. He could live with his child having a piece of paper that said they left the military. Hell, he'd *frame* that piece of paper.

The call came one month and four days after Disney. January 30, 2016. Him, Stephanie, and Cassie were shopping in Nashville, like two hours away. Good stores. Something to do. And at some point Courtney, their oldest daughter, in Texas, called to say, "I can't reach Crissy. Something feels weird."

And then it was just tiny bits of information. Basically nothing. They were shopping. They were starting to get worried. It was hours later, in the car headed home, that Stephanie got the Facebook message. "I'm so sorry about what happened to Crissy. I wish I could have done more."

What? What happened to Crissy?

They pulled the car over into a parking lot. A mall. They called everywhere. "No additional information at this time." They called the Red Cross. "Can you get us information?" They kept calling the military. "No additional information at this time."

Stephanie gets up, leaves the room.

He finally got on Twitter. He found Crissy's Twitter name. He found her partner's Twitter name. He tweeted. "Please call us. If you know what's going on, please call us, because no one will give us any information." Five minutes later the partner calls. Stephanie answers. Shane knew just by her face. Then she collapsed. Him calling the military again. "No information at this time." Stephanie talking to Crissy's partner. They weren't together anymore. She was the one who found Crissy. Stephanie collapsing. Him throwing up. Cassie in the back seat watching all this.

He doesn't remember driving home. He remembers the airman coming to the door. He felt sorry for that airman. Nobody should have to do that job. He remembers sitting in his room all alone. Roast beef. No one he felt he could talk to. He's not a person who talks to people, not like that, not about pain. And ugliness inside you.

Why she did this makes no sense. If she left a note even. If she had said something. They took her weapons away. Did they even talk to her? They treated it like it was the flu. She's in their hands. You would think they would want to protect their investment.

Greetings Mr. President and First Lady,

I know my letter will 99.9999% never get read by either of you, but I feel like for the first time in my adult life I must reach out to someone. My 19 year old daughter is dead. She took her own life Jan 30th at Lackland Air Force Base. She left home in 2014 the most happy girl you'd ever meet. If I could attach photos I'd show you a smile that would melt your hearts. I feel like the military failed her on many levels. She had made comments that screamed "get me help" and yet all they did was DNA'd her twice (took weapons away) for like two weeks at a time.

They advised her to get some help but low and behold her "amazing" military insurance would not cover the costs of speaking with

someone weekly, if it had my daughter may still be able to pick up a
phone and call home, but instead she's laying in Lackland, waiting
on a plane ticket home in a casket. Like I said I understand you wont
get this, or be able to personally reply to me, I'm sure I'll get an au-
tomatic reply, because what's my daughters life worth to anyone
who isn't her family? Nothing. She isn't a priority to anyone in
Washington DC, but if it was your family member laying in a casket
you'd be upset to. I did not vote for you, I didn't vote for anyone, but
I believe your family is the best, and most truth worthy family that's
been in the White House since our founding fathers. I believe you all
have tried very hard to correct the wrongs in our country and with-
out hidden agenda. I don't care about oil, immigration, or any of
that stuff. What I care about is another family doesn't get a knock
on their front door letting them know our Military Failed to help
their own. We send our babies to you, and you sometimes send them
back to us in a casket. Mr. President, and First Lady, I thank you for
your time if by any chance you see this.

—Cristina's Dad

Reading that now, he's surprised. It's not a good letter. He wishes
he would've been angrier. If he wrote it now, it would have been
angrier.

She had her weapons back. She wasn't DNA'd anymore. But she
didn't use a weapon. That's not how she did it. That's where you
think, *Well, was she just staging something to get someone's attention,*
and then . . . slipped? You come up with all kinds of explanations. If
she left a note. A clue. Something.

They waited for the military to send Crissy's body back. The
waiting was a lot of extra pain. Over a week. That's too long to make
a family wait to bury a child. "We'll call you when we know when
we're sending her back."

They sent a video of a memorial they did at Lackland. The main
guy over at the base talking about Crissy. Stephanie watched it. She
told Shane, "Don't watch it." She said the video implied that a person
who resorted to killing herself was maybe somebody who was weak.
She said, "Don't watch it," and so he hasn't. He doesn't want to put
himself in a situation where he would go down to Lackland and con-

front a man with that much power. It would not end well. Shane would end up in jail.

The military preys on people who don't know what the military is. That's how they do it. If you're wondering how they do it, that's how they do it.

He doesn't blame President Obama, which maybe is odd. If anything, he felt like Obama would be on his side. It's weird to think about. He felt the Obamas were human beings, at least. He did not know he felt this. It's weird to discover. You're alone in your room, numb. You're not a guy to talk, but you need to talk. You pick the president of the United States to talk to?

Maybe father to father, is what he felt. He never uses that computer. He doesn't know what compelled him. He doesn't remember hitting send.

The military did an investigation into what exactly happened. They haven't sent the report yet. It's been two years, and they still haven't sent anything. She wasn't DNA'd anymore. That's not how she did it. There were no signs. She spent the two days before cleaning her car. Playing with the dog. Just out of the blue. She wrote something on Twitter about missing her mom.

The recruiter who told Crissy about Germany, about Paris and Japan, he never said anything. He lives like fifteen minutes away, and he never called to say he was sorry to hear that Crissy killed herself.

August 5, 2016

Dear Shane:

Thank you for your heartfelt email. I was deeply saddened to learn of the loss of your daughter, Airman First Class Cristina Silvers, USAF. As the father of two daughters, I am profoundly and personally saddened by your loss.

Too many Americans suffer from depression, and our service members are no exception. Cristina's suicide is tragic and a powerful reminder of why we must continuously work to improve access to mental healthcare. It is still not a perfect system and we are working every day to close the gaps so we can move toward a future where other military families are spared the pain suicide has brought them. I will continue doing everything in my power to help ensure other families do not have to endure the terrible loss you suffered.

At this difficult time, Michelle and I hope cherished memories of your time with Cristina help temper your grief. You and your family will remain in our thoughts and prayers.

Sincerely,
Barack Obama

Shane put the letter away. It wasn't like he showed it around. The main thing he took from it was Obama spelled "Cristina" right. Most people put the *h* in there. The guy that has more power than anyone. More responsibility than anyone. For that brief moment, he's thinking about you and your family. Your daughter is in his thoughts.

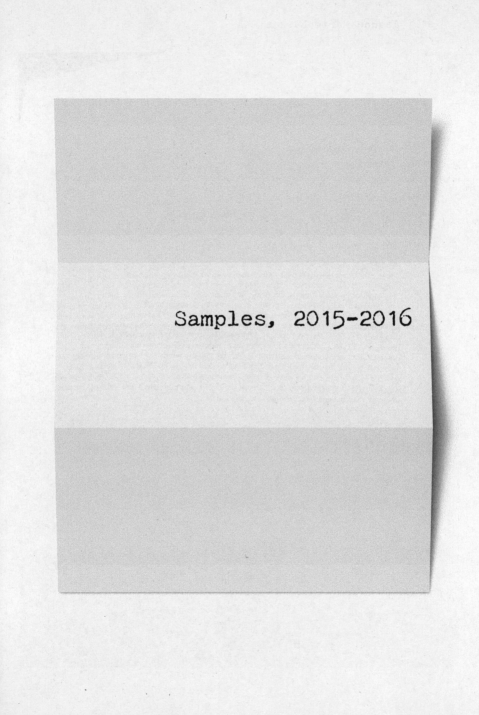

Samples, 2015-2016

3/25/16
8:14

3/29/16

Reply personally

From: Mr. Patrick Allen Holbrook

Submitted: 1/14/2016 10:37 PM EST

Email:

Phone:

Address: Honolulu, Hawaii

Message: Dear, Mr. President

It's late in the evening here on Oahu, and the sun will soon be sinking behind the horizon into the ocean. I sight that gives me comfort when times are confusing, and peace at the end of a long day. Sir, I was injured in Afghanistan in 2011 it was my first deployment, and my last. I was medically retired from the US Army, and after some discussion with my family moved here to help heal the wounds-- it is slow in coming, but I remain hopeful. I started college when I arrived here it has been a difficult experience, but this summer God willing; I will be a college graduate. It's a funny thing fear, I wasn't afraid in Afghanistan, but I am horrified at thought of my future. I want to serve my country, make a difference, and live up to the potential my family sees in me. I am scared I think, because I have no plan on what employment to pursue. It is something that is extremely difficult to me, and with my family leaving the island soon; I am truly lost. Sir, all my life I've tried to find what a Good man is, and be that man, but I release now life is more difficult for some. I'm not sure where I am going, and it is something that I can not shake. P.S. I watched your final State of the Union, and I thought it was well spoken. I too dream of a sustainable future for the next generation.

Sincerely,

Patrick A. Holbrook

THE WHITE HOUSE
WASHINGTON

Patrick —

Thank you for your thoughtful letter, and more importantly for your service and sacrifice. I can tell from your letter you are already a good man; you just need to find the calling that will express that goodness — or it will find you. So trust yourself, and remember that your Commander-in-Chief didn't know what he would do with his life till he was in his thirties!

From: Mrs. Kelli McDermott
Submitted: 9/14/2016 12:37 AM EDT
Email:
Phone:
Address:
Levittown, Pennsylvania

Message: Dear Mr. President Obama,

My grandfathers have been shamed, exiled, and ridiculed most of their young lives. What made it more difficult for them is that they were an interracial couple. They do not like to be in the spotlight, but I wanted to share our story.

My grandfather Richard and Vietnam Veteran Grandfather Al have been together for 35 years. I have grown up knowing that there relationship was perfectly normal. Surrounded by friends and classmates who would ridicule and even bully me whenever I spoke up about the LGBTQ community. To me, there was nothing wrong with love and my grandfathers truly love each other. They have been waiting patiently in Georgia to get married and I was so happy to see their wait was over. On June 26, 2015, Richard and Al finally married. However, a month late my Grandpa Richard was diagnosed with pancreatic cancer. He passed on November 22, just five months after they finally tied the knot.

With a sad heart, I can live on knowing that my Grandfathers were able to make their dream reality. They were able to share their bond legally. My family and I miss him dearly, but it helps to know that Grandpa Richard passed as a married man to the love of his life. I wanted thank you, President Obama and all the politicians involved that made marriage equality leg from the very bottom of my heart. You truly changed the world for the better for my family I. Thank you.

With the Deepest Appreciation,
Kelli McDermott

William Johnson 961072
SCCI
295 Justice Blvd
Griffin, Ga 30224

ATLANTA METRO 300

05 JUL 2016 PM 5 L

FOREVER USA

White House
President OBAMA
1800 Pennsylvania Ave N.W
Washington DC 20500

485

20500-

JUL 15 2016

485

✓ #035

JUL 15 2016

QC ✓ #028

SPALDING COUNTY CORRECTIONAL INSTITUTION

9/17/16
f16

Sample
HR

Dear Mr President

my name is William Johnson. Im In
a Georgia prison Serving a Five year Sentence
For Failing a Urain test. I was Self Medi-
Cating Because I did Not have any Medical
Insurance And I dont qualify For the tax
Break For me to afford Obama Care.
I have been In and out oF Jails and
prison my whole Life All Because oF my
Drug Use. Without Regulations on the
Drugs I have to get on the Street the
quality of the drugs Very and so does
the potency. Whitch makes for a Vary
dangerous Combination. Here is my point
and Why Im Writing you. When I was
working and had Medical Insurance I
Had No problems With Law Enforcement.
When I lost my Job and Insurance, I
Started Buying Illegal Drugs on the Street
For Depresion I use Cocaine and Meth
for my Back pains I Buy pain pills on
the Street to. As Soon as I got Caught
With these types of Drugs I was put
In Jail and then put on probation
the probation Department tells me I
Cant Do any Drugs unless given to me
From a doctor. Here Lies the problem.
No Doctor will See Me without Insurance.

And I Cant Afford Insurance. the
prison System is full of people Just
Like Me when I get out the state will
give Me a fresh Set of Clothes and
25 dollars. With No Medical Help.
Letting Drug Users out of prison Without
ACCsess to Doctors is a huge problem
they Will go Back to Self Medicating
As Soon as they feel Sick. and then
they Will Be Back In prison. In Georgia
you Can Beat Someone to death and
get food Stamps But IF you get Caught
With an once of pot you Cant. I
think the Affordable Care Act Should
Include people Coming out of prison. you
Want to Lower the Repeat Drug offenders
this is a Clear Choice. the Working Poor
Can Not Afford Medical Insurance
even With the Tax Break Most Jobs
are keeping there Employee's under
40 hrs. So they dont have to pay
there Insurance that Loop Hole
Needs to be Closed. More and More
people are buying Street Drugs Because
of these problems.
                    thank You
Can you please   William Johnson
Reply Back With A photo   / 2016

THE WHITE HOUSE
WASHINGTON

January 13, 2017

Mr. William Johnson
Griffin, Georgia

Dear William:

Thank you for sharing your story with me. It's clear you've faced great challenges, and I want you to know I'm listening.

I believe that all people, even people who have made mistakes, have the capacity to make the right choices and to have a positive impact on those around them. Your story shows that improving our justice system will require broadening access to health care and public services, including for those who have been incarcerated. That is why I've worked to support reentry programming for adults with substance use disorders and improve the provision of treatment options. This includes the Affordable Care Act's provision to extend Medicaid to all low-income adults in all States. However, because of a Supreme Court ruling in 2012, each State must choose whether to expand Medicaid. As a result, Republican resistance in some States—like Georgia—has stood in the way of affordable coverage being extended to people like you, even though the Federal Government would cover virtually all of the costs. My Administration has been encouraging States like yours to expand Medicaid so more of our citizens can get the care they deserve, and your message drives us in that effort.

Thank you, again, for your letter. If you have faith in yourself and work hard to pursue a productive path, you can affect not only your own life but also the lives of those close to you. Your story will remain on my mind in the years ahead.

Sincerely,

From: Ms. Yvonne Arnetta Wingard

Submitted: 7/9/2016 3:21 PM EDT

Email:

Phone:

Address: Augusta, Georgia

Message: Dear President Obama,

My name is Yvonne Wingard, and I am an 18-year-old, African American female. With all of the recent events occurring around this country, many people are scared. Many people are concerned. They are afraid and don't know what to do or where to turn. What is even worse, is that many who share the same skin color as me are the most fearful.

I am terrified for my life. As a black youth, it is painful and heartbreaking seeing so many posts and hearing so many news reports of people killed or severely hurt because someone automatically saw them as a threat for being black. It should not be illegal to be black in this country, nor should it warrant suspicion or excessive force.

I am simply asking for change and reform. I am asking that all of the leaders of this nation look at all of the news and terror occurring everywhere and realize that something needs to be done to reform our broken system.

I have the utmost respect for our officers. They risk their lives every day to serve their communities and apprehend those who deserve to face the consequences of their crimes. We need to keep cops armed in case of dangerous situations, but we also need to find ways to train them to know the correct measures of protocol in situations where bullets are not needed to calm the situation.

I have to live my life in fear that an officer will try to kill me simply because he sees me as a threat. I have to fear that someone will think I'm a criminal or thug or thief simply because I'm walking down the street. I have to fear even attending protests or marches because I'm afraid someone will try to shoot me or hurt me simply because they don't want to see me and my people fighting and crying out for justice.

My people are hurting. We are scared. We are afraid to be in our own skin. I am asking simply for our leaders in power to come together and find ways to improve our police and criminal justice system. Thank you for your time and consideration, and I hope that you will find it in your heart to do what is truly best for your constituents, and this nation, as a whole.

Thank You,
Yvonne Wingard

Anne   Bunting   Submitted via whitehouse.gov
                                                    11/13/2016 7:10 PM

Dear Mr. President,
Thank you for saving my life. My name is Anne   Bunting. In 2008, I
was diagnosed with Heart Failure (HF) and had a pacemaker implanted. I was
in the final stages of HF. I did well until 2012 when my heart began to fail
again. By July, 2013, I was once more in the final stages of HF. I was told I
needed a heart transplant and was put on the list. That's when we discovered
that my individual insurance policy (I was self-employed) did not cover a
heart transplant.
The only way to save my life was to implant a Left Ventricular Assist Device
(LVAD - like Dick Cheney). A few hours after that surgery, the doctors
realized the right side of my heart was dying. So they went back in and
implanted a VAD on the right side of my heart. I was the first person at that
hospital to survive this surgery and go home.
My heart was powered by 2 pumps run by computers and batteries which
were attached to me at all times. I lived with those pumps for 9 months.
Then in 2014, the Affordable Care Act came into being and abolished the
restriction on pre-existing conditions. I was able to get an insurance policy
that covered heart transplants and was put back on the list. 10 days later, I
received the gift of life through a heart transplant. So, I tell everyone that you
saved my life and I truly believe that.
You and the First Lady have both been wonderful leaders. Thank you both
for what you have done for our country and its people.
And thank you again for saving my life.
Anne Bunting

THE WHITE HOUSE

WASHINGTON

December 9, 2016

Ms. Anne ▓▓▓▓ Bunting
▓▓▓▓▓▓▓

Dear Anne:

Thank you for your kind words and for taking the time to share your moving story with me. It's clear you have faced tremendous challenges over the last few years, and I am glad to hear the Affordable Care Act helped you to get a heart transplant when you needed it most. Your story highlights how the Affordable Care Act has been life-changing for so many Americans. And in some cases, even life-saving. As a result of so many more people having coverage, we're avoiding an estimated 24,000 deaths annually. And countless other Americans are living better lives because they're receiving the care they need and deserve. It is why I worked so hard to pass health reform in the first place.

Again, thank you for writing and for your support. Michelle and I send our very best.

Sincerely,

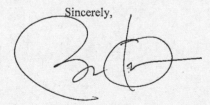

08, 21, 2010

Dear President Obama,
Remember the boy Who Was
Picked UP by the ambulance- in
SYria? Can you please go get
him and bring him to
      Park in the driveway or
on the street and we'll be wai-
-ting for you guys with flags
flowers and balloons. We
~~will~~ Will ~~will~~ give him a
family and he will be our
brother. Catherine, my little
sister Will be collect-
-ing butterflies and fireflies
for him. In my school I have
a friend from Syria, Omar, and
I will introduce him to Omar and

We CAm all Play together.
We can invite him to birthday
Parties and he will teach us anoth
-er language. We can teach him Eng
-lish too, Just like we taught my
friend Aoto from Japan. Please tell him
that his brother will be Alex
who is a very kind boy, Just like
him. Since he won't bring toys and
doesn't have toys CAtherine will
share her big blue stripy white
bunny. And I Will share my
bikke and I Will teach him
how to ride it. I Will teach
him additions and subtraction
in math. and he Smell CAtherine
's lil glass penguin which is

green. She doesn't let anyone touch it.

Thank you very much! I CAn't wait for you to come!

Alex
6 years old

Sample

Donald W. Molloy
United States District Judge

August 4, 2016

President Barack Obama
The White House
1600 Pennsylvania Avenue NW
Washington, DC 20500

     RE: Douglas George Jensen
            Cause No. CR 03-27-M-DWM

Dear Mr. President:

    I assume there is little chance that you will personally see this letter.
Even so, I want to express my gratitude and appreciation to you for
commuting the sentence of Douglas Jensen. On August 16, 2016, I will have
reached my 20th Anniversary as a federal district judge. The life sentence I
imposed on Douglas Jensen has haunted me for more than half of that time.
Your commutation of his sentence finally eases my conscience and the
struggle within me that was caused by following the law even when it was
unjust. Thank you.

                      With great respect,

                      Donald W. Molloy
                      U.S. District Judge

Address:
Email:

From: Ms. Dawn Benefiel

Submitted: 8/12/2016 9:30 AM EDT

Email:

Phone:

Address: Indianapolis, Indiana

Message: Dear Mr. President, I am a 44 year old woman who moved back to her hometown of Indianapolis IN from Southern California three years ago. I come from a mixed race blended family that began back in the late 70's. I was the only white child that walked to school. Back in the day, Indianapolis Public Schools had huge bussing campaigns to comply with desegregation. I was teased by the white kids since I didn't take the bus and I was beaten up by the black kids on the way home from school for that same reason. I still remember my 4th grade teacher who let me stay after school and sing with her until all the kids left. She knew I was tormented. She also had me sing in front of our class. All those kids that did not like me. I sang "The Greatest Love of All". This was long before Whitney Houston recorded the song. But it was my favorite song. I closed my eyes and sang that song with everything I had. For that few minutes, I forgot all the hatred in those staring eyes. I imagine that being the leader of the western world feels a lot like that. I told you that story because it bears reference to something I am about to say. Eight years ago, I worked on your campaign in Orange County CA. Not much, just worked the phone banks, went out to voter registration tables and talked to people about Barack Obama. You spoke to that 9 year old girl in me. You made me believe there is hope for our flawed country. You reminded a very jaded generation x that it is OK to hope, to believe in the good. You were our JFK. After 8 years, you still inspire. You and your wife remind me every day. You did what you set out to do. I just wanted to thank you for leading with grace and dignity. For closing your eyes and ignoring the hate and doing what you felt was right for our Nation. No one knew when you were elected, what we were about to face as a nation. No one knew how badly we needed someone that could ignite and inspire and stand tall. I don't believe there was anyone else who could have done it better. With all of the ugly things you may hear, I just wanted you to know that you have made a difference. Tears filling my eyes right now because I am sure I am not expressing exactly what I set out to. I suppose just to say, thank you for speaking to that little girl who faced so much hate and prejudice and giving her someone to believe in. With much respect and admiration, Dawn Benefiel.

\ //

From: Mrs. Heather Wells

Submitted: 9/21/2016 2:37 PM EDT

Email:

Phone:

Address: Kokomo, Indiana   Valid

Message: Dear Mr. President as you are coming to the end of your second term I wanted to share with you a story about the night you were elected. I am a nurse at an Indiana hospital. Due to being short staffed I was called and asked to work on election night. I agreed to come in as long as I could vote first. Late that night I received an admission from the ER. The patient arrived to the floor and I went in to see him. He was a black man who was about my age that was HIV positive and no longer responding to treatment. When I walked in to greet him he had the election coverage pulled up on the television. I introduced myself and noticed his Obama shirt right away. I asked if he had the opportunity to vote and he said that he refused to come to the hospital before he did. I laughed and pointed to my "I Voted" sticker and told him I said the same thing. I proceeded to pull open my scrub jacket and showed him my "Obama Mama" t-shirt and told him not to worry he was in good hands. We had a laugh and I proceeded to admit him. There weren't a lot of patients on the floor so I was able to spend a little more time just talking to him. He told me that he contracted HIV from IV drug use and that he had lived a rough life. He had two daughters at home and worried about their future. We discussed how much it meant to us for you to win the election. He shared how it gave him hope that his daughters might be able to grow up in a world where it didn't matter what race or background you came from, and that maybe one day they would have an opportunity to be president. We both laughed at that, because who would ever think a woman would get that opportunity (Boy I wish he could be here today to witness the possibility!) We spent most of that night laughing and sharing stories while we watched the votes roll in. When the final votes were tallied and the official announcement was made I am proud to say that I sat in that room with him and we held each other and cried tears of joy. Your election meant so much to me, because I truly believe in you. Your election however meant so much more to him. It meant hope, a promise that his daughters would be ok, security for their future. We spent the rest of the night celebrating he passed away 2 days later. I like to think that the moment we shared was one of his last good times on this earth. I will forever be grateful to that man for all of the hope he instilled in me for the future. Thank you Mr. President for being a part of that.

From: Mrs. Myriah Lynn Johnson

Submitted: 9/22/2016 2:21 PM EDT

Email:

Phone:

Address: Lakeland, Florida

Message: 22 September 2016

Mr. President,

I feel compelled to write you as I sit and watch a great tragedy unfold. You see, I am the one thing no parent wants to be, a Gold Star Mom. On July 12th of this year I lost my son, SPC Alexander Johnson, to a self-inflicted gunshot wound. All I'm left with is to wonder why.

He was a bright and talented young man with a beautiful fiancé and a large & loving group of family and friends. Alex, however, didn't want to address the fact he was suffering from depression. I don't and won't ever know what prevented him from seeking help, but I do know one thing. He was afraid of the stigma around mental illness. He was afraid he would lose something that has been his lifelong dream. That he should just be "Army Strong". To "be a man" and just "suck it up". All of these pressures prevented him from seeking treatment. Treatment which could have saved his life.

I have since been inundated with staggering statistics, that more of the young men and women in our armed forces are taken by suicide than in combat. Numbers range from 18 to 22 per day. 18 to 22 families that are shattered. 18 to 22 parents who lose a child, fiancés and spouses who lose their partner, children who lose their parent, brothers & sisters their siblings. What is worse is I have seen story after story of soldiers & sailors sent away from VA treatment facilities for any number of reasons. This has to stop. We need to destigmatize mental illness. Seeking help is not weakness, it is a show of strength.

As a parent I beg you to consider finding a way to allow both active duty and veterans to seek low or no cost mental health treatment at any available facility, not just a VA facility. If it could save even one family from going through what we are it would be worth it.

Thank you for your time.

Sincerely,

Myriah L. Johnson

Gold Star Mom and Proud American

8/26/16
#9

August 4, 2016

Dear President Obama,

Eight years ago, you came to UNC-Chapel Hill to speak — you weren't president yet, but, after hearing you speak, we all knew you would be soon. I want to thank you for that day. You were running a campaign based on hope rather than fear, and I want you to know that, for the 12-year-old-girl whose father had died suddenly just one week before your speech, your message was invaluable. I can't pretend to have understood, at the time, everything you said — nor can I tell you that I remember all of it. But the message — that we, as Americans, have a disposition that tends uniquely toward a hope that the future can look better — has stayed with me, from that day when I needed most to hear it all the way to the present.

I'm 20 now, and I'm actually a student at UNC-Chapel Hill. Sometimes, when I'm walking across campus, I still think of your visit. This November marks the first presidential election for which I can vote, and it's certainly shaping up to be an unusual one. I wish, of course, that I could vote for you, but instead I'll vote with your message in mind. Some of the popular political rhetoric right now is bent on using fear to create divisions and suggest that the narrative of hope is not worth striving for, and I just wanted to be sure that you heard from at least one more member of my generation that these fear-based strategies are ineffective. One of the reasons for the failure of fear (for us, anyway) is that we got to grow up listening to you.

I hope you never have days where you feel discouraged or ineffectual, but just in case you do, please know — you've done something remarkable for my generation. You helped show us that there exists far more power in hope than there does in fear. We learned that from you, and that knowledge and belief cannot be taken away. (And even if I can't speak for all my peers, I can speak for the 12-year-old girl who saw you that night one April. I haven't forgotten.) I don't know what's coming next or what my generation will one day have to accomplish, but I think you've prepared us well for it. We're not throwing away our shot.

Congratulations on all you've accomplished these past eight years. It means so much, in so many ways. Thank you.

Best,
Nell Ovitt

Chapel Hill, NC

Message: Dear President Barack Obama,

I am Noor Abdelfattah. Born in Chicago in November of 97', I was blessed enough to grow up on Chicago's North Shore. Growing up as child of a Muslim immigrant, I truly realize how privileged I am to live in the greatest country in the world. My grandfather left his homeland in 1951, the year my father was born, in search of his American dream. My father would not meet his own father until he was sixteen years old. Coming to this country with very little, my father was unable to attend college. However, he would spend long hours working low-paid jobs in order to provide for his family. Both my parents and five older brothers faced many difficulties before I was born.

At age seven, my oldest brother was caught in a Chicago gang fight where he took a bullet in the face. Today, that same brother is thirty-three years old and a graduate of University of Michigan Law School. The sacrifices my parents endured for their kids allowed us to prosper within our educational careers. Together, the educational institutions we have attended include University of Illinois-Urbana Champaign, Northwestern University, University of Michigan, and Loyola University Chicago.

Growing up, my parents have always taught us to treat everyone with respect. Although I grew up Muslim, my parents sent my siblings and I to Catholic high schools that placed us in an environment different than our own. Being the only Muslim in my class, I was allowed to interact with people who were raised different than myself. The opportunities my parents have given me allowed me to enter college open minded. I have met people I consider friends from all over the world.

However, with the hostile attitude some people carry towards Muslims, I believe that it is important that we remain together as a nation. I believe that the tradition of hosting an Iftar Dinner at the White House during the month of Ramadan is one tradition that shows the diversity our country holds. We, as Americans, are accepted for what we practice and how we look. On behalf of the Muslims living in the land of the free and home of the brave, I want to thank you for standing firmly with us in rejection of those who are hoping to limit our rights. Additionally, as your term comes to an end, I want to thank you for all the hard work you have done for all Americans and the rest of the world these past eight years as the President of the United States.

All the best,

Noor Abdelfattah

From: Ms. Madison Sky Drago

Submitted: 2/15/2016 7:43 PM EST

Email:

Phone:

Address: Holbrook, New York

Message: I am 13. I am American and I would like to peirce my nose to express myself. My parents disagree with my situation but I feel as I am my own person, I am American and i want to peirce my face. It is my face to show and it represents me and I feel as nobody should have a say against it. What happened to the land of the free? You only live once...who knows when my time will come and I want to make the best of my years.

Done Samantha Frashier incoming.pdf ⬆️

Ms. Samantha Lauren Frashier　　　Submitted via whitehouse.gov
Cincinnati, Ohio　　　　　　　　　　　7/20/2016 10:03 AM

Dear Mr. President,

I know this is a long shot, but I being optimistic and I'm trying. I want to make a change. I may be one person but I've already changed the lives of others. I am 29 years old, the mother of 7 month old twin boys and have almost 3 years clean from using heroin. I have been contacting my local officials and sharing my story of hope with others. I am helping start a non profit recovery home here in Warren County,Ohio by Cincinnati. We have nothing. I spent hours on the phone trying to find a place for a friend. I am watching my friends around me die. And I can't help them because the only option is to send them to Florida, New York, California ect. I remember hearing you speak about putting in some funding into substance abuse and I am curious what it went to? I am also interested in figuring out the best way to help addicts. Prison is not helping and the laws are crazy with this involuntary manslaughter charges. Prison is not the answer. I urge you to please contact me. I have sooo many things I would love to speak with you about. I know it may not be possible, but a girl can dream! Thank you!!

THE WHITE HOUSE

WASHINGTON

August 4, 2016

Ms. Samantha Lauren Frashier
Cincinnati, Ohio

Dear Samantha:

Thank you for writing and for sharing your story. Every day, I am inspired by resilient Americans like you who summon extraordinary courage and strength to live healthy and productive lives in recovery.

Too many Americans are affected by the prescription opioid and heroin epidemic. My Administration has been doing everything we can to increase access to treatment, but it won't be enough without more resources from Congress. That's why I have called on Congress to provide $1.1 billion in new funding to help ensure that all Americans who want treatment for an opioid use disorder can get the help they need. Unfortunately, Congress has repeatedly failed to provide these resources. Congress needs to act quickly because lives are at stake.

My Administration is committed to promoting evidence-based strategies to combat substance use disorders, and to reforming the criminal justice system to address unfair sentencing disparities and provide alternatives to incarceration for nonviolent, justice-involved individuals with substance use disorders. Recovery can transform individuals, families, and communities.

Thank you, again, for taking the time to write. With access to treatment and other supports, recovery is possible for American with substance use disorders, and I will continue to work alongside you until we achieve this reality.

Sincerely,

CHAPTER 14

The Writing Team

"Back from the OVAL" was what the stamp said on the letters Obama had read. They were returned in batches to OPC, and most had some kind of notation in the margins. "What's going on here?" the president may have written, which meant he was requesting a follow-up memo from staff with some broader context—say, in response to a teenager dealing with a trend he didn't understand. He might write, "DOJ, can we help?" which meant he wanted the staff to reach out to the Justice Department to look into the situation by doing something like making sure an inmate was getting the medications he needed. Or he could simply write "REPLY," and if he did that, he would offer notes in the margins for the writing team to use as guidelines for how to respond in his name.

The writing team was not easy to find. They worked in the attic, up on the fifth floor of the EEOB—where most of the elevators didn't go; you had to take a back staircase. It was a tight space with low, slanted ceilings; tiny windows set back in alcoves; people tucked into corners staring into glowing screens. "Even people in the White House don't know this office exists," one of the writers said to me.

They were the elves of the operation. Every thank-you note, gift acknowledgment, condolence letter, congratulations greeting—every piece of typed correspondence with the president's signature on it (the notes in longhand were authored by the president himself) came from the writing team, nine people in all. Perhaps the heaviest lift for the shop was composing the form letters that were sent automatically and in accordance with the way incoming mail was coded. All the form responses the team wrote—more than a hundred of them dealing with specific subject areas like immigration, race relations, climate change—had to be continually updated in accordance with the news cycle, policy changes, topics covered in presidential speeches. Each week a group would comb through and revise the letters, while another, the "conditional language tech team," constantly tweaked algorithms they had designed to allow for personal touches. So, for example, a teacher writing about immigration reform would get the immigration letter, with an added thank-you for his or her service to students; a recent retiree writing about climate change would get the climate change letter and a "best wishes on your retirement." The algorithms allowed for hundreds of combinations.

The goal was to make sure that everyone who wrote a letter to the president got something of substance back. If people believed in this president enough to write to him, that belief needed to be nurtured. The underlying assumption for the writing team was that this president *did* care. If you didn't hold that notion at your core, you wouldn't last. Fiona was at the helm, maintaining quality control and constantly singing her song: This matters. She tracked reader responses to the form letters, organized those into "smile" and "frown" files so the team could gauge its own success rate. "So if someone writes, 'Thank you for the acknowledgment of the death of my mother; your letter really meant a lot,' that goes into the smile file," she told me. "Then another person may write to say, 'Your letter about Syria didn't answer my concern.' That's a frown."

Nobody wanted a frown. Everybody wanted a smile. Everything needed to be perfect. The formatting, the margins, avoiding extra paragraph breaks and random periods, the address label, the printing—it all fell on the writing team, and no detail was too small. This may have been a form letter, but this was a form letter *from the president*. This would be one citizen's proof. It might end up in a frame, hung on someone's wall—passed down to children and to grandchildren. This was an artifact, a piece of American history.

. . .

Kolbie Blume was the person on the writing team in charge of an-swering the 10LADs. If Obama wrote "REPLY" and scrawled notes in the margins of a letter, that meant a personal response had to be created, and those all went to her.

She had a separate office. "I'm *not* the youngest person here," she said when she got up to greet me, as if to preempt an all-too-familiar conversation. She had the clean, unadorned look of an ado-lescent: a neat, short bob; a buttoned-up top with pearls. She was twenty-three. "This is my first job out of college," she said. "I mean, it's a lot of pressure." She'd been at it for two years already.

It took me a moment to do the calculations. Kolbie would not even have been eligible to vote when Obama was first elected; she would have been in high school. "Basically, my job is to channel the leader of the free world," she said. "I'm doing my best to be . . . him," she said, adding, appropriately I thought, "um."

I asked her how she'd learned to write in President Obama's voice.

"Listening to speeches, mostly," she said, sitting down at her desk and motioning for me to take a seat too. She said Obama's speeches were a *thing* for her, ever since she was a kid back in Utah, standing in front of the living room TV. "The way he could master words, the way he phrased ideas . . ." She had never bothered listen-ing to a politician before. Those blah-blah talking heads were for her parents or for other people, not her. But this guy was different. *He's talking to me.* She wanted to learn about him, began reading his books. He was somewhat dangerous: a Democrat. The novelty factor alone could have been part of the appeal. Had she ever met a Demo-crat before? Did Utah even have any? She fell for the cadence and rhythm of his sentences. "The way he could so eloquently, so power-fully, and so poignantly say something and move people to tears." She became a closet Democrat, then an out one.

"I was so excited to vote for the first time in 2012," she told me. "And I remember my boyfriend was like, 'Why? What good is it going to do?' It struck such a chord with me. Something that I'd been so excited for, and here there were so many people so jaded; they didn't think one vote was going to make a difference.

"I mean, you could argue that my one vote in 2012 didn't really help anything. One Democrat in a totally Republican district. Well, it helped *me*. Because I felt empowered. I remember getting the sticker. 'I voted.' I put it on the back of my phone case, I was so proud of it."

The sticker had barely worn off by the time she arrived at the White House two months later, just before Obama's second inauguration, having secured an internship through Utah State, where she was majoring in literary studies. "And I just remember my phone case was still all gummy—"

I was still trying to catch up with the fact that a person this young was the one who wrote all the personal letters that went out with the president's signature on them.

"I love my job," she said.

It turned out that a steady diet of Obama's speeches made you especially talented at this sort of work. "You listen to so many speeches, you just have a running commentary in your head," she said. OPC interns with ambition and drive would routinely apply for staff openings once their internships were completed; Kolbie was just one of many following that path. Fiona recognized her knack early on, hired her to be part of the writing team, and soon put her in charge of the 10LADs portfolio.

"When I draft a letter, I'll sit and read it out loud," she said, trying to explain her methodology. "I'll hear what kind of inflections the president would have. If it sounds like him, I know it's right. If it doesn't, then I'll try to make it so it does.

"I wish I could tell you exactly how to do that, but . . . I just do it every day."

She gave me an example. A letter from a woman in Tulsa sitting on top of her day's to-do pile. "So my job is to take what the president wanted to say to this person," she said, holding it up, "and turn it into the custom response that every letter writer deserves but that the president wanted this particular constituent to have." The letter was about a shooting—a white cop had fatally shot an unarmed black man who, according to the letter, was seen raising his hands above his head in videos released after the shooting. The woman was outraged; she wanted to know why Obama wasn't doing more to repair the growing tensions between police and people in African American communities.

Fiona had chosen it as one of the 10LADs, and the president had read it. He wrote "REPLY" on top, and down one margin he wrote, "I'm mad, too." He underlined various sentences, added exclamation points in the margin, various squiggles, and a few other brief comments.

"See?" Kolbie said, pointing to one of Obama's exclamation points. "See this right here? And this over here—" The markings Obama had scrawled on the letter may have been sparse, but Kolbie understood the code.

She turned to her computer, pulled up a draft of the response she had been working on. It was a Word doc with an array of annotations in rainbow colors running down the side. Footnote everything— that was Kolbie's motto. If she was quoting Obama verbatim from his scrawling on the letter, she would indicate it; if she had borrowed language from a speech he had given on the topic, or another letter on the topic, or a town-hall conversation about the topic, she would indicate those things. She had made it her habit to constantly search through the archives on Whitehouse.gov to gather bits of Obama's language to use in letters. In the end, crafting the responses in his name was one part deciphering, one part collating, and one megadose of confidence that you were just the person to inhabit the mind of the leader of the free world and put this thing together right.

I asked her where she got the confidence.

She grabbed her pearls and twirled them. "It's so easy to think linearly," she said. "Like, okay, here's a person who wrote about climate change, so let's just plunk in some language about climate change here." She said those attempts were all duds. Fiona, the grand pooh-bah of quality control, would toss those right back to her, saying, "No," and "Try again," and "You're not nailing this." Fiona needed to remind Kolbie that this was a *person* she was writing to. And the president was a *person*.

"And I vividly remember, almost like an epiphany," Kolbie told me. "It was like one day I just got it." Every letter coming from the president was ultimately a variation on the same theme, she realized. "It's: 'Look, I hear you. You exist, and you're important, and I care about your voice.'"

I thought about how that underlying message, not cynical, not fancy, not loaded—no baggage—was perhaps best kept in the protective arms of a person not far from childhood.

Kolbie flipped through the pile of letters she needed to get through that afternoon, about fifteen in all. Back from the OVAL, Back from the OVAL, Back from the OVAL, REPLY, REPLY, REPLY. "A few of these will be easy," she said, pulling out one. A person was writing to give advice to the president on what he should do after he retires. "'Ride a bike daily. Volunteer. Don't be afraid to day-drink. Go out to lunch as often as possible with Mrs. Obama.'" The president had written little more than "Thanks for the great advice!" in his comments. "I'll probably flesh that out a little," Kolbie said. "I remember recently he joked about wanting to take three or four months to sleep; maybe I'll incorporate some of that language—"

She pulled out another letter. A woman was writing to apologize; she had first written to Obama years earlier accusing him of being anti-Christian. Now she was writing again, having had a change of heart, and saying she was sorry. Obama wrote "REPLY" on top, and along the side: "Thanks for being thoughtful and open to ideas. I'm sure you will do well."

"I have not drafted this one yet," Kolbie said. "But it won't be much more than what he said here. It just needs . . . what he said there." She put it back in the stack, fanned through some of the others. "And you know, the vast majority of these start by people saying, 'I know my letter will never reach you,'" she said. "Or 'I'm sure some staffer will just toss this letter in the trash.' So for me, knowing that the person is going to get a response, knowing that their cynicism or their disillusionment is going to be chipped away just a little bit— that feels like a victory."

I thought about some of the letter writers I had met and what getting a personal letter back from Obama meant to them.

I thought about Shane Darby, who wrote to howl in the aftermath of his daughter's suicide; the thing that soothed him about the president's response was seeing the president spell Cristina's name right. "Most people put the *h* in there."

I thought about Donna Coltharp, an attorney in San Antonio, Texas, who wrote a letter of thanks to the president for commuting the two life sentences of her client. What moved Donna was that the president thought to thank her for her service as a public defender. "No one ever thanks us."

I thought of Bob Melton, a guy in North Carolina who wrote in 2014 to thank Obama for the Affordable Care Act; it enabled him to see a doctor for the first time in twelve years. The president wrote back, and Bob Melton showed the letter to everyone. "I couldn't believe it! I immediately jumped in the car and went down to Walmart and bought a frame." He got invited to the Burke County, North Carolina, Democratic Party meeting to come read President Obama's letter out loud, and everyone clapped, and so now other local groups are asking him to come read it for them too. "I'm just overwhelmed by the whole situation. I mean, little old me, you know? Down here in North Carolina. You know? I never thought I'd get any kind of applause." Because of that letter, Bob Melton will tell you, he now walks as a tall man.

I thought, finally, about Patty Ries, a woman in Dallas, Texas, whom I'd recently gotten to know. She wrote in 2016 because she wanted Obama to see one of her own family heirlooms, a letter her father had once written to President Roosevelt, in 1943.

> I have meant to write to you for some time. Now I am concerned whether this letter will reach you before you leave office. . . . I am deeply concerned about Donald Trump running for President. I sincerely hope that he doesn't win. I fear that our country will go back in time if this comes to pass. . . . My father was born in Germany and came to the United States when he was eighteen. My father desperately wanted to become a United States citizen so that he could join the US army and fight against the Germans during WWII. . . . He was sworn in as a US citizen at two in the morning by a Justice of the Peace after this letter was received in Washington. If Donald Trump was the President, my father probably would not have been allowed in the United States let alone been sworn in as a US citizen. . . . When the war ended he did find his mother who had been a prisoner at the concentration camp Theresienstadt. She too was able to come to the United States after the war and lived almost fifty years in the US before her death at age 99! Unfortunately I did not get to meet my grandfather. He was killed in Auschwitz concentration camp.

THE WHITE HOUSE

WASHINGTON

January 13, 2017

Ms. Patty Ries
Dallas, Texas

Dear Patty:

Your letter reached my desk, and I wanted to thank you for sharing your family's story with me. I was deeply moved by it and by the letter your father wrote to President Roosevelt—what a powerful piece of history.

It's clear you come from a long line of people committed to building a more inclusive, more just future, and your pride in that legacy came through in every word. I hear your concerns about our country's politics. I know it may sometimes seem as if the loudest and angriest among us drive our national conversation, but I firmly believe that the most thoughtful and compassionate voices will ultimately win out and shape the stronger America we all deserve. Hearing from folks like you only reaffirms my optimism for our country's future.

Again, thank you for writing to me, and for your father's dedication to our country. It's been a tremendous privilege to serve as your President these past eight years, and your words—as well as your father's and grandfather's—will stay with me.

All the best,

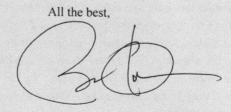

I remembered how proud Patty was of that letter from the president, like Bob Melton, like so many of the others. She put it in a brown frame and hung it over her computer, prime real estate, a new family heirloom to add to a collection that dated back to her grandfather's imprisonment and murder in Auschwitz.

I suppose Kolbie was the one who actually wrote that letter to Patty, and the letters to Shane Darby, Bob Melton, and Donna Coltharp, and so many of the other typewritten responses I had read. I didn't ask Kolbie about any of those letters specifically. This was inching way too deep into Santa Claus territory. I remember Yena telling me that one of the reasons she and other people in OPC didn't like talking about their work to outsiders was because they felt a responsibility to preserve the illusion. Like the magician's pledge—thou shalt not reveal the tricks of the trade. Your silence was your gift.

"Every day I just can't believe that (a) I'm here," Kolbie told me that afternoon, "and (b) that the president cares so much about these letters."

It was impossible not to root for Kolbie. The more time I spent with her, the more I thought there was probably nobody I'd rather see be in charge of the magic than a woman with a tender heart whose still-burgeoning belief in a hero had not been tainted.

I asked Kolbie what she needed to do to finish the letter to the woman in Tulsa who wrote about the shooting, and she went back to her computer, scrolled up, then down.

"Okay, so what I've done here is break down the sections of his thoughts," she said, tapping the screen. "See? It's 'I'm mad, too.' And 'My administration can't intervene in individual cases.' And 'But this is what we are doing.' And 'No one should have to fear being profiled.' And then he ends with 'This is what you need to do.'

"Basically, POTUS has given me topic sentences, and I'm filling in the blanks," she said with a shrug. "I'm an English major. It's what we do."

The final version, including all the annotations, would go to Fiona, who would inspect and edit it, then forward it to the interns who manned the printer. Fiona would inspect the printed version, the margins, the consistency of the ink—no random dots or splotches—before finally sending it back to Obama for his signature. Then the letter would be out the door, destined for a mailbox in Tulsa and, likely, a frame on a wall.

"If my job didn't exist, so many people would have unanswered letters; you know what I mean?" Kolbie said. "They wouldn't know that the president cares. They wouldn't know that their voice does matter. They just wouldn't *know*."

I asked her if she'd ever had a chance to talk to Obama about what it was like to channel his voice.

"I've never met him, no," she said. "I mean, he hand signs these letters, and he knows that they don't just come out of nowhere, so he knows my job exists."

But that was as close as he was to knowing her. She told me that would soon change, however. Every White House staffer was due to get a departure photo taken with the president during his final months in office, and Kolbie's appointed time was just a few weeks away.

"I'm trying to mentally prepare," she said. "It's bigger than anything that's ever happened to me. Sometimes I spaz out in front of people, so I'm trying to prepare.

"I'm going to shake his hand. I'm going to make sure he knows who I am. I'm going to say, 'My name is Kolbie, and I'm your voice.'"

CHAPTER 15

Donna Coltharp and Billy Ennis, August 4, 2016

EL PASO, TEXAS

Billy was fifteen the first time he got kidnapped. It was a Saturday morning, back in the 1980s, in Anthony, New Mexico, just north of El Paso, Texas, where the family moved after they got rich. Billy was asleep in his room. He was a skinny kid who loved motocross and who lived by the rules his parents taught him: If you're hit, hit back harder, and don't go bothering your parents about it. Take care of your own problems.

So this one morning the doorbell rings, and Billy answers it, and the guy asks for Billy's dad. "He's not home," Billy says, and the guy leaves only to return an hour later with more guys who grab Billy by the hair, drag him across the yard, and stuff him in the trunk of a car. Next thing Billy knows he's handcuffed to a bed frame in a house somewhere in Mexico, and everybody's calling him Chester.

"My name is Billy," Billy says.

Chester was his brother, a few years older.

They got the wrong kid. Ransom-wise, a firstborn was worth more. Billy learned a lot just listening. This situation clearly had something to do with his dad's booming drug business, the extent of which Billy was only beginning to grasp. It had always been more of a vague thing. A lot of garbage bags moving into and out of his parents' bedroom, put it that way. After three days with the kidnappers and no ransom coming, Billy escaped in the middle of the night—he tricked the guy with the key to the handcuffs—and ran for his life through the desert. With the help of the Mexican police (who knew Billy's dad), he was deposited at the border, and his dad picked him up.

A few weeks later, Billy got kidnapped again, only this time they took both him and Chester. They came in the middle of the night, and they shot up the house, and they bashed his mom's head in with the butt of a machine gun because she wouldn't stop screaming. They again stuffed Billy into the trunk of a car, which was much more crowded with Chester jammed in there too. Again the kidnappers drove to Mexico. This time they hog-tied Billy and put him face-down on a couch. The guy who had been in charge of the handcuff key beat Billy repeatedly saying he shouldn't have tricked him like that. "You would have done it too," Billy told him. "I wasn't doing anything a normal person wouldn't do." They were so much meaner this time. They threatened to kill Billy's mom, and they beat him and Chester. The rescue, days later, by the Mexican police (who knew Billy's dad), came after a shoot-out.

Nothing was the same after that. Billy was so angry he got kidnapped twice and so was Chester. They wanted retribution. They got guns. They believed they knew who was behind the kidnappings, and they said they were going to go get him. Their dad pleaded with them not to do this. Their mom said, "Well, I'm not letting you kids go alone," so she got her .44 and got in the car with them, and so then their dad got in too—the four of them, off to go get even.

It did not go well. The guy they were after was not home, and so Billy and his parents and Chester took the wife, a maid, and two kids hostage. They took them to a hotel room. "I was an asshole," Billy would later remark, looking back on how he treated them. He did buy them food, though, and toothbrushes. It was a fiasco. Everybody was terrified. In the end, Billy's family locked the hostages in a U-Haul and turned themselves in. His dad worked the deal. Everybody was part of the drug trade. Everybody. Nobody pressed charges. Everyone walked away.

. . .

"I found out later it wasn't a normal childhood," Billy was telling Donna Coltharp in 2002. He was now thirty-three.

It was the first time Donna had ever talked to her client. Billy was calling from the Florence Federal Correctional Institute, a medium-security prison in Colorado; she was a newly appointed federal public defender in the Western District of Texas, and she had been assigned his appeal.

"Nice to meet you," she had said after he introduced himself. "How was your morning?"

Billy told her that his dad was his cellmate, and that his dad snored, so they were moving him.

Donna asked Billy how he ended up in prison with his dad, and Billy was trying to summarize. He explained about the kidnappings, and he told her that by the time he turned sixteen, he was homeless. His dad had been busted—"with ten tons of marijuana," as Billy recalled it—and went to prison. Chester also went to prison, but it was for gang stuff he got involved in. Billy's mom couldn't afford the house, so she took off. She did not take Billy with her. "I was an asshole," Billy said, defending his mom. Billy found a spot under a bridge to live in. The school told him he couldn't come back because he no longer had an address in the district. (He did not tell them about the bridge.) He broke into a vacant trailer and lived there for a while. He stole groceries for food. He met a guy who said there was a better way. It took Billy just a few hours to sell a kilo of coke. He made twelve thousand dollars that first day. From then on it was party central.

Billy put his story on fast-forward and told Donna about the two convictions that had led up to his current situation. He said his teenage cocaine business was wildly successful. When he got busted, in his early twenties, he was full of fury, until he figured out it was the best thing that could have happened to him. In prison he learned about normal childhoods. He got clean. Drug dealing, he discovered, led to one of two possible outcomes: prison or death. He tested the theory when he got out; it took him another round of prison for the point to stick. It was after finishing his second prison sentence that he got it together. He got a job. He had a son.

Billy wouldn't snitch on anybody; that could be part of why the cops got so mad when they came and raided his house in 2002.

They didn't find any drugs. They found diapers and baby toys, and Billy told them to take their hands off his son.

Billy's father was the one they wanted. He'd been free for a few years and had opened a print shop with Billy's mom. Billy suspected his dad was up to no good, but he wouldn't give any information to the cops. When the cops finally busted his dad and a neighbor as part of an organized crime investigation called Operation Power Play, they wrapped Billy into the arrest.

"I had nothing to do with it," Billy said. He confessed to having dealt weed—his occasional freelance work when he needed to make rent. That much he did do. He told them, you can have me for that, but not for this.

They tried three of them at once: Billy, his dad, and the neighbor. The jury came back with a guilty verdict for all but Billy. On his case, they reached an impasse. The judge instructed the jury to continue deliberating. In the end, the jury found Billy guilty, and because of his priors and the "three strikes" law imposing mandatory prison time for repeat offenders, the judge handed him two concurrent life sentences.

"For a drug conviction," Donna said that day on the phone. Two life sentences for a drug conviction was the kind of thing that drove Donna crazy. She was the type of person who thought a lot about mercy and the power of imagination. Warehousing nonviolent offenders was doing nothing to help society.

"Well, let's get to work," Donna said.

Over the years, Donna and Billy grew close, even though they never met in person. Everything they did was by phone. That's pretty typical when you are talking federal appeals court. They chatted about their sons; they both had toddlers. When Donna's son started preschool, so did Billy's. Both boys learned how to tie their shoes and started sports. Donna and Billy would compare notes, as parents do. They became the kind of friends that parents become, sharing transitions. Donna knew that for Billy the transitions were theoretical. She could feel the passage of time in a way Billy could not, and the disparity would eat at her.

Billy's appeal came down to a black-and-white box. At trial, police had testified that they had aerial surveillance of Billy carrying a box into his dad's house. Thirty kilograms of cocaine had been found in a box. Specifically, a Gateway computer box. Gateway was an iconic brand in those days. Its mascot was a Holstein cow, and all its boxes had large black cow splotches on them. Did the guy in the helicopter see the splotches? He should have been able to, the defense said. Could he have instead seen any number of other boxes Billy may have taken over to his dad's? In deliberations at the first trial, the jury was hung up on the question of the box. No fingerprints or other physical evidence had connected Billy to it, just the aerial surveillance. The jury asked to see the box. "Sorry," they were told. The box had been inadvertently destroyed by courthouse cleaning personnel.

Donna thought the missing evidence should have cleared Billy then and that it should clear Billy on appeal.

It didn't.

It was 2005. She called Billy with the news. The denied appeal was three years in the making.

"I'm so sorry," she said.

Billy said he wanted to keep fighting. There had to be *something* they could do.

Donna was out of ideas. She told him, well, we can always appeal to the president of the United States to grant clemency—that's how out of ideas she was.

Unlike presidents before him, Obama had not made use of his pardon power. People said he had pardoned more turkeys than people. In fact, he wouldn't commute a single sentence until 2011, and even then it was just one.

A pardon is forgiveness of a crime, wiping out the conviction entirely, while a commutation leaves the conviction intact but wipes out the punishment.

The idea of the president commuting Billy's sentence was, Donna knew, a fantasy. It was like hoping for the tooth fairy to be real. But it was all that was left. So she prepared the plea, told Billy's story, and contacted a commutation attorney to file it.

It wasn't until late into his second term that the dam burst open for Obama on the issue of commutations. On July 14, 2015, he gave his first major criminal justice speech at the NAACP convention in Philadelphia. "Mass incarceration makes our country worse off, and we need to do something about it," he said. "I'm going to shine a spotlight on this issue, because while the people in our prisons have made some mistakes—and sometimes big mistakes—they are also Americans, and we have to make sure that as they do their time and pay back their debt to society that we are increasing the possibility that they can turn their lives around."

Obama followed the speech with a visit to the El Reno Federal Correctional Institution in Oklahoma two days later. "When they describe their youth, these are young people who made mistakes that aren't that different from the mistakes I made and the mistakes that a lot of you guys made," he said there. "The difference is that they did not have the kind of support structures, the second chances, the resources that would allow them to survive those mistakes."

He was the first sitting president to visit a federal prison. His presidency was coming to an end, and he had certain things he wanted to accomplish; he would use his power of commutation as a form of criminal-justice reform.

Obama granted 46 commutations in the summer of 2015, another 78 in December 2016, and then hundreds more, including 330 on January 19, 2017, his last full day in office. In total, he would grant executive clemency to 1,927 people convicted of federal crimes, more than the past thirteen presidents combined.

. . .

U.S. Department of Justice

Office of the Pardon Attorney

Washington, D.C. 20530

August 3, 2016

FLORENCE
Warden
Florence FCI
5880 State Highway 67
Florence, CO 81226-9791

Re: William Edward Ennis
     Reg. No. 62601-080
     Recipient of commutation of sentence

Dear Warden:

Please find enclosed a certified copy of the warrant by which President Barack Obama has commuted the prison sentence of William Edward Ennis, Reg. No. 62601-080. Please deliver the enclosed warrant to the inmate and ensure he has completed the enclosed receipt acknowledging that he has received the warrant. The receipt should be returned to this office via email to USPardon.Attorney@usdoj.gov. Thank you for your assistance.

Sincerely,

Robert A. Zauzmer
Acting Pardon Attorney

Enclosures

Donna had never wanted to be an attorney. She wanted to be a literature professor. She wanted to teach *Moby-Dick*. Law school was more her mom's idea.

She was in her office when she got the voicemail from Billy. He was weeping. She called him back right away but couldn't reach him. She checked her email and found the list of new commutations there, and she scrolled up and down to make sure what she was seeing was really there.

- William Ennis—El Paso, Tex.
Commutation Grant: Prison sentence commuted to expire on December 1, 2016.

She forwarded the news to everyone in the office, to everyone in the district, to everyone she knew. She couldn't sit still. She kept trying to reach Billy. For a couple of hours, she tried to work, then drove home. She wanted her husband to take her out to dinner. She couldn't sit still. She wondered if Obama knew how commutations affected people. She wondered why he had done it. He would get no political capital for a thing like this. She wondered if anybody in the press would say it was the right thing to do. What an odd, quaint thing to have in America, she thought, the idea that politicians could step outside of the system and say, "Enough is enough." All of these ideas were racing through her mind, and her husband wasn't home yet to take her to dinner, so she was going to just pour herself a drink to calm herself down, but instead she got the idea to open her laptop. She drafted the email, slept on it, edited it the next morning. She wanted to get it just right.

She wondered if anybody ever bothered to thank the president. When a person in a position of power does a powerful thing, the focus tends to be on the thing, not the person who did it.

. . .

From: Donna Coltharp

Submitted: 8/4/2016 12:14 PM EDT

Email:

Phone:

Address: San Antonio, Texas

Message: Dear Mr. President

Yesterday, you announced the commutation of the three-life sentences one of my first clients as a federal public defender is serving. His name is William (Billy) Ennis. No one I have ever represented is more deserving of a second chance. In fact, for this reason, I referred Billy's case to a commutation lawyer a year before our national commutation projects began.

Billy grew up with parents who trafficked in drugs at the border. At one point, when he was a child, he was actually kidnaped by people who were seeking to collect drug debts from his parents. For awhile, as a child, Billy lived under a bridge. It was not surprising that, as a young adult, he picked up two drug convictions -- one relatively minor. Then, he went straight. Quit using drugs. He had a son. But, he got pulled back into his parents' dealings and performed a role in a drug transaction. And, the drug laws put him away for three lifetimes. His son, whom he had custody of, was just a baby.

I lost Billy's direct appeal. But, I have remained in touch with him for the past 14 years. We talk at least once a month. So much has changed. His son now plays high school football in El Paso! His mother passed away a few years after he was sentenced. Billy has participated in every prison program available to him and has the respect of prison staff and inmates alike.

Billy deserved a second chance. But not many people would have given it to him. I am profoundly grateful that you have the courage to look at people whom society has decided are not worth looking at and see an opportunity for redemption rather than just a criminal. Yesterday, the day I heard about Billy's commutation, is the single best day I've had as a criminal defense attorney. I've seen clients walk free because of my representation (not many!), but I have never seen a client handed the gift of grace that you gave Billy.

Billy called me in tears yesterday. I may never hear from him again, but I will never forget him or that call. Please keep him in your prayers as he tries to find a way forward to a better life.

Billy has never met Donna in person. Today she's in El Paso for some kind of meeting, and that's why he's finally getting to meet her. He imagines her with dark hair, probably about fifty. He knows he's put on weight, and he wishes he still had hair. In a few minutes he'll be ready to head out, but first you can look around if you want.

As you can see, the house needs work. When Billy first walked in a few months ago, the cobwebs were like *The Addams Family*. He's tackling the plumbing and the electric first. It's weird being forty-seven and coming back to the house you grew up in. Billy lived here until he was thirteen, back before everything went haywire. His grandmother owned it. When she died, she left the house to Billy, even though he was serving two life sentences. Not three, as Donna says in her letter to Obama. When it comes to multiple life sentences, it's easy to lose track.

Over the years, while the house sat vacant, people came through and trashed the place. But that's okay. As you can see, they left the family photos. Here's one from a vacation at Knott's Berry Farm in about 1980. Billy is maybe ten here. He and Chester and a cousin, Billy's mom and dad, all dressed like cowboys at one of those booths where you get to wear historic costumes. That's Billy's dad with the sheriff badge. Everyone in this picture besides Billy is either dead or in prison.

He's glad he has a house to live in. He's been able to see his son, William, a few times. William is tall and super involved in church and school, so he's busy. He got Billy a dog. They named him Zeus.

Billy's job is in roofing. Metal roofs. He appreciates the guy giving him a chance. After just months on the job, he's already been promoted to supervisor. He sometimes feels like Rip Van Winkle. Everyone now is so obsessed with their phones. When he left for prison fifteen years ago, it was still the flip phone. Billy does not yet quite understand texting. He recently went to his first Starbucks. Also, he recently got a girlfriend. They met in the supermarket.

"Don't I know you?" she said.

"My name is Billy," he said.

"Ennis!" she said.

They recognized each other from seventh grade, before everything happened.

Dear Donna:

Thank you for taking the time to write to me last August. I read your message personally, and it meant a lot to hear your perspective on

Billy's case. People who have made mistakes deserve opportunities to earn second chances, and stories like his underscore why we need to make our criminal justice system fairer and more effective, particularly when it comes to nonviolent drug offenses.

I firmly believe that exercising my power as President to commute the sentences of deserving men and women is an important step toward restoring the fundamental ideals of justice and fairness. Still, there is more work to do, and your experience speaks to the responsibility we have to make sure people who learn from their mistakes are able to continue to be a part of our American family.

Again, thank you for your inspiring message. I am tremendously grateful for your years of service as a public defender, and your message will stay with me.

Sincerely,
Barack Obama

When Billy gets to the office in El Paso, Donna is eating birthday cake. It's awkward. They can hardly make eye contact. She offers him cake. She says there's quesadillas in the back. She finds that she really wants to feed him.

"How is your son?" she asks.

"How is your son?" he asks.

They exchange updates and soon begin showing pictures.

"He looks just like you!"

"I got fat."

"You look fantastic."

He tells her about getting promoted to supervisor on the job; $17.50 an hour is pretty good for El Paso. She tells him she got promoted to supervisor, too, to deputy federal public defender. "It's weird. But I guess it's worth it—"

"Definitely."

"Right."

"Anyway—"

It's hard to find words sometimes.

"I want you to know I appreciate everything you've done for me," he says finally.

"You kept me optimistic," she says, and she opens her arms.

"I'm sorry," he says about crying, and she holds him.

"I'm sorry," she says.

It turns into more of a laugh-cry for both of them.

"It's hard to believe life can be so good sometimes," she says.

CHAPTER 16

Election Day

On Election Day, Hillary Clinton had an 85 percent chance of becoming the next president of the United States, according to The Upshot in *The New York Times*. "Mrs. Clinton's chance of losing is about the same as the probability that an N.F.L. kicker misses a 37-yard field goal," the *Times* reported. Over at FiveThirtyEight, she had a 71 percent chance of winning, and she was predicted to take 302 electoral votes.

Yena and others on the OPC staff were headed over to Lacey's apartment, where they would watch the election results together. There would be champagne. It would be a celebration, albeit a bittersweet one. The last full day of the Obama administration, January 19, 2017, would be the last day for this OPC staff. They could apply for positions under the new administration, but there were no guarantees of anything; this team was breaking up, and everyone knew it.

Much of the focus over the past month had been on preparing transition materials. Fiona remembered 2009 all too well; the Bush OPC staff had left the Obama team virtually nothing in the way of guidance. No procedure manuals, no letter templates, no software, no hardware, no computer, no telephones . . . no paper. Mike Kelleher had had to start from scratch to create the foundation for what would turn into this OPC empire, and Fiona was determined to hand it to the new folks intact—with detailed manuals. She had instructed her staff to document everything: Break down every beat of every process, sorting, sampling (in pencil), dispositions, Red Dots, policy letters, casework referrals, inmate mail, kid mail, condolence letters, emerging issues meetings, the conditional language tech team, algorithms. If they prepared the materials properly, it would be plug and play for the new administration. She organized the materials into binders, and when the transition team came in, as they were scheduled to do sometime soon after the election, she would hand the material over to them and let them know she was available for questions, for training sessions, anything at all.

Fiona wasn't going to Lacey's party. She wanted to watch the results in the quiet of her home with her husband. The next morning was going to be nuts, she warned me. She had readied the staff: Nobody should even bother going to the hard-mail room. She would need everyone, all the interns, all the volunteers, all hands on deck in the email room. Major national events, like State of the Union addresses, always generated massive amounts of email, and this one— the first woman ever to be elected president, the first black president handing the reins over to the first woman president—was sure to blow the circuits.

Cody Keenan was watching the election results at his apartment with his wife and his friends Ben Rhodes and Dan Pfeiffer. His phone rang at about 2:30 A.M.

It was Obama. "You know we're going to need to rewrite this statement for tomorrow," he said.

"Yeah, I know," Cody said, and he turned off the TV.

He scrapped the remarks he had begun drafting for Obama to deliver in the Rose Garden on the day after the election congratulating Hillary Clinton for her historic win.

Donald Trump had won the presidency, and Cody wondered what in the world Obama should now say to America from the Rose Garden.

At six in the morning, Cody sent Obama his revisions.

"A little too dark," Obama told him.

"Yeah, I know," Cody said.

It was raining on the morning after the election, and I arrived at the White House gates early. No one at the main OPC office on the fourth floor of the EEOB was in yet except for Fiona, who was shuffling through papers as I sat on the other side of her desk.

"Well," she said, looking up. Her face held the vague puffiness of a morning after little sleep.

"Well," she started again, bouncing a stack of pages up and down and into order. She was having trouble making eye contact. The sky outside her window was a flat steel gray. I could hear the distant whirr of a printer revving up. There was a wet umbrella at my feet.

"Well, your hair looks great," she said.

I told her, no, her hair did.

"Oh, it's just—" She shook her head to make a swish. We discussed my bangs.

Hair talk is a refuge.

"I'm sorry," she said finally, dropping back in her chair. "It's just that you're the first person I've talked to."

"Same," I said.

We muttered awkwardly about greeting the security guys out at the gate, and did that count? No, yeah, no.

I suppose a lot of people will always remember where they were when the sun came up. The first person you talked to. What you said. The implications, one by one, hitting you. *Wait, what? This wasn't supposed to happen.* How strange it was to feel that reality had gotten ahead of you and now you had to race to catch up. If you even wanted to catch up. The lethargy of not wanting to join the new reality would increasingly feel like a flu spreading.

The email room was in another building, in the satellite office over on Jackson Place, and soon Fiona and I would head over and join the staff and the voices from all the people all over America who had awakened that morning to the results and had the thought: *Today I need to write to President Obama.*

From: Sam K-G
Submitted: 11/9/2016 8:20 AM EST
Address: Granville, Ohio
Message:

Dear Mr. President,

I'm not really the "writing a letter to the president" type. It seems like more of an idealistic gesture than anything else. But this morning, I am frightened for the future of our country. As, I am sure, are you. As any reasonable person would be. What I ask is this: Please please do whatever you can to curtail Trump. Anything you can do to mitigate this catastrophe that is underway.

I'm sorry your presidency has to end like this.
Sam

P.S. To the volunteer reading this: must be a crazy day in there. Keep up the good work

Fiona finally broke down in tears that morning in her office. It was only a matter of time, and now she was getting it over with. "I'm sorry," she said, her head hanging. She talked about her husband, Chris. They were newly married. She reminded me that Chris had worked at OPC and that was where they met; they had trained together, eight hours a day reading hard mail together. An experience like that bonds you, she said.

"I'm sorry," she said again.

So many people throughout my time at OPC talked about the bond. It reminded me of the way soldiers talk, or coal miners: groups of people on the front line of something most people never witness. The mailroom. Who would think something like that would happen in a mailroom?

"You ready to head over?" Fiona said, and we both grabbed our umbrellas and our coats.

I saw Kolbie on the way out; she was leaning against a wall with another staffer who seemed to be consoling her. She was looking down at her shoes, biting the nail on her thumb.

. . .

Jackson Place is the street across from the White House that forms the western border of Lafayette Square. It's lined with cherry trees and stately brick townhouses that were built in the nineteenth century. They were the homes of diplomats and dignitaries, including Henry Reed Rathbone, the military officer who was sitting in the President's Box at Ford's Theatre next to Abraham Lincoln when Lincoln was assassinated; Rathbone never recovered from the trauma—he went mad and lived out his days in an insane asylum. President Theodore Roosevelt and his family also lived in one of the townhouses on Jackson Place while the White House underwent renovations in 1902. The federal government acquired the properties in the 1950s with the idea of tearing them down and putting up a federal office building. In 1962, First Lady Jacqueline Kennedy intervened, said, don't destroy those beautiful old buildings, and the project was canceled. Now the townhouses hold an array of federal offices that feel homey and interesting and full of intrigue.

The email room was on the third floor of 726 Jackson Place; it was a wide open space that could have once been a formal parlor. The ceilings were high, and the windows were encased in ornate moldings, and there were deep window seats. Otherwise it was cubicle after cubicle after cubicle with computer monitors flickering and maybe fifty people jammed in; at either end of the room, the staffers in charge had their computers propped up on boxes so they could stand while they worked.

One of the staffers in charge I'll call John, even though that's not his real name. The weird thing that happened the morning after the election was some people in OPC started to ask me not to use their real names. That had not once happened before. It was as if everyone had been under the protective shield of Fiona, of Shailagh, of Obama; it was as if OPC was a collective, and what was good for one was good for all.

But now there was a feeling of a free fall, every man for himself. People had futures to worry about—jobs—and political affiliations would matter.

John stood to address the packed room of staffers and interns to give them a pep talk. "We're seeing a lot of people in meltdown mode," he said. He was a young guy with a neat appearance and jet-black hair. "Look, the president is counting on us to do this. So let's do this. This is our thing. It's why we're here. It might just be a little weirder today . . ."

He told them if the mail was getting to them, they should go take a walk. He told them to keep the TV off. "It's not helpful. It's not helpful to say, if this person would have run or did this or that. *It's not helpful.*

"Look, we are all processing this."

People leaned their heads away from the rows of screens to listen. There were tissues. People were crying. Extra office chairs had been rolled in, along with donuts, juice, power bars, and when John finished his pep talk, the staffers and interns went back to reading, and talking, and reading, and trying to console one another.

"We just have to go into duty versus feeling."

"Here's one from a fourteen-year-old girl. 'Dear Mr. President, Please help me understand what to do.'"

"Here's two women who got married four years ago and are going to have a baby this week and are terrified to bring a baby into the world now."

"Last night we were watching, and we were like, 'Fine, fine, whoa. Whoa!' We didn't talk at all. At the end someone was like, 'What are we going to tell our letter writers? What are we going to do with the mail tomorrow?' And we all just lost it."

"I was like, 'I need to go see the mail.'"

"It gives you purpose. It all feels hopeless, but this is something proactive."

"It's that sense of responsibility, that we still need to be there for the people who want to reach out to the president."

"I don't know what we're going to tell all these people. But we're going to have to tell them something. . . ."

"I'm seeing fear. Mostly fear."

"I haven't seen anybody saying, 'I'm happy.'"

"It was about twenty of us. A bottle of wine. We cleared out so much vodka."

"It's not even about the results. It's looking at what used to be."

"It's looking at what we see as progress and to have it, in one day, all of a sudden you're saying, Is this even real, or will it still exist?"

. . .

People had questions for John; they were getting confused about how to proceed. Email was the same as hard mail: Each post had to be coded. Immigration. Israel. Economy. The codes corresponded with the policy-response letters that the writing team had ready to go and that the algorithms were set to personalize. But on this day staffers had had to come up with all new codes: Election Pro, Election Con, and Legacy.

"So Election Pro is like, 'Donald Trump is the best, and this is a great day for America,'" John told the group. "And then Election Con is going to be like, 'I'm scared,'" he went on. He was standing in the middle of the room, and you could tell he was not used to having to make his voice carry.

"So, like, 'I don't know what to do. I have a disability. I'm an LGBT family. I don't know what's going on anymore.' That's Election Con.

"Then Legacy is going be 'You know, I was really disappointed about last night; your family is amazing; I think you did great things'—that's Legacy. Some of these things will be a little vague, and I know it's going to be hard, but feel free to ask questions as we're going through this, and let's try to make sure you're being as specific as possible."

"What about people talking about election recounts and fraud and rigging?" one intern asked.

"Election fraud? Just close those out—"

"What about people writing before the results were out?" asked another. "Like people writing in to say, 'I'm looking forward to President Clinton,' but it's clearly obvious that that's . . . not."

"Yeah. We can close those. We can close those out."

"What if they're saying, 'I'm nervous about the election. I don't know what I'll do'?"

"Election Con."

"'Do we need to call up the military?'"

"Election Con."

"'My wife is undocumented; I have three children; I've never been so scared in my life.'"

"Election Con."

" 'I'm disabled; I have seizures. Will I still have healthcare?' "

"Election Con."

" 'Is he going to void my marriage? Am I going to still be with the person I love?' "

Con. Con. Con.

The writing team would have to figure out a response to the election email later that day. What, exactly, should Obama say to all these people?

Three elderly women in pastel blouses came barging in, asking to turn on the TV. "Are you watching Hillary's concession speech?" one of them asked.

"I wasn't sure where you're from?" an OPC staffer said politely.

"FLOTUS! We're volunteers from FLOTUS! Can we watch the speech?"

But the TV wasn't on. Perhaps the polite thing to do was to turn it on. Sure, they would turn it on. But did they have to? There was hemming and hawing, and they put the TV on with the sound down while Wolf Blitzer waited for Clinton and the crawl beneath brought updated margins from Pennsylvania, and Ohio, and Michigan, and most of the people in the email room went back to their screens, to the email and America in meltdown mode.

From: Mr. Martin A. Gleason
Submitted: 11/9/2016 8:07 AM EST
Address: Chicago, Illinois
Message:

Mr. President—I am sorry I let you down.

I know I could only vote once, and that I could not call every unde-cided voter, or fund every down ballot Democrat. Where I, and every other college educated white male who voted for you in '08 and '12[,] failed you, is in our inability or unwillingness to address the struc-tural racism that has given birth to President-Elect Trump.

I have not spoken up—to family, friends, and neighbors—about rac-ism.

I have not fought hard enough for my fellow Americans.

I have not called out, or called in, other white people enough.

In order for the country to heal, well meaning whites like me need to "take the gun away" from white supremacists. Not only did we literally give white supremacists the gun (and the bomb), we also gutted the safety net that you t[ri]ed to repair.

I am sorry. We let you down.

When you leave office, and return to civilian life, I will join you in whatever task you undertake. I will do whatever it takes to keep your legacy intact.

With love and respect,
Martin Gleason

At the end of the day, Fiona had to pick the 10LADs from the email that had come flying in, and a guy on the writing team who sat not far from Kolbie's office was in charge of composing the response to America in meltdown mode.

"I haven't gotten very far," he said, sitting in front of a blank screen. He didn't want me to use his name. He had been up all night, at his parents' house in Ohio, where he'd been knocking on doors to get out the vote, and then he flew back to work, and he had never expected to have to write a letter like this.

"Personally, the worst thing is that it feels like a rebuke of the connection we're trying to make between the president and the people," he said. "Like, if our responsibility in this office is to connect the president to the people, I'm asking myself, 'Did we fail?'"

He looked at me, expecting something.

"And I don't understand it, because he's read more mail than any president in history," he said. "He seems more connected to the people than any president in history."

I felt compelled to remind him that Obama hadn't been running for reelection. Clinton was the one who had lost.

"The bargaining stage of grief," he mumbled.

Some hours later, he would show me the letter he had composed on behalf of President Obama to America in meltdown mode.

Thank you for writing. I understand the feelings of uncertainty many Americans have had lately. But one thing I am certain of is that America remains the greatest nation on earth. What sets us apart is not simply our economic and military power, but also the principles upon which our Union was founded: pluralism and openness, the rule of law, civil liberties, and the self-evident truth—expanded with each generation—that we are all created equal.

One election does not change who we are as a people. The America I know is clear-eyed and big-hearted—full of courage and ingenuity. Although politics can significantly affect our lives, our success has always been rooted in the willingness of our people to look out for one another and help each other through tough times. More than my Presidency, or any Presidency, it is the optimism and hard work of people like you that have changed our country for the better and that will continue to give us the strength we need to persevere.

Progress doesn't come easily, and it hasn't always followed a straight line, but I firmly believe that history ultimately moves in the direction of justice, prosperity, freedom, and inclusion—not because it is inevitable, but because people like you speak out and hold our country accountable to our highest ideals. That's why I hope you continue to stay engaged. And I want you to know Michelle and I will be right there with you.

Again, thank you for writing. Whatever challenges we may face, there is no greater form of patriotism than the belief that America is not yet finished and a brighter future lies ahead.

Sincerely,

Barack Obama

I could hear Yena outside in the hall, laughing and joking with some other people on the writing team; the discrepancy was palpable. Yena was the kind of person you would want at your mother's funeral. She was trying to put a positive spin on the situation.

"Isn't it so cool?" she was saying. "I think we have a real opportunity to hone in on the president's message. But more than that, like, this is friggin' America. Which is like, what an opportunity. Like, what an honor. You know what I mean? Like, woo! What an honor! Like, what? I lived my life!"

She told me about her work helping Fiona assemble the transition materials, said she was determined to feel optimistic about the new team continuing their work on behalf of letter writers.

"It's like, the Obama administration did all this to hear people's stories," Yena said. "How could they possibly not meet us and grow it further?"

I asked her what she thought she'd do after she left this place. She said she was applying to grad school; she wanted to learn about hostage negotiations. It was because of her time in OPC. That letter she told me about when I first met her, about the mother and the kidnapped son—it had changed her. Lacey had had a similar awakening; she was planning to forge a career working with veterans. Ever since the letter from Ashley about her dad and the guns and the shooting. Kolbie wasn't sure what she'd do next. Something with language, something with children and the power of language. Fiona said she wanted to focus on being married for a while.

I stopped by Fiona's office to see how she was coming with the 10LADs. She was already on the couch with her choices on her lap. "I had some rice pudding," she said, managing a smile. The emails had been printed, and she was flipping through the pages considering the sequence. "I think it will hit him like it hit us, a pile of voices that don't follow a tight narrative." She spoke quietly as she sorted, mostly to herself. "People concerned for others," she said, holding a few out. "People concerned for themselves," she said about another group, and when she was finished, she sat up straight.

"Okay, so this is the first one," she said, showing it to me. The writer was cheering Trump's victory. He recommended a fire into which Obama could put all of his executive orders and, together with the rest of the ruinous liberals, watch them burn.

"It's an introduction, because it sort of feels like the day began," Fiona said, and I could tell she had no interest in defending her choice.

"And then I like the personal nature of this one for the second," she said, going through her choices with the satisfaction of an author reading her final draft. "She's married to someone who voted differently from her. But they will continue to be a family. I think it's nice to have something so passionate and uplifting closer to the front.

"Then this is one where I felt it was moving; he isn't sharing his own personal stake; he's saying this is what I hope you'll do with the power you hold right now for others.

"Then behind him this is someone who is in dire financial straits. I felt that was someone whose voice really matters right now.

"Then this is someone with disabilities, a community that has self-identified as vulnerable.

"Then this one is incredible. What a guy. 'I will join you in whatever task you undertake.'

"Then this is a Trump supporter who is making his case. . . . Obviously there are difficult parts of this. But he is someone who volunteers, and he wants to share who he is and why he wanted this outcome. And he also is really frustrated by the presence of immigrants in the U.S.

"Behind him, this is someone who works on tech that he thinks could be dangerous.

"Then a deferred action recipient.

"Then I'll end with this. Because I think so many people are thinking, *What do we tell our daughters today?*"

She gathered the letters. She checked her phone. She jiggled the lid on the glass water bottle that always accompanied her. "So I'm going to hand them off. And they'll get scanned and sent around."

Some weeks later, Fiona got a call from Rob Porter, the person who had been hired to become White House staff secretary for President-Elect Donald Trump. He wanted a meeting, so Fiona went. He asked about the mailroom, how it worked, and Fiona told him about the transition materials, the binders, and she did her best to summarize.

"Ten letters a day," she said, as if that would simply be the normal order of business. The president would be *expected* to read his mail and answer it. Rob took notes. The meeting was maybe twenty minutes. He said someone would be getting back to her for more information.

No one did.

Samples, 2016

11/9/16
fri

From: james
Submitted: 11/9/2016 12:12 PM EST
Email:
Phone:
Address:

Message: Start packing ! Get ready to watch a big bonfire, maybe in the vegetable garden, where Trump will burn the AFA and most of your executive orders. You can watch it from your new residence with all the other liberals who have been trying to destroy the country.

From: **Alessandra Shurina**

Submitted: 11/9/2016 8:08 AM EST

Email:

Phone:

Address: Tallahassee, Florida

Message: President Obama -

My heart is broken this morning. It is so, seemingly irreparably broken. I am trying hard not to wallow in the hurt that I feel and instead trying to channel my outrage in grief into something productive. I have a five month old daughter and this is not the world I want her to grow up in - please tell me there is something I can do to help remedy this situation? To lessen the blow? How can I get involved? What do you recommend that I do to ensure that at the VERY most we only have four years of a fascist demagogue as president? I'm willing to devote my life to volunteering for a cause or a candidate with the promise of defeating not only Trump but the hateful principles that he was elected on. This has been a wake up call for me. I can't just vote. I must DO. Please, President Obama tell me, what do I do?

From: Amanda Bott

Submitted: 11/9/2016 2:29 AM EST

Email:

Phone:

Address: Rochester, Washington

Message: November 8, 2016

Dear President Obama,

Eight years ago on election night I wrote a letter to my unborn children telling them how proud I was to be one of the millions of Americans who voted for you. On that night I cried tears of joy and pride and happiness. Tonight I'm crying tears of sorrow. I'm crying for my beautiful country with its beautiful ideals. I can't see a way through four years of a hatemonger in the oval office. For the first time in my life I am terrified for my country. Terrified. I have two beautiful daughters. I have a two year old and a five year old and they deserve to have a future and I'm honestly and genuinely scared that there may not be a future with this man in office. He has the ability to deploy nuclear weapons and he has said he would use them.

How did we fall so far? How did this happen? Eight years ago we voted for hope and tonight we voted for hate. How is that possible? Eight years ago I voted for you to be my leader. I'm asking you to lead me now. Please Mr. President, tell us what we can do as a nation now? Tell me what to do as a citizen and a mother. Now that this person is Commander in Chief of the largest, most powerful military on earth what can I do? Do I have to write letters to world leaders apologizing and explaining that we really don't want a nuclear holocaust? Should I write to the heads of state of every nation on earth and apologize for the next four years and beg them to realize that this hatemonger does not speak for us? But, doesn't he?

We elected him. We elected him to speak for us. We heard the hate and prejudice and anger and bigotry. We saw him mock the handicapped and prisoners of war and gold star families - things both republicans and democrats alike always treated as sacred, and yet we voted for him. God help us we voted for him. God help us all.

From: Ms. Nicole Davis

nitted: 11/9/2016 12:37 AM EST

Email:

hone:

dress: Tobyhanna, Pennsylvania

sage: Hello President Obama, thank you for all you've done for our country. During your terms you've made me feel safe, and safe to raise my daughter. Now I am entering a stage where I am terrified to survive with Trump. I am a disabled individual as I have seizures. Trumps comments about those who are disabled have turned individuals against those like me. I am afraid he will hurt individuals like myself, is this a rationalized fear? I'm just afraid and would appreciate any type of reassurance he can not hurt me for my sickness. Thank you so much.

2016

From:

bmitted: 11/9/2016 12:01 AM EST

Email:

Phone:

ddress:

essage: Mr President,

First and foremost, thank you for all you've done. I am so proud to call you my president. I have such a tremendous amount of respect for you as a husband and a father. As I'm watching election results, I'm literally in tears. My wife is undocumented. I have three children. I have never been so scared in my life. I know there is very little you can do now for immigration reform, but thank you so much for trying. We've been working on adjusting her status, but I do not know what will happen now. There is now a very good chance I'll be separated from my family and that is terrifying to me. I know you've done all you can do and I thank you for that. I have been so proud of you over the last 8 years and I wish you the best for the future.

Sincerely,

From:

Submitted: 11/9/2016 2:17 PM EST

Email:

Phone:

Address: Santiago de los Caballeros,

Message: Dear President Obama,

My name is _____, I am not from the United States and do not live there.

I know that there is a big chance that you will not read this letter, but there are some things that I would like you to know.

Growing up as a gay man in a country where everything about being homosexual is wrong and embarrassing is hard. Death threats from parents, bullying at school, or just simple "Gay jokes" that make someone of our sexual orientation or with an open mind feel bad.

You gave me hope, reading about everything you did for our people in your country made me realize that, maybe, the world is not as bad as it seems, maybe there is more than being scared and hiding all the time. You inspired me to move on, to be better and to be the change that I want to see in the world, hoping that one day I would live in the United States so that I could have a normal life.

It is heartbreaking knowing that your presidency is coming to an end, and that the LGBT community will suffer a huge impact,

Thank you, Mr. President for 8 years of hope, for helping me growing up and for a doing a great job, not only for America, but for the rest of the world too,

From: ▓▓▓▓▓▓

mitted: 11/9/2016 9:13 AM EST

Email: ▓▓▓▓▓▓

Phone: ▓▓▓▓▓▓

ldress: ▓▓▓▓▓▓

ssage: Dear Mr. President,

I woke up this morning in a state of disbelief. Partly because I only slept 4 hours after drinking down a whole bottle of Jagermeister, but mostly because Donald Trump is President Elect.

My family has been in this country a long time. My earliest family came to this country on the Mayflower. They struggled and worked hard for "The American Dream" and the fruits of their labor was shown through their achievements. Most notably would be ▓▓▓▓ signer of the Articles of Confederation ▓▓▓▓ delegate to the Continental Congress and ▓▓▓▓.

My dreams for what would be a happy and prosperous America are dimmer today. I took a walk this morning to take in the air and just experience the day. I live in ▓▓▓▓ and I heard no birds chirping. Here ▓▓▓▓ it was raining, very fitting in my opinion, because it feels like the world is crying. I keep in touch with pen pals overseas in the U.K. and they're all in disbelief as well.

I just find it hard to believe that we can "Make America Great Again" through the path that Trump is providing. The America he speaks of is a divided America. An America that wouldn't let women and African Americans vote, an America that would have me separated in schools and offices and bathrooms... I feel like I'm playing the 'Trumped up' version of a board game and we had to "Go back 5 spaces".

I never one-hundred percent agreed with everything you said. But I firmly believe that you're going to go down in history as one of the country's greatest Presidents. You've done so much for civil rights and upholding justice. Keeping Americans as healthy as you could. Honestly, my heart is breaking for you and Michelle and your family. I'm so sorry that for the next four years, you have to watch an angry Oompa Loompa with thin wisps of hair attempt to make America "Go back 5 spaces".

Wishing you all the best,

▓▓▓▓

From: Mrs. Katie Lowden Bahr
Submitted: 11/9/2016 10:20 AM EST
Email:
Phone:
Address:
Madison, Wisconsin

Message: Dear Mr. President,

Eight years ago, when you won the presidential election I was elated. I was hopeful. I watched in awe as you took the stage with your wife and daughters. It felt amazing. Four years later, when you won once again, I was relieved. I had welcomed my first daughter two months earlier. A daughter born with a heart defect. A daughter who will forever have a pre-existing condition. Last night I watched in disbelief, as our country elected Donald Trump. I have another daughter now, and I'm sure as the father to two young women yourself, you feel the disgust over Mr. Trumps treatment of women as well.

I'm writing you this morning out of fear. This election was won on fear. Fear of the other, fear of the unknown. Fear of race, sexual orientation, gender, religion. Fear bred of ignorance. And now I too am afraid. I'm afraid of how this will change our country, and the world, in the next four years. You have always given me hope as a leader, and I could use a little of that right about now.

This morning I ask one thing of you; make these next two months count. As much as you possibly can. Secure the next four years for our country. For the American people that don't even realize what a grave mistake they have made. Do what you can to secure health care, foreign policy, immigration, education, the environment, jobs, and all of the other important issues we all know Mr. Trump is hoping to unravel.

Thank you for the last eight years. You will go down in history as one of the greatest leaders our country has known. Your accomplishments and grace under pressure has been a gift to us all.

Gratefully,
Katie Lowden Bahr

1/18/17
JLS

Dec 20, 2016

Dear President Obama,

For five years I was a home health nurse in your old hometown of Chicago. My territory included Rogers Park and south Evanston, one of the most diverse neighborhoods in this wonderful country of ours.

I've been in more homes than most people, and I want you to know, that every African American home I entered had a picture of you in it. Usually it was the entire beautiful Obama family. You have meant so much to so many people — your grace, intelligence and integrity will be so missed.

Like so many other people I am horrified and anxious about the results of the election. I hope you continue to speak out and work for the values we hold so dear — the democratic process, and the equality of all people.

You and your family are truly beautiful, and will be so sorely missed. I certainly don't blame you for wanting to take a break, but this country continues to desperately need you. I hope to continue to see you on the world stage, fighting for good.

Much Love,
Tracy LaRoch

Tracy LaRoch
Evanston, IL

November 20, 2016

Dear President Obama:

In January of 2009, in the absence of ability, time or energy (or all three) to travel to DC for your swearing in, our close-knit group of friends and neighbors decided to throw our own inaugural ball in your honor. We cleared out a living room, dressed to the nines, drank champagne and danced all night. Parents, kids, everyone. Several weeks prior to Christmas, I had been in DC for a visit (I am a DC native) and as I walked through Union Station, I saw Barack Obama in a gift store and knew I had found the perfect "party favor" for our ball. At the party, we hung the American flag from my father's funeral on the living room wall (he fought in the South Pacific in WWII), and stood O up in front of it (see small picture in the enclosed; that's me with you) and party guests "had their picture taken with the President". My father would have been so proud to be a part of this.

On November 13 this year, we had a post-election potluck. Alas, we had anticipated it being a celebration, but reality intervened. We considered cancelling, but quickly realized that gathering our friends around us was what we, and they, needed even more. We brought O down from the attic, and posted a board for all of us to "teach 'em how to say goodbye." (I am obsessed with "Hamilton".) Enclosed are photos of what we want to say to you.

I believe strongly that we will get through this, and that we will come out better on the other side, but it will be difficult, enraging and in many ways sad. Your influence in our lives and in the lives of our children was incalculable. My daughter is a NC Teaching Fellow, and she is in her third year teaching sixth grade math at a Title 1 school in Durham: she can tell by their behavior when her kids return from a school break who had food in their home during the break and who didn't. She recently did a successful GoFundMe campaign and raised money to buy new desks for her classroom: the old ones were falling apart right in front of the children. But she and her ridiculously dedicated teaching peers are the future of this country. (And I know she would welcome a presidential visit to her classroom, should you have future spare time...). We will get through this, in part due to the dedication of people like Millie and her fellow teachers.

Thank you for all that you did. Thank you for your kindness. Thank you for sharing your wonderful family with us. Thank you for being the president our children really knew first, and will always hold as the hallmark of what a president should be. I have your first acceptance speech taped to my home office wall, and read it periodically for inspiration. Your hair may be a little grayer now, but you can be sure that those gray hairs were honestly earned. Thank you.

Maureen Dolan Rosen,

Chapel Hill NC

BARACK OBAMA

April 26, 2017

Ms. Maureen Dolan Rosen
Chapel Hill, North Carolina

Dear Maureen:

Thank you for the very kind note and for passing along the thoughtful messages from those who attended your potluck. Your optimism is inspiring, and I share your hope for our country's future.

Remember that the long sweep of America is defined by forward motion. And although it sometimes seems like we take one step back for every two steps forward, I am confident that so long as engaged and passionate citizens like you keep speaking out and working in earnest to defend the values that make us who we are, our progress will continue.

Thanks again for thinking of me. Serving as your President was the greatest honor of my life—it was worth every gray hair! Please tell Millie I'm proud of her service in the classroom. I wish you and your loved ones the very best.

Sincerely,

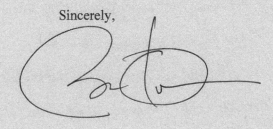

1/18/17
f.6

December 6, 2016
Jaconita, New Mexico

Dear President Obama,

I heard your speech from Florida today and was comforted. I wondered what you did the day after the election to salve your wounds. I baked an apple-cranberry crumb pie and ate half of it that very day. Two friends of mine went out for a salsa lesson. A neighbor down the road read "Hillbilly Elegy" until first light and then threw herself into putting her garden to bed for the winter. A retired teacher friend in D.C. went to her scheduled piano lesson, stopping on the way home for a bottle of bourbon. (She usually drinks a little port at twilight)

At first I swore off watching the news. Then I decided that if I were going to hell in a handbasket

I would need to be prepared. Thus I decided to watch carefully, write down the letters I'm always composing in my head and then post or email when and where needed. I am 84, can look back on 25 years with bright-faced kids in mostly run-down schoolrooms or portables and hope that those kids learned the most important lessons I had to teach: fairness and objective thinking.

Thank you for epitomizing the values a truly just nation espouses. Thank you, Obama Family, for providing a model to embrace. History will treat you well, Mr. President. I am grateful for having lived long enough to see your day.

Sincerely yours,
Roberta Fine

Michaela

601

12 NOV 2016 PM 4 1

President Barack Obama
The White House
1600 Pennsylvania Avenue NW
Washington, DC 20500

20500—

QC✓#020

✓#034

"RECEIVED DAMAGED"
485
NOV 17 2016

Dear Mr. President,

I am writing to you on the morning after the election after a restless night and two hours of sleep. I remember today going very differently eight years ago, when it was announced that you had been elected. I was in my first year at community college, walking through an icy quad in my snow boots with a big, dumb grin on my face, every closed door before me suddenly opening up, like magic. There was so much hope in that moment. It would be another four years before the DACA program would change my life.

I was born in the Philippines to two hardworking, college-educated parents. We lived in Manila, had a house, two cars, a dog I loved more than anything. We'd vacation in Chicago every few years. One of those early trips involved a rare April snow when I was four. One of my first memories was scooping some up in my mitten'd hand and taking it inside, only to watch it melt not two minutes later. It was my first snow. That might have been the moment I fell in love with this place.

When my father was forced into early retirement and unable to find work, my parents spent a year trying to make it on his severance and my mother's secretary salary. In 2000, they decided to leave everything behind and try to make it here. Though we were petitioned as a family through my maternal grandparents, the broken immigration system and extreme backlogs caused all three of us to become undocumented after overstaying our Visas. What followed were 16 of the hardest years of our lives. Countless lost jobs and missed opportunities, the university I never got to attend, the job offers I had to decline, days of staying indoors with nothing to do but wait and worry, depression and anxiety, the isolation of being friendless by choice (too many questions), losing our health insurance and deciding to go without to save money, the foreclosure of our home, my parents' eventual divorce. The pain of those years is still so palpable and raw that I doubt I'll ever be able to let it go.

I was amazed at how fast the transition was for me from "illegal alien" to "real person". Within 2 months of DACA approval I had a social security number, learned how to drive (properly, at 23), got a license and a part time job. Within a year I had landed a full time position   at a firm I still work for today (but never did let go of that weekend job). I started making friends again. I made plans for a future that included furthering my education and skillset   . I happily paid rent, taxes and bills. I jokingly complained about, but secretly enjoyed, being tired from working seven days a week. I enjoyed the minutiae of my daily life. I was a real person, with the luxury of mundane, real person problems. I did not squander this gift. I have savored every last bit of it.

For the past four years, the road for me had been become quiet and predictable. But today, I am terrified. As an early DACA recipient, who has since renewed twice, everything I have worked for is in jeopardy. I grew up here. This has and always will be my home. But today I woke up feeling like I couldn't trust anyone, and have barely been able to eat or speak. It's been very hard to stay positive, but the more I look around, the more I see a community of support building, and with it, there is hope. Struggle has imbued us immigrants (documented or not) with a magic and a fire that cannot be quelled. We are here. Please don't give up on us.

Before I close this, I want you to know that regardless of what happens, ~~████████████████████~~ ~~████████████████~~ I am grateful for everything the DACA program brought into my life. I would not have the courage, nor the will to go on after this election were it not for the confidence this program, my education and experience has given me. Someday I'll teach my future child about the value of compassion, sacrifice and hard work in the face of adversity. And who knows, maybe someday she'll be President.

With great admiration and respect,

Michaela

Darin M. Reffitt

Wilmington, DE

President Barack Obama
c/o Fiona Reeves
Office of Presidential Correspondence
Room 412
Eisenhower Executive Office Building
1650 Pennsylvania Avenue, NW
Washington, DC 20502

November 9, 2016

Mr. President:

I wrote you on this same day eight years ago, which seems to have passed far too quickly and yet feels like a lifetime ago. I wrote the day after the 2008 elections, and was honored to learn recently that my letter was selected as one of the ten that you are given each day to read.

With everything that has happened in the intervening years, I do not expect that you would remember my letter or my specific situation. But on that day I congratulated you on your victory, and explained how—while my heart had soared with pride at you being elected as our 44th President—I awoke that next morning to news of passed ballot measures that had stripped or codified the removal of rights for my LGBT brothers and sisters in California, Florida, Arizona, and Arkansas. I then shared with you the story of my partner's car accident, and how the lack of same sex marriage had impacted us so dramatically as we dealt with everything from insurance companies to cell phone companies to hospitals. I poured my heart out about the frustrations I had faced at repeatedly hearing that I had no rights as his partner, hoping that my story could help you understand why the issue was so tremendously important.

And now, knowing that you actually read my letter within the first month of your presidency, I hope that it in some small way helped to ignite within you the understanding that led to your change of heart on marriage equality, and that my story had something to do with your decision to not defend the Defense of Marriage Act. I cling to that hope today, because the only thing keeping me from brink of despair at the outcome of last night's election is the hope that one person can indeed make a difference.

Because I will be fighting on and I do plan to make a difference.

But this letter isn't about me. It's about you. I am writing today to thank you. To thank you for so many things that you've done over the past eight years, and for the integrity, dignity, and class that you brought to the office of the President. To thank you because you validated every bit of faith that I had in you in 2008, and made me proud that I had been an advocate and volunteer during your campaign.

It hasn't been an easy eight years for those of us who supported you. First, we had to defend you to the people who were sure that you were going to take their guns, turn us into a socialist state, and destroy our economy. Instead, you shored up our economy, pulled us out of the worst financial disaster since the great depression, and fought for people who were less fortunate. Under your leadership, we were able to insure millions of less fortunate people who lacked access to healthcare, we saw the Dow soar to record levels, and we experienced the longest period of job growth on record.

But then, we also had to defend you to our own, to people who voted for you but then didn't think you did enough; people who either don't understand that a President isn't all powerful or who saw you trying to work across the aisle and viewed compromising and negotiation as weakness, instead of an integral part of how things were designed to work by our founding fathers. We had to explain that incremental change is better than no change; that sometimes you don't get perfect, but you accept better and go from there.

We had to watch in horror as Republicans in Congress blocked every initiative, brought us to the brink of defaulting on our debt, and refused to address the growing epidemic of gun violence in our nation. We cried with you as you spoke following shooting after shooting, even as those who opposed you failed to accept that you were expressing genuine sorrow, to our shock and dismay.

They vilified you at every turn, but we loved you through it all, knowing that you would keep fighting for what was right, and just, and fair for even the least fortunate of our citizens.

And through it all, you brought honor and dignity to the White House.

I have many friends in other countries, people who could attest first-hand to me how much you and your team—Secretary Clinton especially—had done to rebuild the reputation of our great nation overseas. I recall a trip we took to Italy in 2003 where our group of Americans was shunned because of the situation in Iraq, so much so that I began telling people we were Canadian to avoid being overcharged and snubbed. But you repaired all of that, and you brought us back to being a nation respected the world over.

And somehow you always stayed positive. You never sank to the level of some people who feel they need to respond to every personal attacks and perceived slight. And that's perhaps the most amazing thing of all.

I cannot remotely fathom what it must be like to see yourself and your family attacked in the vicious ways I've witnessed yours being assaulted online and in social media. I'm sure as a loving father you did your best to shield your daughters from being exposed to the hateful rhetoric lobbed against your family. But I know that at some point they inevitably became aware of it, and I can only imagine the heart wrenching pain it must have caused you to see them hurting as you explained that there are people who simply hate; how they would need to fight against that discrimination for the rest of their lives; and how even becoming the most powerful man in the world can't overcome it or matter to some people—people who will never accept that a man isn't inferior because of the color of his skin.

It wasn't until your wife—a paragon of grace and class as our First Lady—shared the mantra "When they go low, we go high," during the Democratic Convention, that I realized how you kept your beautiful daughters smiling throughout it all: you led by example. It's my fervent hope that they will someday follow in your footsteps and take a role in our great democracy. But whatever they do, I'm sure that they will succeed, inspired by the passion and determination of their father.

But it's not just them that you've inspired.

I'm sure that today you fear for your legacy; that, over the next four years, you will see so much of what you accomplished in the last eight years destroyed. I share your fear.

In Lin-Manuel Miranda's *Hamilton*, Alexander Hamilton asks, "What is a legacy? It's planting seeds in a garden you never get to see." Shortly thereafter, Thomas Jefferson states, "I'll give him this: his financial system is a work of genius. I couldn't undo it if I tried. And I tried."

The coming administration may work to reverse the progress you made. But they cannot undo the secondary impact of those accomplishments, nor the memory of the country as it is today.

Since I last wrote you, I'm pleased to share that my now-husband and I were joined in a civil union in August of 2012, which became a legal marriage in 2013 when Delaware became the 11th state to approve same-sex marriage. We now share full rights and privileges, at least for the time being. But 55% of Americans now support same-sex marriage, and will no longer buy into the hateful rhetoric that it will destroy society or hurt children. That's part of your legacy too. The changes in attitudes and values that your policies instilled won't just vanish overnight.

And unlike Mr. Hamilton, you are still here, still able to plant more seeds.

I have to believe in the basic goodness of Americans, that common sense will eventually prevail. I am sure that you and Secretary Clinton, and others like you, will find ways to bring some good out of what has happened. Whether it's convincing the 33% of eligible Americans who aren't registered to vote to do so, or getting more people engaged in the political process at local levels, or just enabling us to better understand the things that drove us to where we are, we know it's not over.

I had the great pleasure of hearing President Clinton speak at a conference in 2014. One of the things he said that inspired me was this (roughly paraphrased): "I travel all over the world, and one thing is consistently true: in places where people are focused on what they have in common, instead of on what divides them, great things are happening; in places where people are focused on what separates them, instead of what brings them together, great things aren't possible." I was proud to meet him and shake his hand that day, and I hope one day to meet you and shake your hand similarly.

In the meantime, I can only hope that the vast majority of Americans will soon realize how much our next President has driven us to focus on what divides us, and will recognize that we can't survive as a nation and do great things as long as that's the case.

And until then, we will continue to fight for the ideals you put forth eight years ago. We can afford to do no less. And I promise that I'll be here to support you and fight with you when the time comes to do so in the future.

So thank you, again. I've learned so much from you over the past 8 years. You've inspired me to care more and to be a better American.

I remain proud to call you my President.

Sincerely,

Darin M. Reffitt

CHAPTER 17

Vicki Shearer, November 9, 2016

RENTON, WASHINGTON

Submitted: 11/9/2016 12:11 PM EST
Message:
You said that the sun would shine tomorrow. Sir, I live in Seattle WA
and the sun is not shining. In fact it's raining. I am so upset with the
election outcome, on all levels. But, the hardest of all is the division
I feel in my own family now. My oldest son is gay. My younger son is
married to a legal Mexican immigrant. Their newborn daughter was
born just weeks ago. My husband, their father, voted for [T]rump.
Yes, as he keeps telling me, his vote is his right. I do get it. But, in my
heart, he voted against our family. He could have written in a name
or left it blank like George W. Bush supposedly did. I have felt so safe
and confident my family was being looked after and accepted by
your Presidency. I don't have those feelings now. . . .

Vicki has lived in this small ranch house for the past seventeen years
and all her life in Renton, south of Seattle. The hanging pots are
mostly petunias, and as you can see, she doesn't care about a color
scheme. It's just: color! An explosion of color. Tim put in an auto-
matic watering system last year, and that's the reason they look this

good. Gardening is her exercise. That plus her morning walk around the neighborhood, just seeing what's going on.

Before everyone gets here, Vicki, who is in her early sixties, soft and round with a dark pixie cut, would like to say a few words about Tim.

"Tim is a gentleman. Of course he loves our kids and our family. He has a better way of turning things off. He's more logical, and I'm more emotional."

She would like to let Tim speak for himself about why he voted the way he did. "He's explained it to me a hundred times, and I still can't hear it."

Vicki and Tim have been married for forty-one years. They met right when she got out of high school on a summer afternoon. She always tells people how impressed he was with her brand-new car. ("It was a Volkswagen Rabbit," Tim will say. He was not impressed with that car.) They got to talking. They went to the Space Needle. They talked and talked. "You're the first person to hear what I'm saying," he said. "Who doesn't like to hear that?" she said.

Vicki has heard of couples divorcing in the aftermath of the 2016 election. Of families split apart. Sisters avoiding brothers, cousins disinvited, in-laws going silent or into hiding. Vicki doesn't think that kind of thing could happen to her family, but she acknowledges it's been a strain.

"That night was sad and depressing and gray and dark and not happy."

She and Tim were home, tuned in to news. Remember this is the West Coast, so everything is three hours earlier. Both of them were pretty bitter at that point. They missed Bernie. That whole thing with Bernie disappearing the way he did—that had them both raging against the Democratic Party. Which is sad because they were lifers. For example, on Election Night 2008, Vicki had baked an Obama pie. (She is known for her theme pies. "Pies are happy food.") It was strawberry-blueberry. She had tried to carve a likeness of Barack into the crust, but she kind of messed up the chin—"too wide!" Everyone joked that Michelle would have appreciated the big ears because they knew Michelle liked to tease Barack about those ears. Everyone in the family referred to the president as "Barack."

On Election Night 2016, Vicki had no interest in making a pie. She planned to watch Hillary Clinton win and get it over with; she was not a fan. She was disappointed in herself for getting caught up with every twist and turn of the campaign. What a waste of time. It was all so ugly. It took her out of the garden. Tim would be at work at the asphalt plant. A lot of those guys on the crew are Republicans, so maybe that contributed to it.

But really, she has no idea how it happened. One day she looked up, and she was married to a Trump voter. An alien in her own home. *How could something like that have happened?*

She had found out Tim was a Trump voter a few weeks before Election Day when—get this—he filled out an absentee ballot, and—seriously, get this—she was the one making the run to the post office that day. That's what makes this whole thing doubly and triply hard. *She had it in her hand.* She stood in front of that mailbox hemming and hawing. She didn't have to drop it in. Tim would never have known. She thought about secrets. She thought about the boys. The boat. Fishing and hiking and all the love. The happiest life she could have hoped for. She pulled open the mailbox and closed her eyes, and with a flick of a wrist, it was done.

A vote against her family. A vote against her as a woman. Against Neil, a gay man. Against Nick and his wife, Dani, from Mexico. Against Isla too. Against the dog if they'd still had one. How does a family absorb something like that? How does a country? Factions forming, betrayal happening, suspicion and hate popping up.

Forgetting the whole mess would need to happen. That was how Vicki thought about it on Election Night when she sat there watching the results with Tim. Hillary Clinton would win, and Trump would be out of the picture, and the forgetting could begin.

But then of course blue states started going red, and Vicki couldn't believe it, and she went to bed. Pulled the covers over her head. Tim came in later. She has no idea when.

One thing about this house is there's no TV in the living room. That's always been the rule. A living room is for conversation and being together. It's small, just off the kitchen, soft beige wall-to-wall carpet and couches coming together to form an L around an end table.

Most of the decorations are Vicki's crafts, framed embroidery, pots of dried flowers; Tim nailed up that narrow shelf so Vicki could display a row of adorable miniature houses, barns, and churches—a cheerful little town.

Neil, the older son, is first to arrive. He's thirty-eight, tall, with a full beard, a gray cap, the same smile as his mom's. He knows what he wants to accomplish today in the living room. He wants to be forthright. Six months have passed since Election Day, and he wants his dad to know his vote still hurts. "That there was something he would choose that superseded *me*," Neil says. "And I know that's just ego talking. It doesn't mean it's right or wrong. It just means that it hurt."

Neil has always been good at explaining things. It's why he loves his job working with customers at the insurance company. (Even policy language has nuance.) Explaining things is about more than imparting knowledge; it's about having compassion for those who don't yet understand. Neil learned that one the hard way, just after college, when he was struggling with how to come out to his parents. It was not a smooth transition. Out of nowhere a postcard arrived in the mail from a friend, the message referring to some guy Neil thought was cute. His mom happened upon it. *Wait, what?* And should she discuss the matter with Tim? A lot of hush-hush, confusion, and shame.

Neil grew distant, eventually moved away to Olympia. He was determined to live an honest life, whether his parents understood it or not. Soon he came to miss them. He wondered if that part would fade with time. Apparently not. After about six years, he couldn't bear it anymore, and he made the decision to reunite with his parents. His gestures were grand at first—fancy dinners, evenings on the town—one more awkward than the next.

Eventually, Neil decided to just come home, here, to the living room, once a week. Every Friday, no matter what, no matter how the conversation had gone the week before or how they left it. There would always be another Friday. It took the pressure off. They got to know one another again. That was maybe ten years ago. It seems ridiculous now to think there was ever a problem.

.   .   .

Nick and Dani are next to arrive. Nick works with Tim at the asphalt plant. When Nick was little, he played with G.I. Joe. "He's all boy!" his grandma would say. (Neil had a Raggedy Ann doll.) People still say Nick and Neil look like twins, right down to the matching dimples on their chins, except now Nick has a totally shaved head and no hat, so you can see it comes to a point.

Nick and Dani got married last year. Dani does almost all of the talking, which Nick loves. She has added so much pizzazz to this family. For example, no one else in the family curses. ("She can light it up," Tim says.) Dani was twelve when she and her family left Mexico. They had been selling CDs on the street to buy groceries. It took them fifteen years to become U.S. citizens. "They put us through hell." She's a husky woman with thick, dark hair swept to the side and an easy laugh, and she's here on the couch holding Isla, the baby, who's eight months old now. Isla has Nick's complexion—fair, almost translucent skin. When Dani first laid eyes on her, she said she was glad Isla came out that way. Light. It would make her life easier. Vicki can hardly listen to talk like that.

Tim is the last to enter the room. He's a rounder version of Neil and Nick, bald on top, white tufts on the sides. He's any guy you'd see at Home Depot. He's the guy who would let you go ahead of him in line because you only have a few things. When he retires in a few years, Tim wants to stay right here in this house and in this beautiful part of the country. All the outdoors, all the activities. He'll be able to do things during the workweek. No lines. This entire area has become jammed with people and money and huge houses. It was good for the asphalt business, though.

Anyway, it's time to deal with it. The fact of Tim's vote and the pain it has caused. A family has to deal with it. America has to deal with it.

Vicki pulls up a chair so she has a good view of everybody gathered together on the couches. They ordered a fish plate from the local deli—smoked salmon, cheese, crackers—which should be here soon.

"You know, I felt it was a vote against our family," Vicki starts, turning to Tim. It's not the first time she's uttered these words. "I was like, Who am I married to?"

"I know there are people who voted in the sense of, like, trolling," Neil offers, looking over at his dad. "'The election is broken. Let's break it further and *vote for a reality TV star!*'"

"He was against everything that we are as a family," Dani says, the pile-on continuing without interruption.

"What upset me was that Trump *didn't* upset you. He doesn't upset you!"

"He gave permission to people who were on the fence about being racist. He gave them the green light. You see now, like, holy shit, it's still alive and kicking."

"That cynicism—Trump is such a cynical choice. And I don't believe that you are cynical, Dad."

"He's a con man. He conned America. Some people think that makes him a great businessman. He's a con man and a bully. I think you're smarter—I *know* you're smarter."

Tim has his arms folded tight, his gazed fixed on a spot on the carpet.

"I realize I'm the bad guy here," he says. "But somehow this has got to stop."

Nick would like to take a moment to address a related topic. He would like to offer an image of the hell that was his and Dani's house on Election Night.

"Dani's mom was staying with us, and those two got in a big argument," Nick says.

"Huge argument," Dani says. She is happy to tell the story, as many times as necessary if it will help her . . . deal. "So we're watching TV," she says, "and my mom comes into the room. My dad's there too. And I'm like, 'I can't believe this asshole won.' And she's like, 'Well, we voted for him.'

"And I just went, '*What?!*'"

She takes a gulp of air, slides forward on the couch as if needing the proper position from which to gather and emit a high volume of hot steam. Isla, for her part, does not stir. Isla appears prepared to snooze on through her mother in revved-up mode.

"Because up until that point, it was all about *this* family," Dani goes on. She talks fast, a patter that draws people in. "This entire time I was like, *I still can't believe Nick's dad voted for Trump. His entire family is what Trump's trying to fight.* So for my parents to tell me that they had voted for him, to me it was like, *What are you doing? He doesn't want us here!* My brother's not a citizen yet. When he was younger, he got in some trouble with an ex-girlfriend. So I'm telling my mom, 'Do you realize that the president you voted into the White House is probably going to want to deport your son?' I could see the lightbulb going on in her head. I was like, *'This guy's going to deport your son!'* And she said, 'Well, I never thought of it that way.' *Well, what do you think he's been up to this entire time?* Two years we've been hearing Mexican people are rapists. We're criminals. We're drug dealers. We're everything. *What do you think he's going to do?* And she's like, 'I just thought he was a good businessman.' And I'm like, 'Please elaborate.' I just went, like—I couldn't believe it. Even my dad was like, 'Should we leave?' Even Nick was like, 'You need to go easy.'"

"It was pretty rough," Nick says.

"I worry about my brother constantly," Dani goes on. "I'm always telling him, 'You need to have a backup plan.' Go to Canada or Belgium. And now when my mom talks to me about politics, like, 'Did you see what Trump said or what he did?' I'm like, 'Don't even talk to me about it. You have no right to talk shit about him; it's *your* fault. *People like you who are uneducated about the candidates basically made this asshole president.*'"

"It's still pretty rough," Nick says.

The doorbell rings. It's the guy with the fish. Everybody gets a break, bags opening, plates clanking. Vicki fixes the spread so it looks pretty, the lemon-pepper-smoked fillets fanning down the sides, candy-smoked and alder-smoked in the middle, a ring of rosemary and sesame crackers around the edge.

On the far wall in the living room, off in a corner, inside a frame, hangs the letter Vicki got back from Obama in response to the note she wrote to him on the morning after the election. "Remember that although politics can significantly affect our lives," reads the letter, typed on White House stationery, "our success has always been rooted in the willingness of our people to look out for one another and help each other through tough times—rain or shine."

"To get a personal response," Vicki says. "I felt light. I felt heard. It made me feel: There's still goodness out there. That he made it a part of his day. That there was a place for me . . ."

This in contrast to the way her husband made her feel in the aftermath of the election, a point lost on no one.

"A former president writing a letter, though," Tim says, motioning toward it. "He's acting like I don't even live here. It makes it a little tough."

Vicki shoots him a warning glance: *Leave Barack out of this.*

This has nothing to do with Barack. This is about Trump.

"You can't have a conversation about the presidential race without including the people who were in it," Tim announces firmly. "You can't have that conversation with me without acknowledging the fact of who he was running against."

This is not about Trump. This is about Hillary.

"Well, I'm pro-Hillary," Neil says, "which I think is not a common stance in this room."

Definitely not a common stance in the room. Both Nick and Dani voted for Hillary reluctantly, and Vicki, who determined that neither candidate was worthy, did not vote at all. She knows her decision not to go to the polls makes her voice weak. Everybody knows it, but nobody, not even Tim—who could certainly use some firepower—brings it up. *Respect your mother* is the subtext in this house.

"I'm so done with the Democratic Party," Tim says. "I should have been more vocal about that. The reason I voted the way I did was to stop somebody else. It was a protest against the Democratic candidate. That's what it was—that's exactly what it was."

Tim thinks that should be the end of it. What more is there to say? A protest vote. Can't that be the end of it? Why is everyone still so upset about this? Another person might storm off. *You people are being ridiculous. I said my piece. Deal with it.*

"Do you think if we had been a swing state," Nick asks his dad, "you'd have thought about it differently?" If this were Ohio, or Florida, or Pennsylvania, surely his dad would have voted more . . . responsibly.

"No," Tim says. "Not with Hillary Clinton. I thought her story was way outdated, and she doesn't represent—she only represents herself."

"But so does Trump," Dani says.

"Both of them are exactly the same in that respect to me," Tim says.

"That's really fascinating," Neil says. "So like—her experience doing that job, being a politician, doesn't count for anything?"

"It was a direction I didn't want to go in," Tim says. "It doesn't matter how fast you're going if you're going the wrong way."

"Trump's complete lack of experience—did that also not count?" Neil asks him.

"The only requirement is to be a citizen in this country," Tim says. "I disagree that career politicians mean that they're more qualified to represent me."

"I'm just trying to understand," Neil says. "So Trump's plan for the country was the better plan?"

"I felt that he would be pretty irrelevant," Tim says. "But not more of the same; I was not interested in more of the same."

"So it's like you're driving your car," Neil says, leaning to the edge of the couch. His arms bounce up and down as he offers this metaphor, one, two, three: *Get this straight. This is what you're saying, Dad.* "You're driving your car, and you see that you're almost out of gas, so you crash your car into the wall and say, 'Well, now I don't need to get gas because I stopped!'"

"I'm sorry this upsets you at the level that it does," his father replies.

"I think about when Mount St. Helens blew up," Vicki says.

Isla awakens, kicks her legs out.

"Does anybody want more fish?" Nobody wants any more fish.

Perhaps Tim just needs to apologize, admit he made a horrible mistake. Because here's Vicki mad, and Neil working overtime on a metaphor, and Nick throwing out lifelines, and Dani offended. How do you clean this up? Perhaps independent voters across America just need to apologize, whether they think they did anything wrong or not.

Isla clamps her fist around her mother's thumb, pulls it back and forth. Dani jiggles her knee—"Whee!"—while the others look on.

"The thing that's interesting to me is our current state of politics is absolutely against the sense of community," Tim says. "It's separated all things right and left."

"Voting for someone doesn't equal all our problems getting solved," Neil offers. "We start at the wrong end. Even if Sanders had been elected, that's just getting one person in power."

It's one thing, besides Isla, that everyone in the room can agree on. You need a starting point. "My analogy has been we have this big ship, and it has this really small rudder," Tim says. "Turn it all the way one way, it's just going to move a little bit. The presidency only has a certain amount of power."

"I do believe that if Hillary was in power right now and she were involved with the Russians, that it would be ten times the clamor," Neil says.

"She would be out on her ass right now," Dani says. "She would be impeached already."

"So the waste of time would've been comparable," Neil says.

Everyone's trying to make this be okay. Trump is a waste of time. Hillary would have been a waste of time.

Maybe?

"What did Barack say to you?" Tim says to Vicki, motioning again toward the letter. "It's going to be all right. He believes it; I believe it too. Democracy is messy. It's loud."

Maybe.

"What about the *Access Hollywood* tapes?" Vicki says. It's the one thing she'll never get past. "What did you think when you heard that statement?" she asks Tim. "When he said that about women?"

"To hear he's got those kind of standards didn't surprise me a bit," he says.

"But what he said against *women*," Vicki repeats. "It upset me so much." Does that not matter to him?

"This is a really bad thing to say out loud," Tim says. "But there's a certain kind of language some people on the East Coast have. They seem to be— Howard Stern is really welcome there. It's more typical and more common in New York than it is out here. Their culture's different. I never gave it much thought."

"I just know how much you respect women and how polite you are," Vicki says. "And I would have thought that that would have offended you."

"It most certainly did," Tim says. "The guy's a pig."

This declaration seems to break much of the tension in the room.

"Remember we had the Women's March on TV?" Vicki says as if to verify the fact that Tim thinks Trump is a pig. "I saw one sign that I would have been so happy if you carried it. It said: 'Stop Pissing Off My Wife.'"

"I'd be happy to carry that sign," Tim says.

Well, this is all such a relief. Tim is still the Tim they know and love.

Except, wait, Tim voted for a pig *on purpose?*

What the hell is the matter with him?

Isla screams abruptly.

"She's hungry," Nick says.

"She needs to be changed," Dani says, standing, hauling Isla to the back bedroom, the scream losing volume as they head down the hall. "Niiiiick!" Dani shouts then, and so Nick jumps to his feet, and so does Vicki, both of them heading back to help.

Alone together in the living room, baby clamor in the distance, Neil and his dad lean back on the couch, their heads at the exact same height, underneath the shelf with the row of little houses. They both have their legs crossed the same way, as if one is copying the other. It's like all those Fridays again. Here in the living room. Every Friday, no matter what, no matter how the conversation had gone the week before or how they left it. They got to know each other again.

"I respect you and I love you," Neil says finally. "But there's still, like— That moment, that choice, I wasn't there. And I wonder about that. I trust how intelligent you are and how caring you are and sharing and giving. But can you see where I would just have that moment of, like, *How?*"

"So did Dani," Tim says. "So did your mom. All you guys did."

"Well, I think it's brave of you to be able to talk about how you voted," Neil says. "Like, there's no malice in there. I get that."

"I don't put the weight on it that you guys do, and I never will. And I'm not going to change about that."

"I'm interested in the fact that people who didn't feel heard now feel heard," Neil offers. "And what that means for them."

This is not about Barack, not about Trump, not about Hillary. This, now, is about rebuilding.

"I didn't know that they didn't feel heard," Neil continues. "It wasn't that I wasn't interested. I was maybe oblivious, but I didn't know."

"All these people are vocal now, and none of these people were vocal a year ago," Tim says. "Hopefully good people will stand up, find leadership that makes some sense."

"I'm glad we've gotten to a place where we can continue to discuss ideas," Neil says. "This election changed me. I don't even know if I was prepared for how different I would feel. I do feel differently in this modern world."

By the time Dani comes marching back in, with a cleaned-up Isla and the others trailing behind, the mood in the room has completed its shift. Like an eclipse happened. But it's not just the Earth routinely spinning on its axis. It's all human effort. "For people who are so disappointed," Neil says to the group, "or confused by family members' votes, or the way they're talking about politics right now, I think we all have to listen to each other and admit when we don't understand. I think everyone wants to be heard right now. I even think Trump wants that. I think he just wants someone to say, 'You are the president!' To acknowledge that he *did* that. As a human to a human, I can have compassion for needing to be heard."

"Yay! I agree with you," Dani says. "I love you."

"I have this silly phrase that I like," Neil says. " 'Forgiveness equals fun.' The more forgiveness I can have, the more I get to enjoy things, because I'm not so caught up. Like, the point of contention doesn't have to be where we stop. It's where something new starts."

"Well, I told Nick," Dani says. "I said, 'You need to apologize to your dad.' We need to be more understanding. We've all got to move on. And I feel like we did. I feel like we did a good job. I think we moved on, right?"

"I think so," Vicki says.

"We're still angry," Dani says. "But, like, not at each other."

"I'm not mad at anybody in this room," Vicki says. "But I'm mad at the situation."

"Conflict is a way of demonstrating love," Neil says. "As long as you keep at it. You have to keep the work up."

"I thought that was a pretty gloves-off letter you wrote," Tim says to Vicki, after everyone has gone. "Am I the only person you throw under the bus when writing emails?"

"I didn't write anybody else," she says. "I just wrote to Barack. It was a factual statement. I was telling him that you voted against our family as though he were sitting across from me. It was like a friend thing."

CHAPTER 18

Obama in Jeans

Fiona told me she was nervous, and when I asked her why, she let out a burst of laughter, like, *What a stupid question*. It was a windy day in March 2018, and we were in my hotel room, about to head over to meet with Obama in the postpresidency office he maintains in Washington.

Since leaving the White House, Fiona had become a mom. She and her husband, Chris, whom she had met in her earliest days working in OPC (he was the person assigned to handle mail containing threats to the president), had named the baby Grace.

The fact that Obama had agreed to a postpresidency conversation said more than probably anything he was about to put into words that day. He'd been largely absent from public life since he left office, working on his foundation and his book, offering no comment on the cascading tumult that characterized America's new political landscape. Like Bush before him, Obama had been careful to step off the presidential stage, no matter how weird things got, no matter how destructive the new administration may have been to the accomplishments of the old, no matter how many of his supporters clamored for him to jump in and somehow rescue America from what they came to see as the grip of a tyrant.

At that point in his postpresidency, well over a year in, he had done just three interviews: one about his early days as a community organizer, another that brought David Letterman out of retirement, and a third with Prince Harry.

And now he would do one more: a conversation about the mailroom.

The mailroom, with the mail lady.

It's not as if he and Fiona were pals, not by a long stretch. The divide between a president and the person running the mailroom was, well, a metaphor all on its own. A king and a servant, a rock star and a roadie, a president and the mail lady. If Fiona and Obama had any kind of relationship, it was largely a silent one, restricted to a purple folder in the back of his daily briefing book, an archived sample of voices, a smattering of responses scribbled in margins: REPLY, REPLY, REPLY. I remembered what Fiona had said: It was like passing a tray under a door.

She and Obama had met a few times previously, mostly for photo ops, and he had called her over to the Oval Office during the last days of his presidency to thank her for her service. She told me she had been nervous for that meeting too. "I thought a lot about how I wanted to thank him, and then you walk in, and he completely throws you off, and you don't remember what you were going to say. He gave me a letter. He had folded it, and that's not normal. We don't fold his letters.

"He talked about the unglamorous part of the White House, the idea of service at its core." Then he gave her a hug. "He's a hugger," she said.

I asked her about a letter she had once written to him. It came out of a session at an OPC staff retreat as part of an "empathy-building exercise." The prompt was, "If you wrote to the president, what would you say?" The staff broke into small groups and shared their letters with one another. The point wasn't for the president to ever get those letters. Fiona had thrown hers in a folder, and that was the end of it.

Maybe she wanted to give it to him today?

"Oh, he doesn't need that," she said brusquely, and then she busied herself with her coat and marched toward the door, and she took in a deep gulp of air, let it out slowly.

Again I asked her why she was nervous. "What's the worst thing that could happen? You'll be speechless? You'll say something you'll regret?"

She stood still for a moment, looked at me. I'd forgotten how big and round her eyes were; a person could climb inside those eyes.

"I'll cry?" she said. She reached into her coat pocket, showed me the wads of rolled-up toilet paper she had thought to arm herself with before she left the house.

"Oh, for God's sake." I grabbed a fistful of proper tissues from the bathroom, folded them, and handed them to her.

The suite was bright, airy, and colorful. Large images of the Pacific Ocean adorned the waiting area, along with knickknacks of distinction—the set of Muhammad Ali boxing gloves he used to have on display in the Oval Office dining room, a replica Vince Lombardi Trophy. Heading down the wide center hall toward Obama's office brought you steadily closer to a photograph of Martin Luther King, Jr., featured prominently at the end. The image was of King's back as he stood before a crowd—the point of view of the speaker, not the listener.

Many of the staffers, about twelve in all, had worked for Obama in the White House, and most of them knew Fiona; people stepped out of their offices to greet her: "How's Chris? *How's the baby?*" And Obama appeared just like the rest of them, like any old worker taking a break; suddenly he was with us, smiling wide, saying he had just finished filling out his March Madness brackets and was feeling good about them, really good. You don't realize just how lanky he is until you see him in person, a long, flat physique; he looked fit, even youthful, his hair cut super short so that all the new gray he'd famously acquired during his presidency was less pronounced. He walked up to Fiona with his arms outstretched and asked about her family, and she sheepishly stepped in for a hug.

"I'm great. She's great. We're just great. . . ."

"Well, we've got babies popping out," Obama said, referring to a staffer who was due to deliver any day. "It's the best thing. I've got all these staff who started with me when they were like twenty. And now suddenly it's like they've got kids everywhere. It's sweet. And a bunch of them, you know, a number of them met on the campaign or at the White House. But nobody yet has named a child Barack—"

"A lot of letter writers did," Fiona offered, perhaps too quietly for him to hear.

"I'm a little frustrated about that," Obama continued with a laugh. "I'm like, 'Come on, people!'"

We followed him into his office. It was a wide space done in shades of tan and brown, earthy, warm, and welcoming. Zero razzle-dazzle. He offered us a seat on the couch, and he sunk into the chair at the end. He was in jeans and a light blue shirt unbuttoned at the top. He put his feet up on the coffee table, crossed his legs at the ankles; overall this was the portrait of one relaxed man. Pete Souza's book of photographs was on the coffee table; family pictures were everywhere, on end tables, on the walls; and Obama's expansive desk on the other side of the room was covered in paper, piles, books—a place of activity. He mentioned the book he's been working on, said it was . . . difficult. "Writing is just so hard. Painful. It's—everybody thinks it's, you know. But it's work. It's like having homework all the time. Yeah, it's hard.

"I should mention to you, by the way, Fiona," he said, as we were getting settled, "we're still getting like two hundred fifty thousand letters a year. It's a lot—"

"I was really excited when Emily told me that you were going to keep getting mail after you were president," Fiona said. "Because people weren't just writing to you as president—as sort of like this guy who got elected, so now my problems are his problems. Like, I think people thought that you might *believe in them*. And so I'm not shocked that they're continuing to write."

I thought Fiona was masking her jitters remarkably well, or else they had already dissipated. She wasn't the mail lady. He wasn't a king. I told Obama about Fiona's image of a tray passing under a door, asked him if he ever had that same sense of a kind of silent relationship with the strangers over there in OPC.

"One of the things I learned fairly early on about the presidency is that people change around you," he said. "They're constantly watching you and measuring your responses, and—you can tilt the field. And so I actually liked the fact that Fiona and the other people in the office were not inhibited or constrained by trying to think about *What would he like?* or *What would he want?* But rather they were in some ways helping to channel, through all the sifting that was going on, something that was representative of the mood of the moment, the emotions that were bubbling up through all the mail that was coming in."

I noticed that over by his desk, on a wall, he had hung the same framed letter he used to have displayed in the corridor between his private study and the Oval Office. Natoma Canfield, a cancer survivor from Medina, Ohio, had written in 2009 about her ballooning health-insurance premiums; Obama had said she reminded him of his mom, who died at age fifty-two of a similar cancer. The letter had stood as a reminder to him of his commitment to healthcare reform.

"The only instruction I gave was that I wanted every packet to be representative," he continued. "And understanding that it wouldn't be perfect. It didn't mean that, you know, out of every ten letters, there had to be two positive and two negative and three neutral and one funny. It wasn't formulaic like that. But that was the one thing I insisted on—that this is not useful to me if all I'm getting are, you know, happy birthday wishes. And I think they did a wonderful job of channeling the American people in that way."

"It wasn't just me," Fiona said. "It was this big group. And folks in the office came from different backgrounds. We had our volunteer workforce. And there were some old people in the mix too. So we had a lot of people putting stuff forward for you, a lot of people interpreting what 'representative' meant."

"I will say this does also have to do with a culture that we tried to develop early on in the campaign," he said. "Which was putting a lot of confidence in a bunch of young people to fairly, meaningfully, and passionately reflect the people they were interacting with. Whether that was on a campaign and they were out there organizing or in the office."

That would be a theme that would come up repeatedly during our time together that day. The continuum. The values established in the earliest days of campaigning, maintained and carried forward in the hands of people like Fiona, who may not even have understood, when they first got started, what drew them in.

. . .

"So this is Marnie," I said, placing a file on the coffee table and reaching inside. The folder was filled with some of the letters I hoped to talk about, along with photographs taken during visits with letter writers.

"I reviewed the letters and the responses in preparation for this meeting," Obama said. "I didn't memorize them. . . ." I wondered how to tell him it was okay he didn't memorize them. (Memorize them?) Here was a guy committed to excellence in homework.

I reached for a photo and handed it to him. "Marnie Hazelton," I said. He studied it closely, leaning in. In the photo Marnie was seated behind her big, impressive desk at the Roosevelt Union Free School District administration offices, looking every bit the superintendent.

"She's an example of someone who was writing to you for help," I said. "And your response, the words 'I'm rooting for you'—she carried them everywhere. She read them out loud to Meredith Vieira on *Who Wants to Be a Millionaire.*"

"I didn't hear that!" he said. "That's cool."

"But she choked. She missed a question. It was 'Rub-a-Dub-Dub—'"

"Oh."

"But now she's the *superintendent* of the entire school district!"

"That's pretty cool!"

"I wonder if you have any sense of the power of your responses to these folks," I said.

"I think I understood that if somebody writes a letter and they get any kind of response, that there's a sense of . . . being heard," he said, carefully considering my simple question. I knew enough by then to not be surprised by Obama's exceedingly slow delivery, but that didn't stop me from continuing to marvel at it. He's a ponderous man; he is a person who ruminates. It's not the sort of blathering a person does to hear his own voice or to fulfill some need to command the room; he's not a mansplainer. He is, rather, thoughtful to the extreme. A person who would memorize homework. His words are precise, and the sentences are . . . dense. It's like you could add water to them, and they'd keep expanding.

"And so often, especially back in 2009, 2010, 2011, a lot of people were going through a lot of hardship," he said. "And a lot of them felt alone in that hardship. They were losing their homes, or they're dealing with somebody at the bank and the bank saying, 'There's nothing we can do. You're going to lose your house.' Or they've got a pink slip, and they've lost their job, and they're going to interview after interview after interview. Over time, I think it's easy for folks to feel a little invisible, as if nobody's paying attention. And so I did, I think, understand that if I could at least let them know that I saw them and I heard them, maybe they'd feel a little bit less lonely in those struggles."

I wondered if this might be the sort of stuff that made Fiona reach for the tissues. The raw kindness. It's wonderful to behold it in anyone, let alone to hear that it was a value at the core of a president.

"Certainly what I learned during the presidency was that the office of the president itself carries enormous weight," Obama went on. "And, sadly, probably where I learned that best was in moments of tragedy where you'd visit with grieving families. Sometimes they were in places where—I think it's fair to say—I didn't get a whole lot of votes. You know, after a tornado or a flood or a shooting. And what was clear was that my presence there signified to those families that they were important. Their loved ones were important. The grief they were feeling was important. That it had been seen and acknowledged.

"That was fairly consistent throughout my presidency," he said.

I thought about President George W. Bush and the ways in which he'd botched that particular presidential duty in the aftermath of Hurricane Katrina and how damaging his perceived lack of compassion for flood victims was to his entire presidency. I thought about the ways in which Bill Clinton was the opposite; there was a president who glopped it on thick. "I feel your pain," he'd say, and he did that little bite of his bottom lip. People came to mock him for it, or at least distrust it. Maybe he wasn't being sincere. Maybe there was nothing behind it. For Clinton, the "maybe" took over.

I don't think that happened for Obama. Whatever people thought of his presidency, I think he was given credit for being a man who brought a solid well of empathy to the office.

But since when did empathy become a requisite trait for a president? Sympathy, the capacity to feel compassion for others, is perhaps the baseline expectation we have of any good neighbor, let alone leader. Obama was the first modern president to explicitly and repeatedly raise that bar. Empathy, he said, in *The Audacity of Hope*, "is at the heart of my moral code, and it is how I understand the Golden Rule—not simply as a call to sympathy or charity, but as something more demanding, a call to stand in somebody else's shoes and see through their eyes."

In his presidency he would demand it of himself—what was the 10LADs experiment if not a daily reminder to experience the world as others did?—and his expectation seemed to be that a call for empathy would trickle down to those who served in his administration.

"That notion of being heard," I said about his response to Marnie's cry for help. "That message that you matter. It seemed to be embedded throughout all of this." I told him that Pete Rouse had talked about it, about how it spread through the staff. If the mail mattered, the people reading it mattered. I told Obama it was the message that so many people, so many letter writers and Friends of the Mail, kept hitting when I talked to them. "You matter."

"I still believe it," he said.

It's hard to argue with empathy. It's a deeply admirable trait. It's Pope Francis. It's a tenet of Christianity. It's a mindset religious leaders throughout the world have sought and taught followers to seek.

It made you a good person. But a good president? Obama had been criticized bitterly by conservatives, in 2009, for perhaps taking the call for empathy too far when he said it was the thing he was looking for in a U.S. Supreme Court justice. "I view that quality of empathy, of understanding and identifying . . . people's hopes and struggles as an essential ingredient for arriving at just decisions and outcomes." Conservatives had called it "the empathy standard"— Obama's personal litmus test—and said it was an awfully "touchy-feely" reason for choosing Supreme Court Justice Sonia Sotomayor. "Empathy," said Utah senator Orrin Hatch, was "a code word for an activist judge." They said relying on personal experience would lead judges to reach subjective interpretations of U.S. laws. We're supposed to have impartial judges sworn to provide equality under the law, independent of the whims of personal preference. The word "empathy" does not appear in the U.S. Constitution.

Moreover, Obama's empathy, you could argue, was what begot Trumpism. Its opposite. We now had a president who seemed to go out of his way to remind us how little he cared about the struggles of the less fortunate.

Was this simply a style issue? A caring, thoughtful president versus a wild and oafish one? Perhaps leadership styles fell on a continuum, and people oscillated between a preference for one or the other. It's hard to imagine, though. We don't want a president who cares about people?

"Where does this even come from?" I asked Obama—that focus on empathy as a core value for a president.

"I think this whole letter-writing process and its importance reflected a more fundamental vision of what we were trying to do in the campaign and what I was trying to do with the presidency and my political philosophy," he said. "The foundational theory, it probably connects to my early days organizing. Just going around and listening to people. Asking them about their lives, and what was important to them. And how did they come to believe what they believe? And what are they trying to pass on to their children?"

When he talked like that, starting to dig in deep, he didn't make eye contact. He looked straight ahead, at a spot somewhere near his feet propped up on the coffee table, brown leather boots, like the desert boots the boys I knew in seventh grade used to wear.

"I learned in that process that if you listen hard enough, everybody's got a sacred story," he said. "An organizing story. Of who they are and what their place in the world is. And they're willing to share it with you if they feel as if you actually care about it. And that ends up being the glue around which relationships are formed, and trust is formed, and communities are formed. And ultimately—my theory was, at least—that's the glue around which democracies work."

"Listening," I said.

"Yeah," he said, and he looked up at me, into my eyes, as if he were coming up for air.

"I don't want to suggest that I would have necessarily described it in a sort of a straight line from when I started running," he said. "But I do think that that was pretty embedded in our campaign philosophy. I think that's how we won Iowa, was having a bunch of young kids form those relationships because they were listening to people. It wasn't us selling a policy manifesto, and it wasn't even because we were selling *me*. It was because some young person in a town they've never been to went around and talked to people, and listened to them, and saw them. And created the kinds of bonds that made people want to then try to work together."

I could tell he was talking about Fiona and all the people like her who knocked on doors. I looked over. She had her eyebrows up. I wanted to say, "So how does that make you feel?" I don't know how it was that we got tiptoeing toward therapy.

I referred back to the picture of Marnie on the table. She was wearing a black suit, and her hands were folded neatly on a desk covered in piles of paperwork, Post-it notes, files—a place of work not unlike Obama's desk on the other side of the room. Next to the photo was a copy of Obama's response to her. "I'm rooting for you."

"When I think about somebody like Marnie in particular," he said, "it was important, because based on what she had written, I felt fairly confident that this would be a temporary rather than permanent circumstance."

As he continued talking about his correspondence with Marnie, I came to realize that what he zeroed in on was not "I'm rooting for you"—which to me, and to Marnie, and to Meredith, and to a live studio audience and all the folks back home was the important part. No, what Obama was focused on was the blah-blah-blah part, the what-a-president-*should*-say part in his response to Marnie.

I know that things seem discouraging now, but demand for educators and persons with your skills will grow as the economy and state budgets rebound.

"Part of what happened during the early parts of this Great Recession," Obama said, "was state and local governments were seeing their budgets hemorrhage. And a big part of the Recovery Act was getting money to states and school districts so that they would not lay off massive numbers of teachers, firefighters, and cops. And given what Marnie was describing, I felt as if, if she could stay at it, that, like in school districts across the country, there'd be the opportunity for her to be rehired at some point."

The Recovery Act. That note about rooting for Marnie was about the American Recovery and Reinvestment Act? In his mind apparently it was. It wasn't just "I hear you," or "I feel your pain," or even "I'm rooting for you." It was, "Hang in there; I've got this."

"It's the power of empathy not as an end-all, be-all," he said. "Because even after you've listened to somebody or seen them, they still have a concrete problem. They've lost their house. They've lost their job. They disagree with you on abortion. They think that you're pulling troops out of Afghanistan too soon and, you know, potentially betraying the sacrifices that have been made by the fallen. There are all these concrete issues that are real. And there are real conflicts and real choices.

"But what this form of story sharing and empathy and listening does is it creates the conditions around which we can then have a meaningful conversation and sort through our differences and our challenges," he said, "and arrive at better decisions because we've been able to hear everybody. Everybody feels heard so that even if a decision's made that they don't completely agree with, then at least they feel like, *Okay, I was part of this. This wasn't just dumped on me.*"

"Well, now you sound just like Neil," I said.

He had no idea who Neil was, of course. Neil's mom, Vicki Shearer, had not used his name in her letter to the president.

I pulled out Vicki's letter. Here was a family trying to keep it together after the 2016 election when one of them, the father, had voted for Trump against the perceived interests of the rest of the family. I had a photo of the group gathered around the couch in their living room. "Here's Neil," I said, pointing. I told Obama that the whole Shearer family were supporters of his to the core. "In fact, when you won in 2008, Vicki baked an Obama pie."

I had a picture of the pie too.

"Oh, that's a good pie," Obama said, reaching for the picture. "That's excellent. Thanks for the ears there—"

"Yeah, Vicki thought Michelle would appreciate the ears."

"She got it just right."

I read him some of the things Neil had said about the transformative power of listening.

For people who are so disappointed or confused by family members' votes, or the way they're talking about politics right now, I think we all have to listen to each other and admit when we don't understand. I think everyone wants to be heard right now. I even think Trump wants that. I think he just wants someone to say, "You are the president!" To acknowledge that he *did* that. As a human to a human, I can have compassion for needing to be heard.

"Exactly," Obama said. (He offered no comment on the part about Trump needing validation.) "Which is why I wanted to offer that corrective to the idea that, you know, empathy—putting yourself in somebody's shoes—somehow solves all the divisions and conflicts we have in the country. That's wishful thinking. But what *is* true is that if a person is recognized, and how they're feeling is validated as being true for them, then they are more prone to engage. And open up to the possibilities of other people's perspectives and maybe even at some point say, 'Hmm. I didn't think of that. Maybe I'm going to rethink how I think about certain things.'

"I will tell you—and Fiona will recall this—some of my favorite letters were actually to people who violently disagreed with me. So, okay, you want to call me an idiot. Well, I want you to know there's a person at the other end of this thing who's listening to you, and here's why, actually, I did what I did. And I can see why you're thinking this way, but here are some countervailing facts for you to consider.

"Those letters I always hoped got into circulation. Right? That there were entire communities or families or schools where people looked at that and they said, 'Huh. I still disagree with the guy, but the fact that he bothered to write back—that's interesting to me.' And maybe then it starts breaking open some new possibilities. Maybe not immediately. Maybe it's in the future. Maybe it's a kid notices that, and they say, 'Huh, there's actually this human who's in the White House. And if you have something to say, he's supposed to listen to you.'"

"I think that worked often," Fiona chimed in. "And sometimes it got back to you, and you personally got a follow-up where, after you sent a handwritten letter to someone who disagreed with you, they wrote back either saying, 'I still disagree and here's why' or 'You know what? I'd like to rescind my earlier statement.' And in other cases where it didn't make its way back to you, we got word in our office that, you know, a letter had been put up in a faculty lounge or sort of small conversations started out of something that began with a pretty angry late-night email."

"It goes both ways, right?" Obama said. "I want to emphasize the degree to which this was important and useful to me doing my job.

"There was a sizeable percentage of the letters where, if they were critical, I'd read them and say, 'Well, that's not fair. I don't think that's true. They obviously don't know this.' But there were times where somebody would write a letter, and I'd say, 'I can see their point.' And I'd circle it, and I'd write it on the margins: 'Is this true?' or 'Can you explain why this is?' or 'Why don't we fix this?' "

We talked about two other letters that day, and both pointed him in that same direction—the degree to which the letters helped him do his job. The emphasis surprised me, although I suppose it shouldn't have. I remembered that he had brought it up the last time we had talked, when he was still in the White House. We'd been discussing some of the mail he got in the wake of the 2016 election. "There was a lot of anxiety and sadness I had to respond to," he said that day. "I remember one that said, 'Pack up your bags because, thank goodness, we're about to undo everything you've done; it couldn't have come a moment too soon,' something along those lines. I don't think I responded to that one. . . ."

I remember that I had asked him then how he might advise President-Elect Donald Trump on what to do with the mail.

He had laughed. I think it was more out of awkwardness than because of any sort of image the question may have conjured, but I can't say for sure.

"But, um, it, ah," he said about the idea of President-Elect Trump reading the mail. "You know what, this is a great habit. I think it worked for me because it wasn't something I did for anyone else. I did it because, as you said, it sustained me. So maybe it will sustain others in the future. Okay?"

Okay. But I never used the word "sustained." I remember wondering how that word had popped up.

"I can tick off the bills and the policies and the accomplishments," he said. "But I tell you one of the things I'm proud of about having been in this office is that I don't feel like I've . . . lost myself."

Like everything else, that thought came out slowly. But I suppose not losing yourself is a big thing to think about quickly.

"I feel as if—even if my skin is thicker from, you know, public criticism, and I'm wiser about the workings of government, I haven't become . . . cynical, and I haven't become calloused, and I would like to think that these letters have something to do with that," he said.

The letters as sustenance was the same idea he came around to when we talked about the letter from Donna Coltharp. "She's the attorney who wrote to thank you for commuting her client's two life sentences," I said, handing him a picture.

"Is this Billy here?" he asked.

"That's Billy!" I said. "And there's Donna. They had never met in person before this. They had this really wonderful Oprah moment."

"Is that right?" he said, looking deeper into the photo, smiling wide. "How *cool* is that?"

I told him Billy was doing great. He got a job as a roofer. He got promoted to supervisor. He got a girlfriend. Obama's action had given Billy a second chance at life, and he was determined to make the most of it.

"That's wonderful," Obama said. "That means a lot."

I told him the reason Donna had told me she wrote. She'd wanted to acknowledge that there was a human being behind all those last-minute sentence commutations; forgiveness was, after all, a personal act. "She wanted to thank you."

"That means a lot," he said. "I will say, selfishly, that the number of people who would write letters acknowledging the meaningful difference that a policy had made in their lives—making it real as opposed to abstract—was sustaining.

"The numbers are telling you twenty million people got healthcare through the ACA," he said. "But that's not the same as a mom writing a letter saying, 'My son got insurance. He got his first physical in a decade. They caught a tumor. It's out. He's fine.' And you go, *Okay,* that *is the work we're doing.*

"And the same is true in this circumstance. You read not only that Billy had contacted Donna to say thank you to her but that he's rebuilding his life."

"When you wrote back to Donna, you thanked her for her ser-vice," I said. "That was what meant so much to her. She's like, 'No one ever thanks us.'"

"Well, she was deserving," he said. "It was a little lovefest."

"A thank-you loop."

"A loop!"

He could see another photo popping out of my file folder. He tilted his head up as if to peek.

"That's Marg," I said, handing the photo to him.

"Marjorie? Look at Marg! Marg is pretty cute. I love the pictures behind Marg too. And the little dolls—"

"She was writing to tell you that she was listening to you."

"It's a beautiful letter."

She was writing about trying to expel the racism she believed was lodged like some kind of poison in her heart. She had discov-ered it and wanted to get rid of it.

"And now here's Marg starting a chapter of the NAACP in her town," I said.

"What a great story."

"She went for it. She wanted to tell you that."

"It makes me proud," he said. "My grandmother, who loved me more than anyone, had an initial reaction like Marg to young black men approaching."

He sat for a moment before finishing his thought, his gaze going back to the spot in front of him occupied by his shoes. He had told the story about his grandmother publicly back in the earliest days of the presidential campaign, in a speech during the 2008 primary against Hillary Clinton. Afterward, he had been criticized for his candor about a topic as sensitive as unconscious bias. In a radio in-terview later, he tried to explain what he had meant, which made it only more controversial. "The point I was making," he said to the host, "was not that Grandmother harbors any racial animosity. She doesn't. But she is a typical white person, who, if she sees somebody on the street that she doesn't know, you know, there's a reaction that's been bred in our experiences that don't go away and that sometimes come out in the wrong way, and that's just the nature of race in our society."

"Typical white person." You're not supposed to say stuff like that, especially not as the first black candidate ever to run for the office. The Clinton campaign pounced. Obama was clearly new at this game.

As he sat in silence and thought that day with me and Fiona, the room felt static, like we weren't supposed to move. Behind him was a large window with wooden shades blocking some of the light. Behind that the March winds were whooshing; you could hear them. I thought about how people talk about a person having the wind at his back, and they talk about having it in front, fighting it. But here was a man with neither. Here was a person set apart from a current violently streaming by. The world out there in tumult. The calmness in here.

All that listening he'd been talking about—eight years of it—was just history. All those letters he'd received during his presidency, millions of them, had been shipped off to the National Archives. I was glad that he, or someone in his administration, had thought to save them. They'll live on, artifacts for a museum exhibit someday. Here are the voices of America, from 2009 to 2017. This is *us* during the Obama years, surviving an economic crisis, a healthcare overhaul, a couple of wars, mass shootings, a government shutdown, heartache at our borders, hurricanes, the ravages of climate change, and all the rest of it. This is who we were, and there is an innocence about it, as there is always an innocence when you look back at yourself. Get too close, and it hurts, depending on your point of comparison.

Wallowing in the sorrow of what's lost is always a temptation.

But the letters offer more. They reignite the imagination. They remind you that kindness matters (seriously, we can all use a palate cleanser on that one alone), whether it's in style or, as it may appear to be under the Trump administration, it's out. They remind you that government *can* work and that people committed to public service really do exist. Moreover, there is the deepening discovery of what used to be. All that was right under your nose that maybe you hadn't noticed. I'd had no idea, not until the last few months of Obama's presidency, that a place like the mailroom even existed. I had never known that all those quiet conversations between the president and his constituents were going on, that there were all those random people believing they had the president's ear or believing that they could have it by simply jotting him a note. I'd had no idea that there was an entire army of caretakers reporting to duty each day to make sure the conversation kept going.

A discovery like that can give you hope. We *had* this, which means we can have it again. "And, you know, right now," Obama said to me, finally looking up from his shoe trance and meeting my eyes, "a lot of people who have worked with me in the past or supported me or voted for me, you know, can get discouraged by the news day to day. And that's understandable. I always have to be careful in not sounding as if I am Pollyannaish about the future."

The future. I hadn't said the word out loud. But it was, of course, the elephant in the room. America was not, as of late, aging gracefully. Did he feel responsible? Did he want to get back to it?

"A better future is earned," he said. "It's hard work. And democracy in a country this big, with such a diverse population, is especially hard. And complicated. And there are times in our history where we've had bad, ugly stretches. And so it's important not to ever forget and to recognize that the ideals and the best version of America isn't preordained.

"But I do think that when you hear someone like Marjorie, at her age, just take a leap of faith like that, then you can't help but feel as if it is worth the effort.

"If we duplicate enough of those moments, enough of those interactions, enough of those shared stories, over time we get better at this thing called democracy. And that is something that all of us have the capacity to do. That's not the job of the president. That's not the job of a bunch of professional policy makers. It's the job of citizens."

Over to you, citizens.

. . .

"You didn't cry," I said to Fiona afterward.

"I welled up," she said.

I asked her when. And why?

"The parallels between knocking on doors and answering letters," she said. "This idea that first we're going to ask something of you, and then you're going to ask something of us."

She said that part cut deep. "That he draws that connection on his own. We were a bunch of young people who had never worked in government. We were given the gift of his signature and trusted to know what we were doing. And we were winging it to some extent, just watching what he did and mirroring those values without hearing him expound on them. We only had the behavior to watch. Not some process document. So then hearing the 'why' behind it and hoping that the whys that were implied and the ones we implemented more broadly were not so off base.

"Treating empathy as a starting point," she said. "Not letting empathy be the end game. His take on the idea that our hearts were in the right place. And the idea of that being something worthy of being proud of in and of itself."

I told her I still wished she had read her letter to him or that at least she had given it to him.

"Oh, he doesn't need that," she said.

Dear President Obama,

Toward the end of my time in college, when I had no plan and no pull in any direction, my mother sent me Kurt Vonnegut's book "A Man Without a Country" with a note in it that said 'You and your generation have a lot of fixing up work to do!' I felt totally at a loss as to how I or even my generation could live up to that kind of task, and I thought that was such a classic mom move to put such an impossible ball in my court.

A few months later, I found myself walking down long New Hampshire driveways to interrupt family meals, first on hot days and later on snowy ones. As I walked by myself, I would repeat a few lines in my best imitation of your voice, which is a horrible imitation but made me laugh to myself and also somehow fortified me. I dreaded every unwelcome interaction, beginning with 'the primary isn't for 8 months' and moving into 'you've already been here too many times,' but I was able to keep going because I felt like I was part of a broader team, a team you understood, needed, and cared about, and a team that made me better than I had been without them. The people who came together for you in New Hampshire and in every state I went on to see made me so much better and stronger, and the road you sent me down taught me, among other things, just how emboldening a clipboard can be.

When your early state organizers fanned out for Super Tuesday and the later primaries, I found myself feeling flanked by your organization even when there were no other organizers in sight. When I stood on a garbage can at Delaware State University to let everyone lined up know there was no more room to see Michelle Obama but I really needed them to write down their contact information and sign up for canvassing shifts, I was able to draw on courage I didn't have but had seen in a Merrimack mom who, on a very rainy Saturday 6 months prior, had put garbage bags over herself and her son so they could spend the day canvassing their neighborhood. She had told me "there's always a reason not to," and she had canvassed every Saturday between that one and the New Hampshire primary. When I felt out of my depth speaking from a pulpit in Akron about the Ohio primary, and later felt like the ultimate enemy of fun while pleading with a group of Alphas hosting a Ted Kennedy speech to stop letting all the beautiful women circumvent the sign-in process, I knew I could do whatever needed to be done because kids like me were in over their heads for you in places all across America, and we owed it to one another to give it our all.

I was just one of many, but that was kind of the wonderful part. Together, we could really do something that mattered. One time before one of my mom's brain surgeries, you called her to wish her luck, and you told her a lie—you told her I was one of the best you had in the field. That wasn't true by a longshot, but man did it mean a lot to her. Thanks for telling her that, and thanks for building a movement that really wasn't about who was the best but rather what we were together. There were these pink and blue-haired teenagers who joined me to make phone calls one afternoon in Fond Du Lac, Wisconsin—they didn't get through many calls, in fact I *~that lowest of volunteer tasks~* have to admit they ended up making posters, but their presence reminded me what I was part of on a day when I needed it. They kept me going, like so many other people along the way.

When I interviewed the person who most recently started in my office, which of course is your office, she told me a familiar story I get the feeling a lot of people have told over the years since you first declared your candidacy. She described the experience of working on the 2012 convention, and the reasons it had felt right for her rang so true for me and should make you feel so proud. She said that it wasn't the work itself that made the job fulfilling, but rather working alongside the people who came together around your presidency and your campaign—people who felt passionate about what they were working toward and who wanted to play a part in making things better. I felt so lucky to know what she meant. *~exactly~*

Thank you for letting me have that experience too, and for letting me make so many people a part of it. Thank you for connecting with so many of us and connecting us with one another, and thank you for reconnecting me with our country and its promise. And most of all, thank you for making me and so many others like me feel like we could really be a part of the fixing up work my mom demanded of us.

Sincerely,

Samples, 2016-2017

Zoe E. Ruff
Bath, ME
BRUNSWICK, ME
NOV 30 2016
USPS 04011
Mr. President
1600 Pennsylvania Ave. NW
Washington DC
20500
485
DEC 07 2016
✓#016

1/12/17
LH 4

Sample
8m

Tuesday, November 29th, 2016

Dear President Obama,

Hello! My name is Zoe Ruff. I am thirteen years old, and I live in Bath, Maine. I wrote you this poem to show you that people care about this election. I think, in the end, it all comes down to pride. Whether someone voting for Donald Trump or for Hillary Clinton, or for someone else, how you take the results is as vital as the results themselves. As an extremely opinionated liberal myself, I believe the citizens of America should be proud. Not that we elected Donald J. Trump into the White House, but that we got to live under the name Obama. That, in and of itself, is an honor. You have taught love and kindness to this country, and that's not something our future president can take away from us. We can make it through the next four years if we can keep our heads up, and not let anyone tell us we should act one way, believe in a certain god, or be threatened because of color. Because if we do, he's really won. And we cannot let anyone as afraid as him win. We have gained too much to go back now.

I wanted to thank you for everything you've done for my home, and more. You have been honest, kind, and smart as our leader, and I couldn't be prouder to be American.

Yours Sincerely,

Zoe Ruff
age 13
grade 8

Election Results
An Abecedarian

A shuffle of slippers awakes me. I arise from my
bed. Mom looks at me through tearstained cheeks. "Honey, she lost.
Clinton lost." I squeeze my eyes shut. I can't even pretend to suppress the
dry sob that
echoes in my throat. Someone
fear-driven will be the head of this
glorious nation, my
home country. How could we have done this?
I convince myself to get up. The days are now numbered until
January 20th, that dreaded day when our true leader is
kicked out, no
longer in the position to
make our country the place we
need it to be. Right now,
only Obama can make me feel better, so I
press the *Home* button on my iPad to watch his speeches.
Quiet tears leak down my face, a whispered
reminder: my Mexican, Asian, and Muslim friends may
soon be leaving me, all because of
Trump, who can't even begin to
understand the rest of the world's point of
view. I thought I
would be angry. Instead, I'm sad that he's brainwashed America with his
xenophobia-ridden lies. I turn back to Obama,
yearning for everything and nothing at the same time. I tell myself,
"Zoe. We can get through this."

—ZOE RUFF

This is an abecedarian. What makes an abecedarian special is that the first letter of each line follows the alphabet.

BARACK OBAMA

May 31, 2017

Ms. Zoe Ruff
Bath, Maine

Dear Zoe:

Thank you for writing to me and for sharing your thoughtful poem. In the letters I receive from young people like you, I see the creativity and patriotism of your generation, and in particular, your reflections on the election and your outlook for the future give me tremendous hope for what lies ahead.

I know it sometimes seems like for every two steps forward, we take one step back. But remember that the course our country takes from here will be charted by engaged citizens like you who step forward and speak out for what they believe in. And I'm confident that as long as you stay focused on your education, set your sights high, and seek out new challenges, you can help shape a brighter future and effect positive change in your community and in the lives of those around you.

Thank you, again, for your kind note. Know that I'm rooting for you in all you do, and I wish you the very best.

Your friend,

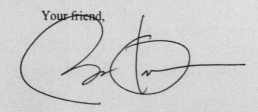

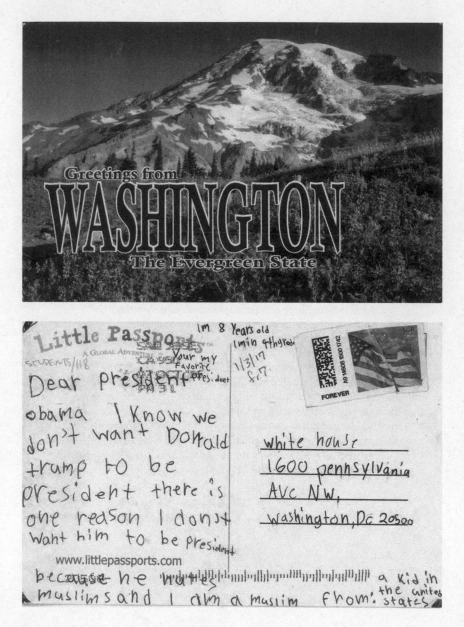

Greetings from
WASHINGTON
The Evergreen State

Little Passports
A GLOBAL ADVENTURE
STUDENTS/118

im 8 Years old
imin 4thgrade
Your my
Favorite
president
1/3/17
f.r7

Dear President
obama I know we
don't want Donald
trump to be
president there is
one reason I don't
Want him to be president

white house
1600 pennsylvania
Ave Nw,
washington, Dc 20500

www.littlepassports.com

because he hates
muslims and I am a muslim from:
a kid in
the united
states

1/19/17
+5

Submitted via Facebook Messenger
Case Number

From: Jamie Snyder

Submitted: 1/12/2017 11:24 PM EST

Email:

Phone:

Address: Los Angeles, California

Message: Mr. President and Mrs. Obama, I am currently VERY pregnant with my second child (and first girl). My husband and I were thrilled to find out that her scheduled due date would be on what we thought would be HRC's historical Inauguration Day. We quickly became distraught knowing that she is now due to come into the world on the day that Trump takes office. After speaking truthfully with my angel of an OB, she rescheduled the c-section to happen on Thursday, January 19th. So my sweet girl will be born on the last day of your amazing presidency! The Snyder Family has the utmost admiration and respect for you both, and we hope to become a fraction of the superb parents you have been to your beautiful and brilliant girls. We thank you for your service and unwavering dedication to our country, and we will miss you dearly. We are excited to think that our daughter will be a small reminder of your legacy. Thank you for everything. Jamie Snyder

Barack Obama

June 14, 2017

Mrs. Jamie Snyder
Los Angeles, California

Dear Jamie:

I read the email you sent just a few days before the birth of your daughter, and I wanted to congratulate you and your husband and let you know how moved I was by your message. Your love for and pride in your children is abundantly clear—a feeling I know quite well—and your kind words meant a great deal to Michelle and me. We hope your family has been able to enjoy some precious time together these last few months.

I know that now remains a time of great uncertainty for many. But I'm confident that so long as parents like you and your husband continue striving to instill in their children the same values, selflessness, and sense of common purpose that came through in your email, the future will be bright. As your son and daughter continue to learn and grow, know that Michelle and I wish the very best for all of you.

Thank you, again—for everything.

Sincerely,

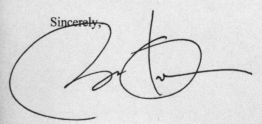

1/19/17
f.s

7:44 am
15 Dec 2016
Marietta, GA

Dear President Obama,
    I'm writing this at the proverbial
kitchen table, after sending my two
boys (13, 16 y.o.) off to school. I haven't
written a letter to a president
for 40 years, since I was 7 years old
and living in Alabama. I wrote
to Jimmy Carter then, excited that
a man my parents had taken me to
visit on the campaign trail was in
the White House. He seemed so kind
and my little-girl self had so many
important things to share with him.
And miracle of miracles, he wrote
me back. Maybe that made me
less cynical* over the years - or a
lifelong Democrat,** which got hard
in a state like Alabama. I'm
picking up a pen to write another
president - you - because I'm
profoundly thankful for your
service to our country and I

*about
government
and the
good it
can represent

**proud
#proud

felt it was important for you to know what good your presidency did in the lives of just one family living in Marietta, Georgia.

and for me to say in writing

When you were first running for office, in 2008, my husband was laid off, with his whole department, from CNN. This was in the spring and we had no idea that the whole economy was tanking. I was working as a teacher (and still do — college) and he got unemployment, which was thankfully extended for almost a year. It was scary — those lean times, but your win and presidency and your personal kindness and decency made us know that times would get better. We were able to put our youngest son in free pre-k, economize, and keep our house. (we always paid the mortgage first) My husband eventually got a job, until the company folded, went on unemployment again (thankfully that safety net was still there) Finally, he got a good job in 2011, and

and has worked ever since. Your
steady leadership through the recession
gave us hope (not just a slogan to us!)
and I was thankful every day that
my boys grew up with you in the
White House,* with you as the
model of a president. Our family
is in a much better place than it
was when you took office — two good
jobs, a nest egg** for retirement, and
kids who have known a president
with a good heart and a work ethic
and vision that made their lives
better. To say that dealing with such
push-back (from congress) wasn't easy is, I'm sure,
an understatement, but we've all
felt that you've put the people first
and done tangible things to make
our lives better. Thank you.
Thank you. Thank you.
    I'm not sure I can love two presidents
as much as I love you and Jimmy Carter,
but I hope all who follow can do
as much good as you have.
                    Respectfully,
            Lynn Murray Luxemburger

*and Michelle too!

**your steady economic policies made this happen

→ my actual tears :) (of gratitude)

BARACK OBAMA

June 19, 2017

Ms. Lynn Murray Luxemburger
Marietta, Georgia

Dear Lynn:

Thank you for sitting down and taking the time to write me a note after sending your two boys off to school this past December. I read it on the final night of my Presidency and just wanted to let you know how much your story moved me.

It's folks like you and your husband who were on my mind every single day that I was President. You're right that "hope" is more than just a slogan, but rather what got so many through such difficult times. It certainly kept me going, and knowing our actions helped so many hardworking families like yours means so much. I'm glad to hear things are looking up.

From my family to yours, thank you—for everything. You have our very best wishes.

Sincerely,

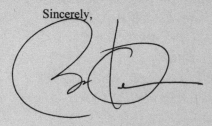

1/6/17
r.S

12-05-2016

DEAR PRESIDENT OBAMA,

I OWE YOU AN APOLOGY.

THERE IS NO QUESTIONS THAT WE ARE AT
DIFFERENT PLACES ON THE POLITICAL SPECTRUM. THERE
FEW THINGS THAT WE AGREE ON WHEN IT COMES TO
POLICY AND THE DIRECTION OF OUR GOVERNMENT.

HERE'S WHERE I WENT WRONG. I LET MY
DISAGREEMENTS WITH YOU TAINT THE WAY I VIEWED
YOU AS A PERSON. I HELD YOU IN CONTEMPT AND
SHARED MY POOR OPINION OF YOU.

BUT THAT WAS WRONG, AND UNCHRISTIAN. AS
THE YEARS HAVE GONE BYE I HAVE TAKEN A CLOSER
LOOK. MY OPINION WAS WAY OFF. WE STILL DISAGREE
ON A VAST NUMBER OF THINGS. BUT YOU, SIR, ARE
A PATRIOT. I HAVE COME TO ADMIRE YOU AS A MAN
OF PRINCIPLE, A MAN WITH A GOOD HEART, A MAN WITH
A TREMENDOUS SENSE OF HUMOR, A FAMILY MAN,
A MAN OF FAITH AND A MAN WHO LOVES THIS COUNTRY.
I HAVE SEEN AND READ ABOUT HOW YOU TREAT OUR MILITARY
AND THE SECRET SERVICE WITH RESPECT. I HAVE SEEN YOUR
GENUINE HUMILITY (AS MUCH AS ONE CAN SEE IN A POLITICIAN).

I DO STRONGLY AGREE WITH YOUR OPENNESS TO CUBA.
I APPLAUDE YOUR CANCER INITIATIVE. SO WE CAN AGREE
ON SOME THINGS.

You will never meet me. You probably won't ever even see this letter. But I judged you wrongly and harshly. My faith and my mother raised me to admit when I am wrong and make amends to the person I've offended. So I thought this the best way to attempt that; a handwritten apology.

So there it is. I want to thank you. Thank you for your example of fatherhood, as a husband and a man. Thank you, Mr President, for your service to this great country.

I pray that God may bless you and your family always and in all ways.

Sincerely,

Patrick J O'Connor

PATRICK J. O'CONNOR

AKRON, OH

Rust Eddy
Canton, NY

The President of the United
States
of America

The White House
1600 Pennsylvania Ave NW
Washington, DC 20500

Hope is a thing with feathers.
                    E. Dickinson
11/14/17
8:5
Dear Mr. President,

Borders seem to be all the
rage these days, mostly strengthening
and reinforcing them. It has
been a gift of my life to live
it across borders. I am a
white man married to a black
woman for 26 years. We live
in a small town in far
northern NY, Canton. My wife,
Dr. Sheryl Scales, teaches
Literacy in the School of
Education at SUNY Potsdam.
My life drifts between the two
worlds of Hillary and Trump;

Sheryl's circle of academia,
and the local small town
friends and acquaintances
who are the perfect microcosm
of Trump voters. Needless to
say living across that border has
caused me more than a little
difficulty in recent days, sometimes
feeling more like a curse than a
gift.

Please know that your example
of strength and compassion,
resolve and empathy, intellectual
curiosity and sense of wonder,
have inspired us throughout
your presidency, and more
importantly will resonate in
your legacy, continuing to
inspire us to persevere.
        Thank You Sir
        Rust Eddy and Sheryl Scales

Sample 11/4/19
f.4

Charlotte Blome

Crystal Lake, IL

18 November 2016

President Barack Obama
The White House
1600 Pennsylvania Avenue NW
Washington, DC 20500

Dear Mr. President,

In this time of uncertainty, I would like to share with you a small, but bright spot that I am sure in not an isolated one.

We are a mixed race family that lives in the reddest county in Chicagoland. I am white. My adopted son Noah is black. His school is overwhelmingly white. Last year, his 7th grade elected him the most likely to become President of the United States, in spite of the fact that he reminded them he is Ethiopian by birth. They did not care. This year, he ran for student council president and won.

It may seem like a small thing on the surface, but I do not think that 20 years ago this would have happened at your typical 98% white school. Noah is likely the first black student council president at his Jr. High, but my impression is it is so normal for him and his fellow students, that it has not even been mentioned! He has experienced quite a bit of racial bias in his 13 years, but never from his peers. Even in a conservative county like ours. I attribute this largely to you. (He gets some credit, too, for being a good, hard-working guy!)

So, I thank you and the First Lady for setting us on the right course. We sure are going to miss you.

With profound gratitude and respect,

Charlotte Blome

BARACK OBAMA

May 4, 2017

Ms. Charlotte Blome
Crystal Lake, Illinois

Dear Charlotte:

Thanks for your note. It's clear you've raised a wonderful young man, and I can tell how proud you are of Noah.

Noah's accomplishments reflect an idea at the heart of our nation's promise: that in America, all people should be able to make of their lives what they will—no matter the color of their skin or the country they are from. The story you shared of his experience in school gives me tremendous hope for our country's future.

Thanks again. You and your family have my very best.

Sincerely,

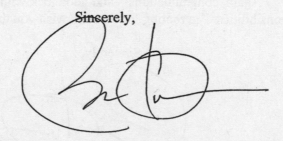

BARACK OBAMA

May 4, 2017

Mr. Noah Blome
Crystal Lake, Illinois

Dear Noah:

Your mother wrote to tell me about all you've achieved in school—congratulations on being elected Student Council President! It's clear your mom is very proud of you, and I want you to know that I am, too.

In the face of challenges, I hope you'll remember that there are no limits to what you can achieve. As long as you hold on to the passion and determination that have brought you this far and keep dreaming big dreams, you can help effect positive change—in your school, across your community, and throughout our nation.

Again, congratulations—and good luck with your new responsibilities. I'm rooting for you and wish you the very best.

Sincerely,

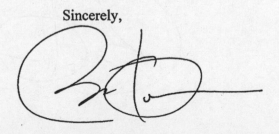

From: Mr. Joshua David Hofer

Submitted:

Email:

Phone:

Address: , Bloomington, Nebraska

Message: Honorable President Barack Obama,

Dear Mr President I appreciate how hard you work and as a former veteran I understand how things you believe get twisted against you by the military. That most saddest thing I see is the hatred towards the Muslim world and the separation our country is going towards. I feel your President Abraham Lincoln and Im watching history repeat itself against color of skin. I served in the military at a young age and being from Nebraska I learned their is no such thing as race. The people who still look out for me today are of different color. I think america is sheltered and needs to see what veterans have seen since the war on Terrorism began. We need more commercials that teach lessons and give other point of views like South Korea does in order to maintain their social customs for their younger youth. I truly believe in what you do buy because I served I saw were the money went to support Pakistan (Terrorism) and Iran. I believe america when you do a presidential speech need to see what life is like when you live in a country that is at war. I have photos of a one girl who reminded me of my sister as I was losing my mind in 2003 in Iraq. I never will leave me but I wanted to change lives for them. Their country has oppressed them to where they were starving. I gave her chocolate and all kinds of stuff but I realized the error in my ways. As I would try to help her out predators because she was a female made an example. As we were leaving I saw that an older child saw what I have done. She cared for her younger brother as well. He was stomped to death and she was being dragged down the street. I care her picture with me to this day. I didnt see Muslim or Christian, I saw human. When you oppress someone and kill their family, they grow up in a world of hate. I believe I have many more things to offer my country then retired veteran but in this new world where your born into privilege it is hard for a veteran who cries from his nightmares to separate. This country is filled with so much hate it kills me. I dont see black and white I see my brothers. I have been wronged and you are the only one who could help me move on. Like people that are angry I feel I was wronged but by leaders in my military service.

From: Mr. larry wright

Submitted: 1/11/2017 7:17 AM EST

Email:

Phone:

Address: Greensboro, North Carolina

Message: Mr President

For 8 years you were loved, hated, mistreated and berated. For 8 years you sung, danced cried and amazing graced us when racism and hatred came knocking at God's door. You was a Muslim, Terrorist, half bread, African but never American. You help two industries that were on the verge of collapse and pulled this country out of its worse recession in years. We seen you go from dark hair to gray hair, we seen your kids grow and become beautiful young ladies and your wife is the woman most admired by many women around the globe. I credit your wife for restoring pride in all women especially black women. You gave people the opportunity to be insured and feel safe when it came to the safety of this country. I'm sure there are things that you are not proud of and wish you could go back and fix them, but we all have things we would love to fix in our lives as well. In closing I would like to say this. There may never be another face like your in the white house, there may never be another family like your in the white house and there may never be a husband and wife team like you and your wife that lived a scandal free campaign in the white house. The one thing that will be missed when you close that door behind you will be Mr. Barack Obama our 44th President of the United States.

From: **Marjan Schneider Carasik**

Submitted: 12/24/2016 12:36 PM EST

Email:

Phone:

Address: Ithaca, New York

Message: Dear Mr President,

Thank you for standing up for the rights of Palestinians as well as Israelis. Answers to all questions lie somewhere in the middle.

I am the child and grandchild of Jewish refugees who suffered greatly before coming to America. It causes me much pain to see Palestinians sometimes being mistreated as my family members were mistreated before arriving on these shores.

I am grateful to you for your courage in standing where you do. This does not make you an anti-Semite, but rather pro-All Human Beings.

With Much Admiration and Affection, and Thanks,

Marjan S. Carasik

Ithaca, N.Y.

Mr. President and Mrs. Obama,   11/18/17
                                   f. 20

I cannot tell you how much I have loved and appreciated your work in the White House for the last 8 years.

As a daughter of immigrants and a woman of color, your actions in office have given me so much hope. Thank you for leading an America that was inclusive and that craved justice.

I got to attend your inauguration in 2008. I still have a lot of the cheesy keepsakes Pepsi was handing out that week. I remember that it was freezing, and that it hurt to cry because of that. I remember being stranded at the Air and Space Museum for 4 hours while we waited for our charter bus. I was interviewed like 3 times that week by Latin American news stations. I cried in all three as I explained that your presidency validated my dreams.

As you transition out of the presidency, I want you to know it was worth it. It was worth all the Fox news attacks. It was worth it to honor and respect Muslims. It was worth it to champion the rights of women. To cry out against injustice. To mourn the loss of black lives at the hands of law enforcement.

Your courage and humility in leadership will be sorely missed. But not forgotten. All the voices you've pulled out of silence — we're all in unison and ready to rally for justice, unity, and equality.

So when you move out of the White House, go on vacation. Drink some margaritas for me. We'll be here fighting the good fight till you get back.

So much love,
Mary-Beth Johnson

MILWAUKIE, OR

BARACK OBAMA

June 14, 2017

Mrs. Mary-Beth Johnson
Milwaukie, Oregon

Dear Mary-Beth:

Thanks for sharing your reflections on the last eight years, including my first inauguration, in the letter you sent me—I agree; it was all worth it.

I was moved by your kind words, and I am inspired by your commitment to continue stepping forward, speaking out, and working to defend the values that make us who we are. As you do, please know Michelle and I will be standing right alongside you, as we always have been, fighting for the America we both know is possible.

Thanks again for writing—you, Benjamin, and Estel have my very best.

Sincerely,

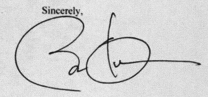

Frank Heimbecker
De Forest, WI
21 DEC 2016 PM 5 L

FOREVER
USA

President Barack +
First Lady Michelle Obama
The White House
1600 Pennsylvania Ave
NW, Washington, D.C.
20500

✓ #023
QC✓ #020
485
DEC 3 0 2016

President Barack &
First Lady Michelle,

    This modest card probably
will not get to you. I want to
thank you for the last eight years.
It has been a honor. You started
out with a part of my heart, and
you leave with the whole thing.
    Frank Hernbecker
Detroit MI

1/19/17
fr10

BARACK OBAMA

June 19, 2017

Mr. Frank Heimbecker
DeForest, Wisconsin

Dear Frank:

On the final night of my Presidency, I read the
handwritten card you sent me, and I wanted to reach out to
thank you. Your kind words were deeply moving, and while I
appreciate your thinking of me, please know the honor was all
mine—it was the privilege of my life to serve as your President.

There are certainly milestone moments we will always
remember from the past eight years, but for me, it was hearing
from people like you that kept me going every single day. My
heart has been touched time and again by the daily acts of
kindness that embody the American people at their core, and as
I take some time now to rest and reflect on all we achieved
together, know that your thoughtful gesture will stay with me.

Sincerely,

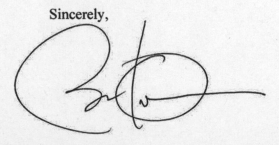

Epilogue

Benjamin Durrett (page 4), twenty-eight, is married and living in Oregon. He works as an office administrator for a water company, and is not registered with a political party.

Despite their differing views of government, Richard Dexter (page 5) treasured Obama's response to his letter, and plans to pass it on to his daughters.

Jeri Harris (page 7) kept her promise to pray for Obama every day of his two terms. His letter hangs inside a frame on a wall in her living room. She wrote a letter to President Trump after the 2016 election, saying she would pray for him too.

J. Martin Ball (page 9) died in 2011. His daughter, Natasha, remembers the day her father wrote to Obama—it was her son's eighteen-month birthday. Her father was overjoyed knowing that his grandson would grow up knowing a black president.

Shailagh Murray (page 12) is not writing as many letters as she believes she should. She thinks often of Bobby Ingram and the thousands of Americans whose stories lived in binders in her West Wing office, and whose voices and conviction were her guiding force.

Every day at about three o'clock, Bobby Ingram (page 23) watches his cat, Purdy, step out on the back porch, hop onto the railing, and begin nudging morsels of cat food off of it. The food drops into the yard below where BooHiss, the fat turtle, awaits with contentment. "Purdy is just fascinated by that," Bobby reports.

Linette Jones (page 34) is glad she shot her angry email to Obama, and would do it again; his response was comforting. Her daughter Sophia, who was stationed in Kabul when Linette wrote to the president, is safely home, living close to her mom in Florida.

Michael Powers (page 36) allowed White House staff to share his letter publicly, along with Obama's reply. The letters showed up on a conservative blog where Obama's handwritten response earned a place as one of the top ten gaffes he made during his first six months in office. (He misspelled "advice," or at least didn't properly curve the "c.")

Kenny Jops (page 48), twenty-two, graduated from Northwestern University in 2018 with a double major in math and environmental studies.

Fiona Reeves (page 64) works for a Democratic communications firm, and her husband, Chris Liddell-Westefeld, collects oral histories for the Barack Obama Presidential Library. Their daughter, Grace, has a letter from Obama framed on her bedroom wall. Her parents report that Grace goes canvassing with them every chance she gets.

Yena Bae (page 67) is pursuing a graduate degree in international security studies at Columbia University. She is a frequent host of wine nights, potlucks, and get-togethers where stories of #teamlittle-people continue to be shared.

Thomas and JoAnn Meehan's (page 74) son, Daryl, named one of his three daughters after Colleen.

Pete Rouse (page 83) delights in watching the young people who came of age under "the Obama experience" continue to contribute to civic engagement. He's enjoying quality time with Buster, his Maine Coon cat, who now weighs twenty-seven pounds so Pete's putting him on a diet.

Mike Kelleher (page 88) works in the United Nations liaison office at the World Bank in Washington, D.C. He also composes, arranges, and performs music professionally; his 2015 jazz album, *Mélange*, is a collaboration with his wife, Karin, a classical violinist.

Laura King (page 96) is now legally married to Lisa.

Robert B. Trapp (page 97) is still the managing editor of *The Rio Grande Sun*.

Retired U.S. Air Force Staff Sergeant Robert Doran (page 98) discovered that his fiancée, Jana', had not been taking her blood pressure medication before she died; she was unable to afford it. SSgt Doran gave Obama's reply to his letter to Jana''s daughters.

Chana Sangkagalo (page 108) enjoys continued success at his popular hair salon in Rhode Island.

Regina Bryant (page 109) received a recipe from Michelle Obama for a vegetarian bean dip. "Some serious spices!" Her letter and the Obamas' reply are saved in an album for her daughter, Caitlin.

Jason Hernandez's (page 112) life sentence for a drug conviction was commuted by President Obama on December 19, 2013. He lives in Dallas, where he is writing a book about the justice system and where he assists federal inmates serving life sentences with clemency petitions.

A campaign staffer was so moved by Sandy Swanson's (page 113) letter that she sent the family a pizza, and then President Obama called her from Air Force One to thank her.

Bill Oliver (page 116) and his wife, Sandra, host a weekly philosophy study group at their home. Quique plans to go to culinary school. Quique's wife, Rebecca, is a premed student in college. Bill and Quique talk daily.

In July 2016, Darin Konrad Brunstad's (pages 129 and 134) husband, Senior Master Sergeant and two-time Airman of the Year awardee David Lono Brunstad, retired from the military after twenty-two years of service. Darin and David rode on an F-15 fighter jet to celebrate. They are now foster parents.

Marnie Hazelton (page 138) is starting her fourth school year as superintendent of the Roosevelt Union Free School District. In 2018, she shared her letter to President Obama with a third-grade class to demonstrate the importance of writing well.

Erv and Ross Uecker-Walker (page 151) will celebrate sixty-one years together and four years of marriage on November 30, 2018.

Jordan Garey (page 160) lived in eleven foster homes before his two dads adopted him. He got invited to the White House for its 2015 Easter Egg Roll, and met the First Lady.

In June 2014, Danny Garvin (page 162) was invited to attend a White House reception celebrating LGBT Pride Month. Obama asked for a picture taken beside him. Danny died in 2015. He was honored by several publications for his activism and his demonstration at the Stonewall Inn.

Tom Hoefner (page 164) is a stay-at-home dad looking after his two girls. He works weekends at a residential facility for disabled people, and is drafting the second volume of a serialized adventure/comedy book series, *The Unlikely Adventures of Race & Cookie McCloud*. He is still looking for full-time work in his field.

Bob Melton (page 166) continues to read his letter from President Obama at the monthly Tuesday meetings of the Burke County, North Carolina, Democratic Party. He lives with his wife, Tammy, in their home of twenty-five years, where they ride and maintain dune buggies.

Shelley Muniz (page 171) is the author of *Eagle Feathers and Angel Wings: Micah's Story*, which chronicles her son's illness and struggles with healthcare coverage.

Since Ronn Ohl (page 173) wrote his letter to Obama, his son's friend, now thirty-four, was granted DACA status, allowing him to obtain a green card, get a driver's license, attend college, and land a full-time job.

Joelle Graves (page 180) became email buddies with an OPC staffer, who relayed to her that Obama was so moved by her letter that he read it to his family in the White House residence. Joelle went on to write a letter to the queen of England, who also responded personally.

Marjorie McKinney (page 181) renovated her house to welcome her daughter Rachel and granddaughter Kirby, who now live with her. She has begun attending a church in Janaluska, one of the region's oldest historically black neighborhoods.

Ashley DeLeon (page 191) got engaged to be married in May 2018, on the same day she graduated from the University of North Carolina Wilmington with a master's degree in marine biology. She gets her love of the ocean from her dad.

Lacey Higley (page 192) works for the United States Digital Service at the Department of Veterans Affairs, building and modernizing digital tools that enable veterans to discover, apply for, and track the benefits they've earned.

A year after sending her 2015 letter to Obama, Alisa Bowman (page 204) and her transgender son addressed their local school board in support of trans students. In 2017, Alisa was elected to the board, which went on to pass a comprehensive nondiscrimination policy that protects students' gender identity. Alisa wrote another letter to Obama in 2018, saying she was "embarrassed" by the anger in her first one. "You gave me the courage to put an end to living small," she told him.

Rev. Christine G. Reisman (page 206), the pastor of Newbern Christian Church in Newbern, Virginia, and her husband moved into a new condo on November 9, 2016, the day after the presidential election. The mover who packed her framed letter from Obama wrote "**Fragile! Historical artifact! Letter from Obama!**" many times on the box.

As a result of her letter to Obama, Sue Ellen Allen (page 208) was invited to attend the 2016 State of the Union address as a guest in the First Lady's box, where she met Attorney General Loretta Lynch. Sue Ellen told the attorney general about her efforts back home to reform the culture of incarceration. "Can you imagine, I'm a felon meeting with Loretta Lynch?"

Mary Susan Sanders (page 211) is the author of three books, including *Solo,* about losing her late partner, artist and wood carver Kathy Ruth Neal. Mary Susan used Kathy's paints to paint her lawn jockey.

Delaney (page 213) wrote a thank-you note back to President Obama with a sticker on top that said "My Fave Person."

Gretchen Elhassani (page 215) is a screenwriter for Georgia Film Company.

Sheryl Cousineau's (page 218) neighbor who helped in the orchard remains in Mexico after his deportation. He drives a taxi. His daughter, Janitza, works near Sheryl at a real estate company.

Heba Hallak (page 220), twenty, is studying biochemistry at Drew University. She plans to become a pediatrician.

Cody Keenan (page 228) is helping President Obama prepare his next book.

In May 2018, Shane Darby (page 233) received a mysterious package in the mail. It was from an anonymous airman who had served with Cristina. Inside the package were an American flag, a hat, and a patch with Cristina's name on it, along with a certificate from the 494th Expeditionary Fighter Squadron of the U.S. Air Force dated May 4, 2018—her birthday. "This flag was proudly flown in an F-15 E Strike Eagle on a combat sortie over Syria and Iraq in support of OPERATION INHERENT RESOLVE. Flown in memory of: Cristina Danielle Silvers. For her smile was strong and true."

William Johnson (page 248) was released from prison on parole. He has a handyman business with his sons.

Yvonne Wingard (page 251) is a junior at Brown University, where she studies public health, serves on the student council, and works as a peer counselor.

Anne Bunting (page 252) shared President Obama's letter with her heart-transplant surgeons. Now, four years after her operation, she enjoys hiking and traveling.

Alex Myteberi (page 254), eight, has a LEGO White House in his bedroom that he will not let anyone touch. He is learning to play the piano.

Myriah Johnson (page 260) continues to raise awareness about veteran suicide in memory of her son, U.S. Army Specialist Alexander Johnson.

Noor Abdelfattah (page 263) was invited to a White House dinner celebrating Muslim Americans as well as Eid al-Fitr, the holiday marking the end of Ramadan.

Madison Drago (page 264), sixteen, received a reply from President Obama advising her to listen to her parents. She got her nose pierced anyway. "And a lot more," her mom reports.

Kolbie Blume (page 269) works in media relations at the Association of International Educators, the world's largest nonprofit dedicated to international education and exchange. She made a present for Fiona Reeves's baby, Grace: a framed calligraphy drawing quoting the speech Hillary Clinton gave on November 9, 2016. "To all the little girls: Never doubt that you are valuable and powerful and deserving of every chance and opportunity in the world to pursue and achieve your own dreams." It hangs on the wall near Grace's crib, next to the letter Obama wrote to Grace.

Patty Ries (page 273) suffered a house fire in January 2018, losing almost everything. But a few of her father's photos and writings, along with his army discharge papers, were found intact in the rubble. Patty felt it was a miracle, the work of her long lost grandmother. "I survived a concentration camp; you'll get through this," she imagined her grandmother saying.

Billy Ennis (page 277) got another raise at his roofing job. He is still with his girlfriend, the woman he recognized from seventh grade in the supermarket. He talks to his dad, who is still in prison, weekly. When Billy watched his teenage son take fourth place in discus at the state track and field meet, he broke down in tears. His son called him a big baby.

Since receiving President Obama's message to "stay engaged," Alessandra Shurina (page 305) went back to school at Florida State University, graduated, and began a master's program in political science and public policy.

"At the risk of sounding hokey, this whole thing has rejuvenated my faith in people and in this country," Maureen Dolan Rosen (page 313) said of receiving a personal response to her letter from President Obama.

Roberta Fine (page 316) enjoys planting flowers and maintaining her vegetable garden. She is the proud great-grandmother of two.

Vicki and Tim Shearer (page 324) bought an RV and frequently go camping together.

Joshua Hofer (page 377) served in the military for ten years. He recalls busting up human trafficking operations in South Korea. He has struggled with the effects of traumatic brain injury.

Mary-Beth Johnson (page 380) keeps Obama's letter framed next to her bed, beside a hand-lettered print that says "I am with you always," a quote from the Book of Matthew. She enjoys writing *Heart of Celebration*, her food blog.

President Obama still receives five thousand letters a week.

Acknowledgments

To Obama grew out of a story for *The New York Times Magazine* that my longtime editor and friend Mike Benoist encouraged me to pursue. My thanks to Mike for his early belief in the wisdom of the mailroom, to Jake Silverstein for his support and willingness to showcase it, and to President Obama for his generous response to the article, for taking the time to meet with me—and for allowing me to keep digging through his mail.

This book was an entirely collaborative effort. Fiona Reeves was its guiding light from the outset; she inspired me with her quiet and determined service to the president and to the country, and my gratitude to her lead is boundless. Researcher Rachel Wilkinson was on the case from beginning to end, and I could not have written the book without her. Her compassion and intelligence are all through these pages, and I'm deeply grateful to her. My thanks also to audio producer Erin Anderson, who along with Rachel trekked across the country talking to people about their letters and whose wisdom guided so many editorial decisions, and to the rest of the people at Cement City Productions—Tim Maddocks, Erin Kello, Tyler McCloskey, Rachel Mabe, Rachel Brickner—whose efforts kept the engines humming. In addition, I would like to thank Michael Lewis for helping me find the courage to take on this book project.

I would like to thank Eric Schultz, Obama's postpresidency senior advisor, for his trust and support and for being so much fun to work with; communications director Katie Hill for her kindness and persistence in providing materials; Mike Kelleher for his insight and generosity; Shailagh Murray for her vision and guidance; and all the people in the mailroom who shared their stories of extraordinary service and who helped track down letter writers from all over the country. Every effort was made to remove all identifying information from any letter whose author requested anonymity and from those whose authors were unreachable; samples from the archives at obamawhitehouse.archives.gov were cleared prior to appearing in this book, and I'm indebted to these letter writers (especially Emily, whose letter is featured on the back cover of this book) who contributed their words and stories to Obama's legacy and to the embrace of history.

My agent, Elyse Cheney, was a ferocious advocate for the book. My ongoing thanks to her and everyone at the agency, especially Alex Jacobs, Alice Whitwham, Claire Gillespie, and Natasha Fairweather.

Andy Ward, at Random House, is the kind of editor every writer dreams of having; he's a writing partner who demands more and makes everything better than you knew it could be. He has shaped my books and articles over the long arc of my career, and as always I can't find words big enough to adequately express my gratitude. I would like to thank the entire team at Random House for their support, notably Susan Kamil and Tom Perry, and the heroic production efforts of Chayenne Skeete and Loren Noveck, Anna Bauer for the beautiful cover, Debbie Glasserman for the interior design, Matthew Martin for protecting the work, and Cindy Murray for her creativity in spreading the word.

I get tremendous support from the people at the University of Pittsburgh, and I would like to say a special thanks to them for the work they do. Pat Gallagher, chancellor of the university, offered helpful insights into this project, and Provost and Senior Vice Chancellor Patty Beeson, along with Executive Vice Provost Dave DeJong, provided especially helpful encouragement and care. John Cooper, deputy vice chancellor for research, remains an enthusiastic supporter; my sincere thanks to him and to Kathy Blee, dean of the Dietrich School of Arts and Sciences, and Don Bialostosky, chair of the department of English, for their ongoing kindness and generous patronage. I'm grateful to my colleagues in the writing program, notably Peter Trachtenberg, Michael Meyer, and Maggie Jones for filling in the gaps while I took leave, and I would like to extend a special thanks to Kit Ayars, my longtime friend, who guided the ship at the Center for Creativity while I took the time to write this book.

I would like to thank my husband, Alex, whose love and support makes all this work possible, and my daughters, Anna and Sasha, who endured my absence during all that time back in the hole.

Finally, I offer my ongoing gratitude to all of the letter writers who gave permission to reprint their letters, and who allowed me the privilege of hearing and sharing their remarkable stories.

Permission Credits

Letter written by Benjamin Durrett reprinted by permission of Benjamin Durrett.

Letter written by Rust Eddy reprinted by permission of Rust Eddy.

Letter written by Gretchen Elhassani reprinted by permission of Gretchen Elhassani.

Letter written by Rebekah Erler reprinted by permission of Rebekah Olson Erler.

Letter written by Samantha Frashier reprinted by permission of Samantha Frashier.

Letter written by Jordan Garey reprinted by permission of Jordan Garey, Matthew Garey, and Jeremy Garey.

Letter written by Danny Garvin reprinted by permission of Debra Carey.

Letter written by Martin A. Gleason reprinted by permission of Martin A. Gleason, MS.

Letter written by Joelle Graves reprinted by permission of Joelle Graves.

Letter written by Heba Hallak reprinted by permission of Heba Hallak.

Letter written by Jeri Harris reprinted by permission of Jeri L. Harris.

Letters written by Marnie Hazelton reprinted by permission of Dr. Marnie Hazelton.

Letter written by Frank Helmbecker reprinted by permission of Frank Helmbecker.

Letter written by Jason Hernandez reprinted by permission of Jason Hernandez.

Letter written by Tom Hoefner reprinted by permission of Tom Hoefner.

Letter written by Patrick Allen Holbrook reprinted by permission of Patrick Allen Holbrook.

Letter written by Bobby Ingram reprinted by permission of Bobby Ingram.

Letter written by Mary Beth Johnson reprinted by permission of Mary Beth Salguero Johnson.

Letter written by Mrs. Myriah Lynn Johnson reprinted by permission of Mrs. Myriah Lynn Johnson.

Letter written by William A. Johnson reprinted by permission of William A. Johnson.

Letter written by Linette Jones reprinted by permission of Linette St. Pierre Jones.

Letter written by Kenneth Jops reprinted by permission of Kenneth P.T. Jops.

Letter written by Dane Jorgensen reprinted by permission of Dane Austin Jorgensen.

Letter written by Sam KG reprinted by permission of Sam KG.

Letter written by Laura King reprinted by permission of Laura A. King.

Letter written by Tracy LaRock reprinted by permission of Tracy LaRock, R.N.

Letter written by June M. Lipsky reprinted by permission of June M. Lipsky.

Letter written by Lynn Luxemburger reprinted by permission of Lynn Luxemburger.

Letter written by Kelli McDermott reprinted by permission of Kelli McDermott.

Letter written by Marjorie McKinney reprinted by permission of Marjorie J. McKinney.

Letter written by Thomas Meehan and JoAnn Meehan reprinted by permission of Thomas Meehan and JoAnn Meehan.

Letter written by Bob Melton reprinted by permission of Bob Melton.

Letter by Michaela reprinted by permission of Michaela.

Letter written by John Mier reprinted by permission of John M. Mier.

Letter written by Judge Donald William Molloy reprinted by permission of Judge Donald William Molloy.

Letter written by Timothy Mullin reprinted by permission of Timothy Mullin.

Letter written by Shelley Muniz reprinted by permission of Shelley Muniz.

Letter written by Alex Myteberi reprinted by permission of Valbona Myteberi.

Letter written by Patrick O'Connor reprinted by permission of Patrick J. O'Connor.

Letter written by Ronn Ohl reprinted by permission of Ronn G. Ohl.

PHOTO: © SCOTT GOLDSMITH 2018

JEANNE MARIE LASKAS is the author of eight books, including the *New York Times* bestseller *Concussion*, the basis for the 2015 Golden Globe–nominated film starring Will Smith. She is a contributing writer at *The New York Times Magazine*, a correspondent at *GQ*, and a two-time National Magazine Award finalist. Her stories have also appeared in *The New Yorker, The Atlantic,* and *Esquire.* She serves as Distinguished Professor of English and founding director of the Center for Creativity at the University of Pittsburgh, and lives on a farm in Pennsylvania with her husband and two children.

jeannemarielaskas.com
Twitter: @jmlaskas

ABOUT THE TYPE

This book was set in Scala, a typeface designed by Martin Majoor in 1991. It was originally designed for a music company in the Netherlands and then was published by the international type house FSI FontShop. Its distinctive extended serifs add to the articulation of the letterforms to make it a very readable typeface.